STRIKE!
THE TOUR THAT DIED OF SHAME

John Coffey

STRIKE! THE TOUR THAT DIED OF SHAME

Scratching Shed Publishing Ltd

Rugby League Classics

Published by Scratching Shed Publishing Ltd, 2012
Registered in England & Wales No. 6588772.
Registered office:
47 Street Lane, Leeds, West Yorkshire. LS8 1AP

www.scratchingshedpublishing.co.uk

Strike! The Tour That Died of Shame © John Coffey

Unless otherwise stated, all photographs are from the personal collection of John Coffey.

Cover image: Captain Bert Avery, *left*, and vice-captain Neil Mouat did not present a united front for long into the tour.
Back cover: Hec Brisbane kicks ahead at Oldham.

All rights reserved. No copyrighted part of this publication may be reproduced in any form or by any means without the written permission of the publishers.

A catalogue record for this book is available from the British Library.

ISBN 978-0956804365

Typeset in Warnock Pro Semi Bold and Palatino

Printed and bound in the United Kingdom by
L.P.P.S.Ltd, Wellingborough, Northants, NN8 3PJ

Rugby League Classics

Strike! The Tour That Died of Shame is the sixth in a series of historically significant Rugby League Classics, rescued, rebranded and re-issued in paperback, often after having been long out-of-print. Each edition comes complete with the original manuscript intact and contains a wealth of new and updated material, including an introductory overview written by a modern-day expert, evocative photographs, appendices, and the recollections of those closest to the book's primary subject, i.e. family members, former team-mates and other contemporary figures.

In a break with tradition, this particular Rugby League Classic is published as a book for the first time; its contents having originally been the basis for an article in one of Bernie Wood's New Zealand Lion Red Rugby League Annuals.

Scratching Shed Publishing Ltd

Scratching Shed Publishing Limited is an independent publishing company founded in May 2008. We aim to produce high-quality books covering a wide range of subjects, including sport, travel and popular culture, that are of interest to the world, yet which offer a distinctive flavour of the North of England.

The All Blacks' War Cry

A brochure compiled by Fred Marsh of the *Athletic News* and published for the 1926-27 All Blacks tour of Britain included the following rendition of their war cry, 'Tankatan'.

> Te Mapu Racana - ee Ngu - Ngu nei Anu - Anu - Anu - Ha Wacane Takakahia, Ah Takahia Kia Kino Ah, Kinga Keiwaho mantonu.
>
> Tankatan hei hei hei Tankatan Kiumiga ote whira whangaiamara nge - nge - nge - ara tu ara tu ara tan.
>
> Tahi Kariu toru Ka wha Homai okupau Kia wete - wete - a Hi - Ha - He.
>
> Buhi Kuia Kuia Kuia Hi - Ha - He.

It gave the meaning as:

> 'The assembly of the human lions.'
>
> 'They are roaring.'
>
> 'Welcome'.
>
> 'We are going to win.'

Photographs taken of the New Zealanders performing the war cry invariably showed the opposing teams standing behind the tourists rather than facing the challenge, which has generally been the custom.

Contents

Introduction *by John Coffey* ix

Strike! The Tour That Died of Shame
1. James Carlaw's Dream Tour 15
2. The Galloping Clydesdale 31
3. Trials and Tribulations 49
4. The 1926-27 All Blacks 68
5. Mutiny on the High Seas 87
6. 'Smooth as a Billiard Table' 106
7. The Games Begin 117
8. Roller-Coaster Ride 135
9. Seven Men Out 149
10. From Mair to Nightmare 167
11. Torn Apart Forever 188
12. 'Loyalists' Threaten Strike 207
13. Banned for Life 226
14. The Aftermath 248
15. Disqualifications 'Uplifted' 268
16. Statistics 277

Bibliography 284

Members of the New Zealand League Team.

INTRODUCTION

In recent times several cricket tours have been blighted by accusations of match fixing. Over the decades individual players have been sent home from rugby league and rugby union tours for behaving badly. But there has never been, and never will be again, such a tortuous sports tour as that undertaken by the 1926-27 New Zealand rugby league All Blacks in Britain.

Seven of the twelve forwards were involved in an increasingly divisive dispute with manager and coach Ernest Mair, an Australian who had convinced the New Zealand Rugby League (NZRL) that his radical tactics and training methods would inspire the amateur tourists to overcome the British professional club, county and national teams on their home soil.

The tour was controversial from its inception. New South Wales and Queensland rugby league authorities were outraged when New Zealand was invited to visit Britain

Strike! The Tour That Died of Shame

ahead of Australia. They were further angered when the NZRL insisted on sending a truly national team instead of following the pattern of selecting Australasian touring teams. At home, the New Zealand Rugby Union threatened legal action if the NZRL persisted in using the name of All Blacks.

But the eruptions which eventually wrecked the tour were internal, starting with such a seemingly minor matter as to whether the players should pay their own laundry bills out of their weekly allowances. The rift between a group of seven strong-minded forwards and the management widened as the team travelled across two oceans and overland in Canada, so much so that some players requested their return tickets upon arrival at Southampton.

With an increasingly alarmed English Rugby League - which was paying most of the tour costs to assist a destitute NZRL - looking on, and then attempting to mediate, the 1926-27 All Blacks split irretrievably apart. The seven forwards refused to train or play under Mair, meaning that backs had to pack down against rugged, specialist opponents in fourteen of the thirty-four fixtures. No replacements were available. New Zealand was weeks away by boat.

For five games in mid-tour and then for the last nine matches the playing ranks were reduced not only by the 'strikes' but even further by inevitable injuries and illness, sometimes to the bare minimum. Brave men climbed out of their sick beds to make up the numbers. In between those periods, Mair himself relinquished his coaching and selection duties for one month. He claimed he sacrificed himself for the good of the game and his adopted country; his detractors within the touring team and on the English council were adamant he had been suspended.

Similarly, there were accusations the 'malcontents' went on strike a second and final time of their own accord, and counter claims they were locked out and their allowances

Introduction

stopped by a vengeful management. All of this was conducted against the backdrop of a crippling miners' strike in the north of England. The widespread unemployment in rugby league's heartland, and the highly-publicised problems within the New Zealand team, ensured crowds fell below expectations and the game in both nations suffered heavy losses in finances and image.

Meanwhile, the nineteen 'loyal' players soldiered on through a merciless winter. There were many remarkable acts of courage. Individual players made up to thirty appearances in a total of thirty-four matches and backed up for as many as fifteen consecutive games. Starting on Christmas Day, the remnants of the team slogged their way through five games in only ten days while travelling to and from South Wales and throughout Yorkshire and Lancashire on a railway system also severely disrupted by the coal miners' industrial action.

On return to New Zealand after their seven-month odyssey the seven alleged strikers were disqualified for life and told they had no right of appeal. The inquiry was held in camera and all records were buried. When another NZRL council sought to reopen the case in 1962 nothing could be found. The nineteen 'loyal' players were awarded medallions which entitled them to free entry into matches anywhere in New Zealand. They swore an oath never to talk publicly of what had occurred. There were to be no death-bed confessions or explanations.

As a sidelight, the tour coincided with Wigan and several other ambitious and cashed-up clubs seeking to abolish the two-year residential qualification rule which deterred Australian and New Zealand players from joining British clubs. That Wigan were intent on signing three of the All Blacks only hardened the famous club's determination to change the rules. So serious was the situation that Australia and New Zealand threatened to break off all relations with England.

Strike! The Tour That Died of Shame

The main characters in one of sport's most incredible sagas included NZRL president James Carlaw, who dreamed of a successful tour to finance the acquisition of grounds throughout the country, Ernest Mair, the fast-talking Queenslander who took his wife on tour and looked on benignly as she led the team onto English playing fields, Bert Avery, the captain and arguably the finest footballer of his time, and Neil Mouat, appointed vice-captain despite an abrasive background and accused by Mair of leading the mutiny.

In the fall-out from the tour and inquiry, a depressed Carlaw stepped down from his post at the 1927 NZRL annual meeting. Mair was to gain further notoriety in his native Australia. Avery, having set try-scoring records on the tour which will never be bettered by another forward, has been lauded as a legend of the game. Mouat, branded as the chief villain and banned from ever again setting foot inside a rugby league ground, returned to Westport and carved out a successful and varied business career.

In reconstructing what went wrong, the author has gathered match and news reports from many contemporary newspapers in Britain and New Zealand. In an era when coaches were never interviewed after matches, Mair conveniently took time out from his other responsibilities to compile detailed summaries for afternoon newspapers in Auckland and Christchurch, while generally avoiding any revelations about the internal 'troubles'. Despite the so-called oath of silence, All Blacks financial manager George Ponder and some players were provoked into making statements several months after the team returned home.

The author is indebted to Ipswich historian Joy Christison and also Terry Williams, of the New South Wales Rugby League, for finding previously unpublished information on Ernest Mair. British historian and memorabilia collector Richard Bailey unearthed tour programmes which have survived more than eighty years.

Introduction

Bailey and fellow historian Professor Tony Collins supplied information on New Zealand players with English clubs. Former Kiwis captain Don Hammond provided access to scrapbooks and photographs held by the NZRL Museum, of which he is curator. Elspeth Orwin, of Auckland City Libraries, kindly traced and scanned rare tour photographs. New Zealand historians Bernie Wood and Peter Kerridge dug into their files and came up with valuable information and illustrations. And the whole project started when Australian historian Sean Fagan suggested it might be a good idea.

John Coffey, September 2012

John Coffey is New Zealand's most experienced rugby league writer, having covered more than 100 Test matches during 44 years with *The Press* newspaper in Christchurch and as a touring New Zealand Press Association correspondent. His previous books have included *Canterbury XIII* (1987), *Modern Rugby League Greats* (1991), *Being Frank, the Frank Endacott Story* (2002), and major publications to mark the centenaries of the Kiwis (2007), New Zealand Maori Rugby League (2008) and Auckland Rugby League (2009).

Members of the New Zealand League Team.

1

JAMES CARLAW'S DREAM TOUR

New Zealand Rugby League president James Carlaw was a happy man when he learned an invitation had been extended for a national representative team to tour Britain in the 1926-27 northern season. He and his officials had lobbied hard to be invited ahead of the Australians and Carlaw regarded the anticipated tour profits as a means of clearing debt and securing desperately needed grounds around the country.

The lobbying began as early as 1923 when the NZRL decided to press ahead with a plan to request a tour during the 1925-26 British season. The English Rugby League fended off that plea, preferring to wait until the fourth Lions tourists completed their 1924 Australasian campaign before making a decision.

In that era England still ruled the international rugby league scene. The game itself had been born out of the great rugby schism of 1895, when twenty-two powerful Yorkshire and Lancashire clubs broke away from the autocratic London-based Rugby Football Union over the vexed question of making broken-time payments to working-class players who could not afford to take Saturdays from their employment without some compensation.

The originally named Northern Union intended little more than to stage its own fifteen-a-side competitions without being burdened by strict amateur regulations. But it was soon realised that if players were to be paid then the sport had to be made more attractive to spectators. It was not long before the laws were changed to put more emphasis on scoring tries and keeping the ball in play and in sight of the fans in the grandstands.

By the time the 1907-08 New Zealand All Golds arrived to transform rugby league from a regional to an international sport, team numbers had been reduced to thirteen players, lineouts were abolished, all goals were worth only two points (tries remained at three) and play-the-balls had become the distinctive method of restarting the game after a tackle.

The All Golds had stopped over at Sydney en route to Britain, playing three rugby union games and stirring the simmering rugby rebellion in that city. By the time they returned to display the new rugby league rules eight months later the Australians had already launched the Sydney inter-club competition which evolved into the National Rugby League. The All Golds also promoted the breakaway game in Newcastle and Brisbane.

All Golds organiser Albert Baskerville is rightfully revered as the father of international rugby league, but his tragic death from pneumonia in a Brisbane hospital left the game in New Zealand without a natural leader. Many of Baskerville's team members had been signed by British or Australian clubs and the others - all banned for life by the powerful New Zealand Rugby Union - faced a tough task to establish a rival sport in their homeland.

Despite the All Golds having triumphed in three-Test series in both Britain and Australia, it was no surprise that

James Carlaw's Dream Tour

New Zealand was destined to be a poor relation to those two. Huge crowds flocked to Championship and Challenge Cup fixtures in the north of England, where clubs had the money to attract star recruits from Down Under and Wales. Rugby league became the dominant winter sport in Sydney when most of the 1908-09 Wallabies changed their allegiance, and that situation quickly prevailed in country districts and Queensland.

Auckland was an exception. Its own inter-club competition was up and running in 1909 and there was a steady influx of players eager to try the new rugby. But it was proving difficult to lay foundations in other areas. Taranaki and Wellington fielded representative teams against Auckland and each other as early as 1908, when Otago and Southland also met home and away, but it was not until 1912 that rugby league officially joined the winter sporting scene in Christchurch and Wellington.

The Carlaw family - James and his nephews Arthur Edward Carlaw and William Owen (Owie) Carlaw - featured among the rugby league pioneers. Arthur was one of Ponsonby's original players and in 1909 he toured Australia with another privately-organised team. He was to cross the Tasman again with the official New Zealand teams of 1912 and 1913.

Owie Carlaw found his niche in administration. After being the Auckland Rugby League auditor in 1911, he was NZRL treasurer, either side of four years of war service, from 1913 to 1920 and its secretary from 1921 to 1948. Owie's long and dedicated service covered two world wars and extremely difficult economic times.

But James was undoubtedly the elder statesman of the Carlaw clan. Born in Newcastle-upon-Tyne, England, in 1854, he was nine years old when his family immigrated to New Zealand. James was employed by the Auckland City Council for forty-six years, most of them as a waterworks engineer in a rapidly growing city.

Strike! The Tour That Died of Shame

Lawn bowls had been his first sporting passion, but he was soon taking a keen interest in young Arthur's burgeoning football career and readily accepted nominations for high office. James Carlaw served as NZRL president from 1914 to 1919, Auckland Rugby League chairman from 1918 to 1921, and national president again from 1921 until the disastrous 1926-27 tour proved too much for him.

His first great ambition was to establish a headquarters for the game in Auckland, which had relied on leasing Victoria Park and the Domain Cricket Ground for matches against the first two British Lions teams in 1910 and 1914 and had no charge ground for fixtures at provincial and club levels.

By 1914 Carlaw was casting a far-sighted eye over a Chinese market garden in the lee of the Domain and within easy walking distance of the city centre. Carlaw wanted to negotiate a sale but was cautioned to wait until after the war by fellow rugby league enthusiast Arthur Myers, who was then Minister of Munitions.

Carlaw became Auckland Rugby League chairman at war's end with the prime purpose of purchasing the property of Mr Ah Chee, who lived on the land and was an understandably reluctant seller. Again Myers urged a delay, until he could navigate a Bill through Parliament legalising an exchange of land which would allow room for two playing fields.

Carlaw's dream was realised when possession was obtained in January 1921. He and secretary Ivan Culpan oversaw voluntary 'working bees' every Sunday for six months to transform the land into the stadium which was fittingly named Carlaw Park and hosted international, provincial and major club fixtures for the next eighty years. That mission having been accomplished, Carlaw returned to the New Zealand Rugby League presidency.

This time Carlaw had set his sights on sending a national

James Carlaw's Dream Tour

team to Britain and thus retracing the sprig marks of the All Golds. It was an ambitious plan, for not even the Australians had achieved that. Four teams from Down Under had gone 'Home' - as newspapers of the day affectionately referred to England - but none of them were totally representative of New Zealand or Australia.

The All Golds had been privately assembled by Baskerville and famed All Blacks wing George Smith, who invited champion Australian centre and goalkicker Dally Messenger to accompany them.

The 1908-09 original Kangaroos were also privately-organised, by entrepreneur James J Giltinan and renowned cricketer Victor Trumper, and included Australian-domiciled former All Blacks forward Bill Hardcastle. Those tours occurred before the New Zealand and Australian leagues were formed in 1910 and 1924, respectively.

When the 1911-12 and 1921-22 Kangaroos toured Britain they were actually Australasian combinations. Current New Zealand representatives Arthur Francis, George Gillett, Charles Savory and Frank Woodward, plus New Zealand-born forward Con Sullivan, toured in 1911-12. Bert Laing was the sole New Zealander ten years later.

It was also fact that the 'England' teams of 1910, 1914, 1920 and 1924 were bolstered by sturdy Welsh stock. But it was not until after the Second World War that the Lions changed their official name to Great Britain. The New Zealand Rugby League was trailblazing when it advocated the despatching of a fully Kiwi combination to Britain.

Carlaw and his fellow officials had been satisfied with the steady improvement of New Zealand teams against their overseas opponents. The First World War had taken a severe toll on a fledgling sport which had no deep roots and relied on young men to not only play the game but also administer it. New Zealand won one of four home Test matches against the 1919 Australians and Auckland had beaten England in 1920 with a team described by fullback Bill Davidson as being comprised of 'beer truck forwards and racing car backs'.

It rankled that the Australians - then administered by separate parochial state bodies in New South Wales and Queensland - had not arranged Test matches for any of the five New Zealand teams which toured their country between 1911 and 1921. New Zealand was being downgraded as just another state of Australia. Despite repeated requests for international matches, that situation was to exist until the 1948 Kiwis played Tests at Sydney and Brisbane.

Carlaw and company were not impressed that Auckland back Bert Laing was the only New Zealander chosen for the 1921-22 Kangaroos tour. Laing appeared in just ten of the thirty-six fixtures, scoring four tries. At least he played in more games than some of the true-blue Australians. South Sydney forward Ted McGrath approached manager George Ball in England and said he was thinking of writing him a letter asking if he knew he was on the tour, while North Sydney's Clarrie Ives actually wrote to the New South Wales Rugby League post-tour demanding to know why he had played only six times!

In September 1923 Australian newspapers picked up on the NZRL's aspirations of mounting a stand-alone tour. Officials there were in the process of setting up the Australian Rugby League board of control to handle international matters and were confident that in a two-sided contest they would bolt in with the next invitation to send a team to Britain. The rugby league 'Ashes' had been lost, two matches to one, by the 1921-22 Kangaroos but they were convinced Australia would do better than New Zealand against the 1924 Lions.

They were in for a shock, though not only from their own team's inability to regain the Ashes Cup. England won the first Test match 22-3 and the second 5-3, both at the Sydney Cricket Ground, to retain that prize. But New South Wales

James Carlaw's Dream Tour

had won one of their two fixtures against the Lions, who were also beaten by the formidable Queensland and Toowoomba sides up north. Australia then achieved a ten-point victory in the third Test match at Brisbane. The Lions sailed on to New Zealand, where their predecessors had been unbeaten in a total of five Test matches spread over three tours.

On consecutive weekends the Lions accounted for Auckland (24-11) and Auckland Province (28-13) to avenge the shock loss of four years earlier. But alarm bells started ringing in the Australian Rugby League boardroom when New Zealand, fielding a new-look team, led throughout to win 16-8 in the first ever Test match played at Carlaw Park. With 22,000 enraptured fans cheering them on, Carlaw's team had won on Carlaw's ground. No prizes for guessing the identity of the happiest man at the park that afternoon.

Australian jaws dropped when New Zealand clinched the series by winning 13-11 at the Basin Reserve in Wellington four days later. But this time it was far from clear-cut. The Lions led 11-0 at halftime after benefiting from a near gale force wind. When the teams changed ends New Zealand claimed an early unconverted try. A freak converted try followed after a kick rebounded from an upright. It was still 11-8 until the last minute when the British failed to secure a tactical kick and New Zealand centre Hec Brisbane dribbled the ball over the goal-line to level the scores. Fullback Craddock Dufty's conversion won the match 13-11 and the series.

Looking on from afar, the Australians would have noted British complaints about the standard of refereeing in New Zealand. In particular, they contested the legitimacy of two of New Zealand's three tries in the second Test. Tour captain Jonty Parkin, the pivot of the British backline, and great fullback and goalkicker Jim Sullivan were unavailable for the first two Tests, having contracted diphtheria during the voyage from Australia. Restored to health, Parkin and

Strike! The Tour That Died of Shame

Sullivan starred in a 31-18 victory in the third Test in Dunedin. This time co-manager Harry Dannatt praised referee Jim Stevens for his interpretations.

On the eve of their departure from Wellington, the Lions management gave very different statements to journalists. Ted Osborne, who was to be English Rugby League chairman during the 1926-27 All Blacks tour said New Zealand sportsmen had lived up to the high pre-tour opinion he had of them. He was thoroughly complimentary and conciliatory.

But Dannatt was in a different frame of mind. 'I will make this statement,' he said, 'that the treatment we have received in some towns in New Zealand is not likely to bring about any more visits from England. The Chinese footballers have been received with open arms, but the treatment shown by Britishers to Britishers has been disgusting. I do not think there will be any more tours. We had a nice civic reception here at the station - in the rain. We are leaving tomorrow and we will not be sorry.' When asked if he felt the standard of play in New Zealand was as good as that in Australia, Dannett replied, 'No, not by a long way.'

Parkin repeated previous comments that New Zealand standards had improved from his previous experience with the 1920 Lions team. But he inferred if England had been free of illness and injury then the outcome of the Test series would have been different. Playing all three Test matches within eight days, and travelling from Auckland to Wellington and on to Dunedin, also prevented the tourists from having the time for any worthwhile training.

Yet Dannatt's damning comments about the tourists' reception 'in some towns' might have played into Carlaw's hands. The 1924 Lions were among many overseas rugby league visitors annoyed that New Zealand's major sports stadiums were off-limits to them. Because rugby union authorities controlled Athletic Park in Wellington, Lancaster Park in Christchurch and Carisbrook in Dunedin, Parkin

James Carlaw's Dream Tour

and his players were diverted to secondary playing fields. An ongoing controversy over grounds culminated with a right rumpus in Dunedin when local sports enthusiasts tried to stage the third Test match as a promotional vehicle for setting up an Otago Rugby League. Humble Tahuna Park was far from a first-choice, or even a third-choice, venue.

The Otago Rugby Union's hold on Carisbrook was watertight and that was never a possible venue. The Caledonian Ground, Culling Park and Forbury Park were other options which came to nothing. Rugby union authorities even issued a writ to prevent a sympathetic Forbury Park Trotting Club from permitting the Test to be held on its ground, arguing that they held the principle winter lease. Public protest meetings were held against the union's attitude and eventually Tahuna Park was begrudgingly made available provided fees were paid to both the Otago Rugby Union and the Agricultural and Pastoral Association.

The Union also deliberately arranged a counter-attraction between Otago and Southland. But that move backfired when the 14,000 crowd at Tahuna Park was several times bigger than the modest assembly at Carisbrook. Some people were even reported to have left Carisbrook when they heard what was happening at Tahuna Park. An Otago Rugby League was subsequently formed on the wave of publicity generated by the controversy and the incontestable fact that the Test match, although resulting in a loss to New Zealand, proved to be a thoroughly entertaining encounter.

Osborne's favourable opinion of New Zealand evidently prevailed over that of Dannatt, a Hull man who had already served his one-year term as English Rugby League chairman, in recommending where the 1926-27 tour invitation should be directed. Osborne, who hailed from Warrington, could not have been blamed if he subsequently regretted the part he played in choosing New Zealand ahead of Australia. He was to be in the hot seat when the tourists

Strike! The Tour That Died of Shame

caused him and his administration to lose so much sleep, not to mention money. During that troubled time Osborne renewed acquaintances with NZRL councillor George Ponder, who was manager of the 1924 New Zealand Test teams and financial manager of the 1926-27 tourists.

James Carlaw, having carved out a stadium for rugby league in Auckland, was aghast that his sport struggled to find suitable facilities for major fixtures in other parts of the country. The problem had been emphasised repeatedly during the 1924 Lions tour.

Athletic Park was the venue for the very first rugby league game on New Zealand soil, a 1908 benefit match for Albert Baskerville's widowed mother featuring the returning All Golds. But that was also to be the last played at Wellington's main football ground for eighty-two years. Most of Wellington's problems in establishing a rugby league club competition resulted from a reluctance of local bodies to upset the rugby union monopoly.

After being used as a potato patch during the First World War, the multi-purpose Lancaster Park was reopened in 1920 by Dr Henry Thacker as Mayor of Christchurch rather than his dual capacity as president of the Canterbury Rugby League. Thacker announced the ground would be available to all of the city's sportsmen and citizens. Lions matches against New Zealand and Canterbury were held there during that winter, before the gates were locked to rugby league until 1996.

Then there was the extraordinary story of the 1911 New South Wales touring team's match against Hawkes Bay at the Recreation Ground in Napier. Hawkes Bay Rugby Union officials condemned the arrival of the 'professional' code in the province but were not averse to demanding a fee for use of a temporary grandstand which had been erected for a previous fixture. When the demand was not met they had the grandstand dismantled. Upon hearing what had happened, rugby league enthusiasts, sympathetic

James Carlaw's Dream Tour

townspeople and even the New South Wales players assembled at midnight and rebuilt the stand in time for kick-off a few hours later.

Carlaw was aware the 1907-08 All Golds had made a handsome profit while in Britain and Australia, which was shared among the players themselves. Their contracts had been similar to those drawn up for early Australian cricket tours of England. The All Golds each stumped up the sizeable sum of £50 towards the tour costs and reaped the benefits of their success. The NZRL was formed in 1910 at the behest of Northern Union authorities who needed a comparable organisation to liaise with about the pioneering Lions tour.

But Carlaw should also have been aware that Giltinan, the promoter of the first Kangaroos tour a year later, had gone bankrupt. Those 1908-09 Kangaroos struck what was described as 'the blackest northern winter in years'. They battled their way through forty-six matches in ice, snow and rain. A general strike had closed down the cotton mills of Lancashire and Yorkshire and a big percentage of the working population was laid idle with no money to spend on such luxuries as attending sporting fixtures.

There were varying reports circulating about the financial outcome of the 1911-12 Australasian tour of Britain, ranging from an overall loss of £400 to a small profit. If there was indeed a surplus it was insufficient to pay bonuses to the twenty-two Australian and four New Zealand players. More likely, Carlaw would have been dazzled by the success of the third Kangaroos in 1921-22, the team which included Aucklander Bert Laing. Despite losing the Ashes, they returned home with a handsome profit of £6197, and the individual players took home bonuses of £150 each. It was surely those figures upon which Carlaw based his estimate of what a tour to Britain could provide for the game in New Zealand.

Even before the English and Welsh were reminded of

Strike! The Tour That Died of Shame

New Zealand's rugby prowess by the deeds of the unbeaten 1924-25 rugby union All Blacks, Carlaw was convinced a rugby league tour of Britain was the means of raising money which could be channelled to districts seeking to establish their own grounds. He reasoned that with the English Rugby League offering such favourable terms, the players being paid a set allowance while on tour and no post-tour bonus, there could be a surplus of £7000 for that purpose.

The NZRL was in no position to make even modest loans to its affiliates. On occasions loans were financed by individual officials making personal contributions at council meetings. Indeed, so poor was the governing body and so successful was the embryo Otago Rugby League under livewire secretary Harry Divers, who had organised a substantial lottery, that the latter was able to make the NZRL a loan of £847. That, Carlaw and his councillors expected, was also to be repaid by the profits from touring Britain. Ironically, the sport in Otago faded into recess a few years later with the NZRL still in its debt.

When Carlaw began agitating for New Zealand's tour invitation he had no idea that rugby league in his country was about to experience the biggest influx of prominent rugby union players since the formation of the All Golds team almost twenty years earlier. By the end of 1924 the depth of talent was considerably greater than it had been twelve months earlier.

Perhaps significantly, four of the pivotal figures in the strife which disrupted the 1926-27 tour had previously thumbed their noses at rugby union officialdom when changing codes. Canterbury forwards Bill Devine and Lou Petersen and West Coasters Neil Mouat and Jack Wright became rugby league players during the infamous Payne Trophy Affair which killed off the Marist rugby union clubs in Christchurch and Greymouth.

Marist was so dominant in the Canterbury Rugby Union senior competition that it had won fifty-eight and drawn

James Carlaw's Dream Tour

one of its sixty-two matches over three seasons. In 1923 that dominance was further emphasised when the club won all five open grade championships. Christchurch publican and Canterbury union committee member George Payne, who was also a Marist man, donated a trophy to be contested by the champion clubs of Canterbury and Otago. Payne unwittingly triggered a time bomb.

Between the end of the local competition and the scheduled date for the Payne Trophy fixture Marist gained two more top-line players. Bill Devine was a policeman who had been transferred to Christchurch and Harry Mullins, who had played for Marist in the past and been close to All Blacks honours, returned to the club after working in Wellington during the winter.

Just as that news became common knowledge, the Canterbury union received a letter from Otago recommending a qualification rule for the Payne Trophy making players ineligible if they had made less than three appearances for their clubs during the season proper. Years later a newspaper investigation revealed Otago had been tipped off about Devine and Mullins by Samuel Wilson, who in 1923 was not only chairman of the Canterbury union but president of the New Zealand Rugby Union. Wilson was a stalwart of Albion, a fierce rival of Marist.

Marist stubbornly refused to replace Devine and Mullins in its announced team and relations with the Canterbury union quickly soured. Canterbury replaced Marist with Merivale, which suffered to a 27-3 thrashing by University, the Otago champion. As the wrangle became more heated Wilson's union suspended Marist and demanded an apology for the tone of the club's letter refusing to drop the contentious twosome.

The stalemate dragged on until April 1924, when Marist's affiliation to the Canterbury union was cancelled. Next day, a record attendance at the Marist Old Boys Association annual meeting voted unanimously to set up rugby league and soccer clubs, entering seven teams in each of those codes.

The Canterbury Rugby League overnight found itself with a powerful new club bringing with it an influx of potential representative players. Marist Old Boys proved to be very competitive, winning Canterbury championships in 1924 and 1925, losing out to Hornby in 1926 and 1927, then winning again in 1928. The club was to last only until the 1930 season but lingering resentment continued between the Catholic Church and the Canterbury Rugby Union. The name Marist did not reappear in the latter's competitions until 1945.

Various selectors were keen to give the Marist men their chances at representative levels. Before the 1924 season was over six Marist players had worn the Kiwis emblem against England: Bill Devine, the unrelated Charles Fitzgerald and Ted Fitzgerald, Terry Gilroy, Harry Mullins and All Black Lou Petersen. All but Ted Fitzgerald appeared in the second Test team which clinched the series over the Lions at Wellington. The Fitzgeralds, Gilroy and Mullins were all backs who could not withstand the challenges of northern rivals for future New Zealand selections. Club-mate Jack Ellis, a forward, toured Australia in 1925.

Another outcome of the Payne Trophy controversy was the formation of the Greymouth Marist Rugby League Club. Marist had beaten the Kiwi club in Hokitika in the opening round of the 1924 West Coast rugby union season a few days before Christchurch Marist's affiliation was cancelled by the Canterbury union. Greymouth Marist promptly seceded from the West Coast union. On 19 April the same team that had beaten Kiwi at rugby union two weeks earlier made its rugby league debut with a 13-8 loss to Runanga. Star forward Neil Mouat seamlessly adjusted from one code to the other and marched imperiously into the New Zealand team, where he was to be joined by fellow forward Jack Wright in 1926.

James Carlaw's Dream Tour

There was controversy of another kind in Auckland leading up to the club championship final between Marist and Devonport in late September 1924. Outstanding rugby union centre Jack Kirwan, considered unlucky not to have been chosen for the All Blacks tour of Britain, had switched to rugby league and was rushed into the Marist line-up for the big showdown. More than 17,000 fans flocked to Carlaw Park to watch Kirwan play a prominent role in Marist's 20-17 victory. The *Auckland Star* accused the club of lacking sportsmanship by playing the new recruit. Kirwan, grandfather of future All Blacks and Auckland Warriors wing John Kirwan, made his New Zealand debut in Australia in 1925 and was to be a team-mate of Devine, Petersen, Mouat and Wright in Britain in 1926-27.

Rugby union was still the major source of proven footballing talent for rugby league scouts in the 1920s, as much out of necessity as anything else. The rugby union exerted a powerful influence over the school winter sporting scene, while using the threat of life bans to deter adult players from code jumping. Any who did, whether motivated by monetary inducements, the disappointment of missing out on national or provincial selections, or attracted by rugby league's boast that it was a more open and enjoyable game, knew they were at the point of no return when they signed on.

It was not quite all one-way traffic. Brilliant centre Karl Ifwersen, whose international rugby league career extended from 1913 until 1920 and was described by renowned All Black Mark Nicholls as 'the greatest footballer New Zealand has ever produced', had been granted a rugby union reinstatement in 1921. Ifwersen was chosen for the deciding third Test against the Springboks at Athletic Park but even his unique talents could not conquer a sodden playing field in a scoreless draw. He was subsequently ruled out of the 1924-25 All Black Invincibles because the Rugby Football Union in England would not accept a former rugby league player. By 1926 Ifwersen was an Auckland rugby union selector.

Such had been the turnover of international players in the early 1920s that only Bert Avery, Frank Delgrosso and Jim Sanders of the twenty players from the 1921 New Zealand team which toured Australia also made the 1926-27 trip to Britain. But there were to be only six debutants among that twenty-six. The other seventeen players had been given international experience during the 1924 home series against England, on the 1925 tour of Australia and in two home fixtures against Queensland later that year.

The results achieved in that period, with the exception of the Queensland section of the 1925 tour, encouraged Carlaw and those he consulted that New Zealand was capable of mounting a strong challenge to the British. New Zealand had the better of New South Wales but had bowed to Queensland. However, Queensland had also beaten the 1924 Lions and dominated New South Wales, winning ten of eleven matches at one stage. The northern state was enjoying an unprecedented run of success with a remarkably powerful playing roster drawn from the Brisbane, Ipswich and Toowoomba city and district leagues.

Carlaw was indeed a contented man. The invitation from the English Rugby League had been received and accepted and the playing ranks were such that many in the game were convinced the two-one Test series win achieved by the All Golds could at least be replicated. What is more, New Zealand was to be guided by a coach who claimed his revolutionary tactics would bedazzle and bewilder the British. He was Ernest Hartley Mair, a product of that great Queensland nursery.

2

THE GALLOPING CLYDESDALE

Queensland city Toowoomba was the centre of the rugby league universe in 1924 and 1925, as its representative team, the Galloping Clydesdales, fashioned an unbeaten record against England, New Zealand, New South Wales, Victoria, fierce Bulimba Cup rivals Ipswich and Brisbane, and Sydney champion Souths. The Queensland state team was also riding the crest of a wave, winning ten of eleven matches against New South Wales over four seasons from 1922. Rugby league ruled in the north, for the Queensland Rugby Union had gone into recess in 1916 and did not re-emerge until 1929.

Ernest Hartley Mair, originally from Ipswich before becoming a prominent hotelier in Toowoomba, revelled in the midst of all this success. Born on 15 January 1891 of a Scottish father and English mother, Mair's own sporting prowess was displayed in the swimming pool. He did play rugby league for the St Paul's club as a young man but was destined to be far more heavily involved as an administrator and sponsor, before revealing ambitions to be recognised as a coach.

Strike! The Tour That Died of Shame

Mair was a busy man in and out of the pool. In 1923, as president of the Toowoomba Swimming Association, he not only announced that American Olympic Games medallist William Harris would compete in the city but included himself in a team of local swimmers chosen to race against the distinguished visitor. Five years later, Mair was president of the Queensland Amateur Swimming Association when he welcomed home the Queensland competitors from another Olympics.

His interests extended beyond sport. In 1919 an Ipswich news item in the *Brisbane Courier* reported 'Messrs J Shaw and E H Mair supervised the dancing' during the City Viceregal Band's annual ball at the Town Hall. He had been working for at least the previous six years as a monoline operator for the *Queensland Times* newspaper, which explains his subsequent awareness of the media and how it could promote his profile.

On 24 January 1920 Mair married Mildred Readshaw in Ipswich and his fortunes, and occupation, immediately took an upward turn. Over the next few years Ernest and Mildred Mair were associated with the Caledonian, Empire and Globe hotels in Toowoomba. In 1923 they sold the Empire Hotel for £4000 as a prelude to holidaying in Honolulu. Mair purchased the freehold of the Globe Hotel on his return, renovated it throughout, renamed it the New Globe Hotel, and resold the property for a handsome £16,000 three years later.

Newspaper journalists would have quickly learned that the former monoline operator turned licensed victualler was a more than useful go-to man when there was need for a good story. Within two weeks in January 1924 Mair was able to tell them that two more famous sporting figures were heading for Toowoomba.

One was Arne Borg, the Swedish swimmer who was to go on and break thirty-two world records and strike Olympic gold during his career. He was accompanied by

The Galloping Clydesdale

Australian Olympic representative Keith Kirkland. The *Brisbane Courier* told its readers on the day after the Toowoomba swim meet that 'Mr Mair motored Messrs Borg and Kirkland around the beauty spots.' After visiting a school, 'Messrs Borg and Kirkland were entertained by Mr Mair at afternoon tea at the Picnic Point kiosk. Thence the party motored to Webb Park, the Quarries and Stony Pinch and back to the Botanic Gardens' (where) 'Borg saw emus and kangaroos for the first time'.

Even more significant was the announcement that prodigal son Duncan Thompson was returning to Queensland to continue his distinguished football career. Five years younger than Mair, Thompson also hailed from Ipswich and had also been a junior player with the St Paul's Church of England club. Mair had worn the St Paul's colours in rugby league and swimming, and in 1924 was pleased to have himself described in newspapers as 'for many years a close friend of the crack footballer'.

Thompson had worked for the Australian Bank of Commerce in Ipswich until transferred to Sydney where he inspired the North Sydney club to its only premierships in 1921 and 1922. He was a star of the 1921-22 Kangaroos in Britain and was widely regarded as the best scrum-half in the world. Having captained New South Wales against his state of birth for four seasons, Thompson was angry when he believed he was the victim of a controversial sending-off and subsequent unjustified suspension in a Sydney club match. He vowed to return north and further bolster the Maroons in inter-state competition against the Blues.

But Thompson did not go back to Ipswich. Instead, he headed for Toowoomba, where he was to play out his last three seasons for the then princely sum of £400 per year. When Mair alerted journalists of Thompson's new allegiance he was serving as president of the Valley club, not as an official Toowoomba district league spokesman. That he had such inside knowledge suggests Mair was sponsoring

Strike! The Tour That Died of Shame

Thompson's transition from Sydney bank clerk to Toowoomba sports store proprietor. Mair had taken a firm grip of Thompson's coat tails.

The *Brisbane Courier* chortled that by having Thompson at Toowoomba and fellow international inside back Jimmy Craig at Ipswich Queensland would boast 'the two greatest halves in Australia. Queensland League football last season reached the highest standard in its history, and the advent of Thompson ought to very nearly guarantee success against the Englishmen'.

While the thirteen-a-side code was introduced to Brisbane in 1908 and Ipswich by 1910, the Toowoomba league was not formed until 1919. It had made extraordinary progress to become such a force in a very short time. Thompson was an inspiring captain and playmaker but sole selector Bill 'King' Renwick could also call upon other legendary figures such as Dan Dempsey, Tom Gorman, Herb Steinohrt, Jim Bennett, Vic Armbruster, Mick Madsen, Bill Spencer and Edwin 'Nigger' Brown. (The latter, a fair-haired centre, derived his nickname from the brand of polish he used on his trademark shiny black shoes).

Toowoomba's greatest occasion was the Wednesday in June 1924 that 10,000 fans arrived on special trains from Brisbane, Wallangarra, Killarney, Chinchilla, Pittsworth and Clifton, and by motor cars, sulkies and motor cycles to pack the Athletic Oval and cheer on their champions against England. The Lions had reclaimed the Ashes with victories in the first two Test matches but Darling Downs folk were convinced their team was stronger than the Kangaroos. They were not disappointed as Toowoomba led 23-12 before holding on to win 23-20.

'The match will probably be talked about when the smallest boy who saw it will be white with the snows of time,' said the *Toowoomba Chronicle*. Mayor Doug Annand coined one of the game's great one-liners by saying, 'The men played like galloping clydesdales'. The name stuck and was acclaimed

The Galloping Clydesdale

with pride as Toowoomba fashioned its two-year unbeaten record against all-comers until Thompson and some of the other stars retired or moved on. The nickname was resurrected when Thompson coached Toowoomba to six consecutive Bulimba Cup triumphs over Brisbane and Ipswich in the 1950s and again when the city's Queensland Cup team served as a feeder club to the Brisbane Broncos from 1999 to 2006.

Mair was in his element among all this reflected glory. The after-match celebrations as one victory followed another would have been good for the hotel business, and he was not only chairing meetings at the Valley club but also the Toowoomba Junior Rugby League. Not content with all that, Mair aspired to greater administrative office.

When the Australian Rugby League board of control was constituted in December 1924 to handle international matters, Mair was not one of the three appointed Queensland delegates. But he found another door to the board room. In short time Mair convinced the NZRL that he was just the man to represent its interests across the Tasman and he was never shy to remind journalists and others of his 'official' position when making announcements.

However, in none of those roles was Mair known to be actively involved with coaching. In hindsight, he was a rookie when he assumed control of the New Zealand team in 1925. But the fast-talking Mair obviously believed he had learned enough from the man he regarded as the master, Duncan Thompson, to create a winning team -- and when he felt his time was right he persuaded NZRL officials that his scant credentials were good enough.

Thompson was credited with devising 'contract football', a system which required each player to pledge his support to his team-mates. 'A champion team must be almost obsessed with teamwork. Individual brilliance is expendable,' said the most brilliant player of the era. 'Contract football is flowing football. It has no relation to bash and barge. The player does not die with the ball. It moves on and on, ideally no ball carrier is so smothered that he must play the ball.'

One can imagine Mair spending countless hours with Thompson, absorbing every word from the lips of the maestro and watching his every move in tactical sessions with the Toowoomba team on the training field and around the blackboard. The importance of fitness and stamina would not have been lost on Mair, who was still confident enough in his own fitness levels to compete against overseas swimming champions when into his thirties.

It is not known what prompted Mair to spread the Thompson coaching gospel to New Zealand. As a keen young sportsman, he might have made the trip into Brisbane to see the pioneering All Golds bring rugby league to Queensland in 1908. He would have watched the 1913 and 1919 New Zealand teams achieve their wins over Ipswich, and the 1921 side lose to Toowoomba. The inexperienced 1922 New Zealand Maori touring team also played at, and was beaten by, Ipswich and Toowoomba.

By the time another full New Zealand side returned to Queensland Mair was very much attached to it. Indeed, it was he who announced the 1925 All Blacks - as the NZRL insisted they be called - were coming. This was to be the last tour organised by the New South Wales Rugby League. Queensland officials were initially annoyed at the financial terms offered them and refused to be involved. But in June Mair told reporters the New Zealanders would play four matches in August - against Queensland, Toowoomba and Ipswich and 'it is probable a match will be arranged against Australia in Brisbane'. He also said efforts were being made to stage a Test match in Sydney.

It transpired that the proposed Tests in Brisbane and Sydney became a second game against Queensland and a fourth encounter with New South Wales. Even the persuasive Mair could not hasten the resumption of trans-Tasman Tests on Australian soil.

The Galloping Clydesdale

Mair met up with the New Zealand team in Sydney and featured in several of the traditional team photographs at the Cricket Ground. The most significant shot was that of Mair taken with financial manager Nelson Culpan, team manager Jim Wingham, coach Charles Pearce, captain Bert Laing and vice-captain Bert Avery. In the photograph Pearce is positioned looming up behind Mair, but the order should have been reversed. Before the itinerary was completed Mair had been installed as coach and Pearce was making an early return to New Zealand. Mair presented the NZRL with a montage of the photographs, prominently featuring a studio portrait of himself.

Pearce was a student of the game and wrote extensively of its foundations in New Zealand for the Auckland *Rugby League News*. Unlike Mair, his reputation had been earned on the field of play. Pearce represented Canterbury and South Island at rugby union before answering Albert Baskerville's call to the All Golds. In Britain alone he appeared in thirty of the matches, including all three Tests, and was a mainstay of the forward pack. Pearce captained New Zealand in one of the three Tests against Australia on the homeward journey before finding himself in a football limbo - banned for life by the rugby union authorities who had branded him a professional - when his adopted code was slow to get started in Christchurch.

He was destined to be a pioneer again in 1912, captaining Canterbury against Wellington at the Addington Show Grounds in the first rugby league match staged in Christchurch and also leading Addington in the inaugural Canterbury inter-club competition in 1913. Pearce proved the layoff had not made him rusty, earning New Zealand honours against New South Wales that season. After that he redirected his energies towards coaching, selecting teams and in administration. Pearce was one of the Canterbury pioneers awarded life membership of the NZRL in March 1920.

Strike! The Tour That Died of Shame

In modern times it would have been a media sensation for any national sports team to leave New Zealand under the guidance of a coach regarded as a pillar of the game, only to return with someone else in control, and an Australian at that. But there were no headlines, not even a down-page paragraph added as an after-thought, to inform the public that Mair had displaced Pearce at Ipswich.

When Pearce, Laing, veteran hooker Sam Lowrie and second-row forward Horace Dixon left Sydney for New Zealand by the *Maheno* there was still no fanfare. Nothing more than a sentence at the bottom of a match report. Pearce either offered to, or was given the task of, escorting three of the casualties of an increasingly injury-hit tour. A sturdily-built stand-off half, Laing, then aged thirty-three, had captained his team only during the early stages of the tour. At thirty-six years of age, Lowrie was also nearing the end of a distinguished hooking career. Dixon had missed the last two games in Queensland.

For Pearce, his demise must have been especially heart-wrenching. The 1925 tour started with characteristic optimism and considerable success. This was the first team since 1908 to have the better of New South Wales, winning two of the three games when Pearce was coach and the fourth under Mair. It was customary for New South Wales officials to pitch their top side against New Zealand teams before they could recover from the often rough and debilitating sea crossings. Even the Sydney scribes considered New Zealand unfortunate to lose 7-4 in the tour opener and in midweek there was a 15-13 loss to a strong Combined Universities combination.

Pearce's players then found their land legs, defeating Newcastle and Maitland district 29-11 before returning to Sydney to beat New South Wales 21-13 and 17-10. They displayed great defensive tenacity, an increasingly more effective attack, and considerable spirit to recover from an eight-point deficit in the third state match. As was the

The Galloping Clydesdale

custom of the time, they were reported to have won the 'Ashes'. But, for the first time in eight visits, the real test of New Zealand rugby league standards lay north of the Tweed River.

Queensland, with Toowoomba twosome Duncan Thompson and Tom Gorman ruling the midfield, outclassed a below-strength New Zealand 43-19 at Brisbane's Exhibition Oval. To put the result into context, Queensland had put paid to England 25-10 a year earlier. But that lopsided scoreline was enough for Mair to relieve Pearce of the coaching clipboard.

It would be surprising if Mair had not already carried out some groundwork with managers Culpan, the NZRL treasurer, and Wingham, the West Coast Rugby League president, for the coaching coup was completed between the Queensland game on 1 August and the match against Ipswich just four days later. Culpan would surely have consulted NZRL president James Carlaw and other members of the national council before confirming Mair as the new coach. The media wire services never picked it up, but Mair himself confirmed exactly when the changeover occurred in an article he penned for the *Rugby League News* on 29 August.

'Since taking charge of the team at Ipswich I have spent the best time of my sporting career,' wrote Mair. 'I found the boys relished nightly lectures on tactics, with and without a blackboard. They have taken to the new system of tactics like a duck to water and have, fortunately for the game in New Zealand, realised to the very full how necessary it is to continue with the tactics that have made Toowoomba and Queensland such wonderful sides.'

Mair's men promptly lost to Ipswich, Queensland in the return match and Toowoomba as they struggled to cope with their long injury list and the very hard grounds. This was the first New Zealand team to leave the northern state without a win. But, considering the quality of the opposition, the scorelines were more than respectable and the performances encouraging. Ipswich won 22-21 through a last-minute try, Queensland was held to 29-20, and Toowoomba went close to having its proud winning sequence broken. The 'Galloping Clydesdales' won 16-14 when New Zealand goalkicker Craddock Dufty managed only one conversion to complement the two tries each scored by Frank Delgrosso and Bert Avery.

Any chance of New Zealand meeting Australia in official Test matches at Brisbane and Sydney, as Mair had hoped almost two months earlier, undoubtedly went with that first loss to Queensland. Instead, there was consolation when New South Wales was edged out 19-18 back in Sydney, in a contest which according to the Press Association 'scintillated with sparkling rushes whenever the Blacks handled the ball'.

Forwards Neil Mouat, who kicked five goals and sent scrum-half Stan Webb across for what proved to be the match-winning try, and English-born Frank Henry were singled out for special commendation. The *Star* in Christchurch later published a comment from Australian sources which claimed 'Mouat and Henry are credited with being two of the best forwards of either code of rugby who have played in New South Wales and Queensland'.

In a bizarre conclusion to the itinerary, the New Zealanders went bush by travelling on an overnight train to Cootamundra. There they lost 26-25 to Southern Districts after the local referee caned them 28-3 in the penalty count. Having expressed strong dissatisfaction with the referee's rulings, the tourists climbed back on the train for Sydney to face the prospect of four more uncomfortable days on the turbulent Tasman Sea.

So Mair arrived in Auckland with a record of only one win from five games, tasked with producing a competitive New Zealand team to confront Queensland in two fixtures at Carlaw Park. First, there was the matter of a warm-up

The Galloping Clydesdale

game against Auckland and he and his supporters must have been buoyed when New Zealand won by an impressive 41-17. Two of the players who had captained the side in Laing's absence, loose forward Avery and stand-off half Maurice Wetherill, crossed for three tries apiece and Dufty was back on form with seven goals.

'The chief trouble with New Zealand football is that it has clung to the orthodox for too long,' wrote Mair after that match. 'When Queensland comes over they will rely on their present successful system of tactics, and our only way of whacking them is to meet them with their own game.' He claimed the New Zealand players were now committed disciples of the Toowoomba tactics as employed by Thompson and company.

'If every man does his duty it would wipe away that great mental strain that teams suffer from when they know there is a player in the side that has a big tendency to let his man through. We lost the second game against Queensland and also the game at Toowoomba principally to this,' wrote Mair. His philosophy was pinched straight from Thompson's coaching manual.

Having dealt with tactics, fitness and mental preparation, Mair stressed how important it was to have 'the right type' of man in his teams. 'Far better (to) have a player of the right type (though) not quite as good, in preference to the better player if the latter sows seeds of discontent and does not carry the manly bearing that prevents his comrades putting him on their own plane.' In his long-winded way Mair was threatening to discard anyone who did not dance to his tune.

He wrote that New Zealand was desperately in need of a scrum-half who could play the role of Duncan Thompson in individual attacking skills and ability to make play for his outside men. Mair's praise for New Zealand team incumbent Wilson Hall was conditional that he be 'coached properly for the next few years'. He felt the other scrum-half on the Australian tour, Stan Webb, was better suited to the centres. Mair advocated that Maurice Wetherill, who had filled in at scrum-half when Hall and Webb had been injured, should move there permanently.

'Duncan Thompson and I have a high opinion of Wetherill as the makings of a fine half - he certainly filled the breach in Australia at a minute's notice splendidly - but the fact that he hates the position makes it unwise to ever think of him playing there again,' Mair said. Maybe it was the implied threat of playing at scrum-half which subsequently persuaded the gifted Wetherill to withdraw from the 1926-27 tour to Britain. Once Mair was out of the picture Wetherill returned to captain New Zealand in all three Tests against the 1928 Lions.

'New Zealand is rich in football natural ability, but she will never reach the great heights of which she is capable until she rings out the old bell of "orthodoxy" and rings in the new,' concluded Mair in what was the first of several long weekly articles in the *Rugby League News*. His byline described him as 'Official Coach to the N.Z. Rugby League'.

Word had eventually begun to seep into New Zealand newspapers of the coaching change during the Australian tour. A comment by West Coaster Jim Wingham in the *Grey River Argus* also testified to the indelible impression Mair had made on the touring managers.

'There is no doubt that the success of the northern state (Queensland) is due to the able management of its affairs, and in that respect they have two very fine men in Mr Mair and (Queensland Rugby League secretary and representative team manager) Mr (Harry) Sutherland. The former is the delegate for New Zealand in New South Wales on the board of management and he will be visiting the Coast with the Queensland team. This man is a football genius,' said Wingham.

A day later, the *Argus* made another favourable mention of Mair: 'During the latter portion of the Australian tour he

The Galloping Clydesdale

acted as coach and lecturer to the New Zealand team and effected wonders in condition and tactics. It is safe to assert that had the team had his services from the commencement of the tour better results would have been attained. This expert will be visiting the Coast and the local centre would be well advised to arrange for a lecture to all players under the league code. Tactics, systematic training, massage etc are the most important adjuncts to the modern rugby.'

(As it happened, Mair never made it to the West Coast nor to any venue except Carlaw Park during the Queensland tour. He coached New Zealand on consecutive weekends and observed and involved himself in Queensland's midweek match against Auckland. Then, having secured his appointment to coach and co-manage the 1926-27 New Zealand team in Britain, he returned to Australia).

The *New Zealand Truth* had hailed Mair as a Messiah in football boots after the 41-17 victory of the 'All Black touring team' over Auckland. Though Mair had no known background as a top-level player or coach, the anonymous *Truth* scribe described him as 'a past master'.

'The tourists for the past three weeks back have had the benefit of the coaching of Mr H (sic) Mair, who came over from Queensland, and if ever any game has benefited by the services of a past master it is League football in Auckland. And when it has benefited in the north it is only a matter of time when the good results of the expert tuition will spread.

'It has always been acknowledged by those in a position to judge that the outstanding fault in the game played in this country has been the entire absence of anything novel or unorthodox. The game had got into a groove, as it were, and nobody saw this plainer than did Mr Mair. Consequently he set about remedying the defect, and this he has accomplished to an extent that must have exceeded the most sanguine expectations.'

According to the *Truth*, the familiar conservative style of orthodox passing and frequent kicking adopted by

Strike! The Tour That Died of Shame

Auckland proved ineffective against the reverse passing and positional switches by the All Blacks. 'The new style of play added untold interest to the exposition, and the endless variety of moves adopted by the winners always left their opponents guessing and the spectators on the tip-toe of expectancy. It was a great display of the game and put it in a new light in the eyes of the fans.'

Rugby League News editor Tom Avery also praised his contributor. 'In the words of coach E H Mair, whose slogan to the New Zealand players is "Don't Kick", the best and quickest way of making the League game in New Zealand the premier code is to give New Zealanders spectacular football! He took a big risk in attempting to change the social system of New Zealand rugby league football, but the way the players have adapted his ideas and the confidence the New Zealand Council have in him should recompense him for all the work he has put in.'

But not everything written about Mair was glowing. Displaced coach Charles Pearce privately jotted down his own predictions for the 1926-27 tourists and did not hide what he thought of Mair and those who had appointed him as coach. 'The majority of the heads of the NZ Rugby League council have the new complaint (of) Mair-itis. Those in the know…say he is all "heifer dust",' wrote Pearce. His prophetic words that the tour was headed for disaster did not come to light until more than eighty years later.

However, that 'heifer dust' initially took on a golden hue when New Zealand roared back from a fourteen-point halftime deficit to upset the vaunted Queenslanders 25-24, the result being clinched by Frank Delgrosso's penalty goal right on fulltime. 'At the opening of the second half, and from that point onwards, the game was a continuous sensation,' reported the Press Association.

Mair's revolutionary tactics had produced five tries to Queensland's four and the visitors made no complaint at being frequently penalised for scrummaging and off-side

The Galloping Clydesdale

illegalities. Queensland dominated the legitimate scrums and the New Zealanders were staunch in their defence against a team which - even without Duncan Thompson - was decades later still being described by many who had seen them as the finest to visit New Zealand.

During the week Mair looked on as Auckland grabbed its own piece of history by drawing 18-18 with Queensland. Outstanding Auckland loose forward and captain Bert Avery claimed two more tries to add to the two he had scored for New Zealand in the first 'Test'. There were no interviews with Mair after either match but he shared his thoughts with all who bought the match programme published for the second 'Test'.

'This is the chrysalis period for the trip to England next year,' he wrote. 'The New Zealand players have christened me their "Rock of Gibraltar", but all the success attending the efforts of the teams representing the Dominion is due to the players, for had it not been for their wonderful enthusiasm and loyalty to me it would not have been possible to have secured the results of the last two matches. Certainly no side in the history of New Zealand rugby league ever took the field more confident, more happy or fitter than the present side.'

'Twenty-six New Zealand players have to be selected to go to England next year and if type and physical fitness are taken into consideration when the ability of the players is being gone over the tour will be a success. Many columns appeared in Australian newspapers of the unwiseness of sending a New Zealand team to England, no doubt inspired by people who have an axe to grind. They short-sightedly judged the standard of New Zealand football by the results of the recent touring party and never made allowances for the many unfortunate occurrences that would have marred the success of any touring side.'

Yet again Mair emphasised the right 'type' of player was required, 'for one white ant will shake the foundations of a team's success'. He announced his intention to spend two months in both the North and South islands during the first half of the 1926 season searching for the talents and temperaments needed to conquer England. He reiterated that the twelve weeks he had spent with the New Zealand players - 'a perfect happy family' - in Australia and Auckland had been the most enjoyable of his sporting career.

Mair was confident New Zealand would beat Queensland in the return fixture at Carlaw Park, the third showdown for many of the players within one week. He planned to counter Queensland's ascendancy in the scrums by replacing Auckland hooker Neville St George with former rugby union All Black Alphonsus Carroll from Wellington. But Carroll sent Mair a telegram regretting he could not travel because of work commitments and St George was reinstated to the pack. Queensland blitzed New Zealand 35-14, scoring the last seventeen points as the home side wilted under pressure.

There was a markedly different tone to Mair's summery in the next issue of the *Rugby League News*. He reminded readers that his prediction of victory had been based on having Carroll at hooker and the expectation that 'certain New Zealand players would be occupying positions most suitable for them. Both these things missed fire. On Friday Carroll wired that his man did not turn up to relieve him and that he was unable to come. Secondly, the players took the field in positions different to where I would have placed them and, furthermore, were persevered with instead of being changed at halftime.'

He then revealed an interesting insight to the contemporary workings of New Zealand teams playing at home, and the role of the coach. Contrary to modern practice, the coach's influence effectively ended when the players ran onto the field. Any mid-match or halftime variations were left to the captain and selectors to implement. Mair was angry at the system then in operation.

The Galloping Clydesdale

'It was my privilege to watch the games on the recent Australian tour and I should have a fair idea of the right positions to play players in. I did appreciate the action of the three Auckland selectors on the Wednesday in allowing me the privilege of shifting Delgrosso to the halfback position at halftime in that game, for it proved the principal factor in the second spell that secured the draw and nearly victory.

'Last Saturday our team were like the thirteens in many cases that represented New Zealand in Australia this season. They were under a mental strain right through the game, and it became so acute in the second half that it put them off their game. It was anyone's game (at 18-14 during the second half). Then came the Maroon avalanche over the last third and our players went to pieces.'

Mair did not accompany the Queenslanders when they went south to rack up mammoth scores against provincial and combined teams. Instead, he boarded the *Maheno* bound for Australia. But not before he had met with James Carlaw and the other NZRL councillors, who 'unanimously' extended his term as New Zealand coach to embrace the 1926-27 tour of Britain. Provinces other than Auckland had cause to feel somewhat aggrieved that Mair did not take the opportunity to see their top players in action against Queensland, or even familiarise himself with the state of the game in their districts.

While aboard the *Maheno*, and suffering from seasickness, Mair was still brooding that the dressing room door had been closed to him at halftime during the two-match Queensland series. In particular, that decisive loss in the second 'Test' - 'when my tactics were not considered wise by the selectors, and the unfortunate result is now a memory. At the very least a coach should have the same power as one of the selectors. I had won the confidence of the players, had made them happy, and they were enthusiastic about their work,' he wrote.

Mair had received an assurance from the NZRL that he

Strike! The Tour That Died of Shame

would be one of the selectors in 1926, along with Ces Hardingham, Thomas 'Scotty' McClymont and Dick Stirling. 'Naturally, before devoting such time away from my various businesses in Australia for the benefit of rugby league football in New Zealand, it was only reasonable that I should know where I stood,' wrote Mair. He was obviously looking forward to having sole command when challenging the best of Britain. And not just Britain either, as the following paragraph testified.

'As I always held up the trip to England as an inspiration to the boys when giving them lectures, so by the same plane will I live to achieve the greatest of my ambitions – to see that the 1926 New Zealand team go to England and come back with the greatest record of any visiting side, and to see that they play the game on American soil before returning to their magnificent Dominion,' he wrote, before, seasick or not, adding another thousand or so words about continuing to adopt the tactics which had made Queensland great and how important it was to send the right 'type' of player on tour.

3

TRIALS AND TRIBULATIONS

The vexed question of which nation should have the right to tour Britain in 1926-27 just would not go away, at least not in Australia and England. It was believed that New Zealand had been preferred as the invitee by the English Rugby League in recognition of its home Test series triumph over the 1924 Lions, who had already beaten Australia. But according to an English newspaper report published in early 1925, during the British tour of the unbeaten rugby union All Blacks, that was not the only reason.

'In deciding to invite a New Zealand team first, the (ERL) Council were not unmindful of the fact that it was New Zealanders who first took the risk of sending a professional side to this country; hence they have the prior claim over the Australians. The team is to be a purely New Zealand side; it will not include Australian players,' it reported.

'From the Council's decision it is easy to deduce two facts - (1) that there is a direct challenge to Rugby Unionism in New Zealand; (2) that the Council are hostile to any attempt on the part of home clubs to attract New Zealand talent to this country. They wish to foster their game in the Dominion, hence those home clubs who wish to see the two years qualification removed will need to show the Council how the Rugby League game in New Zealand can be improved by depriving it of its best players.'

It might have been strange logic allowing British professional clubs to run their predatory eyes over the New Zealand representatives they were being prevented from signing, but English Rugby League officials obviously had faith that the majority of their affiliates would toe the line. Wigan was then leading the call to again permit the wholesale signing of Australian and New Zealand players.

The original All Golds had been targets for British clubs, to the detriment of the code in New Zealand. Lance Todd (Wigan), George Smith (Oldham), Duncan McGregor (Merthyr Tydfil) and Joseph Lavery (Leeds) never even left Britain, while Edgar Wrigley, William Trevarthen and Con Byrne (all Huddersfield), Massa Johnston (Wigan), Arthur Kelly (Leeds) and Jum Turtill (St Helens) were all back in Britain by the end of 1909.

By their very personalities and influence, Todd, Smith and McGregor would have been authoritative figures in developing the game in New Zealand. Of course, they were not to know of the fatal illness that tour organiser Albert Baskerville was to contract in Australia on the homeward journey which left the pioneers leaderless. The 1908-09 Kangaroos were also pounced upon by the British scouts, and rugby union players such as great All Blacks flanker Charlie Seeling - another Wigan recruit - joined the exodus to play for pay.

In 1913, in the face of pleas from Down Under, the English Rugby League had introduced a two-year qualification period before any overseas signings could actually take the field. That was removed in 1923, but only for a few weeks before the ERL reimposed it after further protests that its clubs were harming the sport in Australia

Trials and Tribulations

and New Zealand. Wigan, backed by other like-minded clubs, was waging another campaign in 1926 to drop the two-year stand-down. No doubt they were watching the rugby union All Blacks, and so was the media.

'When the time comes for the New Zealand League team of 1926-27 to be chosen football men in this country will be specially interested to see whether the visit will have an attraction for any members of the present All Blacks team,' speculated one English writer. 'Of the first All Blacks of 1905-06, the members who came here with Mr A H Baskerville's team two years later were D McGregor, G W Smith, three-quarter backs, and W Johnston, W H Mackrell, forwards - four in all out of twenty-eight.

'Mr Dean, the manager of the present team, has stated that they "hate professionalism like poison". That is a statement which, it is safe to say, will be put to the proof when the players get back to their Dominion. Financial inducements are certain to be offered, and some League people at home believe that the pill can be sufficiently gilded to be swallowed without even a wry face by some members of the present touring party. That, however, is only an opinion. The proof has to come.'

Later in 1925, in the aftermath of the New Zealand team's Australian tour, the question was raised in England why none of the 1924-25 All Blacks had changed codes. 'It was pointed out that only in two or three cases were any of those rugby union players inclined to join the League organisation, "and I can tell you that they would not have been good enough for this team", added another in authority. Competition will be very great for places in the team to tour England.' Perhaps the 'authority' was Ernest Mair, the Australian who had taken over as New Zealand coach and would not have been in tune with the rugby union scene.

By early 1926 there were forces in both England and Australia questioning whether the essentially amateur New

Strike! The Tour That Died of Shame

Zealanders would be able to match it with the semi-professional British clubs, not to mention the county and national teams. In early January the NZRL was moved to release a statement that it was committed to sending a solely New Zealand team. Mair spread that message from his home in Toowoomba.

'Mr E H Mair, the Australian representative of the New Zealand Rugby League, has returned to Toowoomba after an extended visit to the Dominion,' reported the *Brisbane Courier*. 'Mr Mair said today that various statements appearing in the Australian and English newspapers, to the effect that there was a doubt that the New Zealanders would visit England, and that it was possible Australian players would be included in the team were entirely without foundation.

'Mr Mair stated definitely that the team to visit England would be composed entirely of New Zealanders, and already passages had been booked for the team by the Shaw Savill steamer *Tainui*, which would travel to England via the Panama Canal. The team would sail on July 28, and three matches would be played against England.

'The conditions offered New Zealand by the English Northern Union were the most generous ever allowed any Australasian touring League team. The English authorities would pay all expenses, and, in addition, the New Zealanders would receive 75 per cent of the profits. Married and single players would receive the same liberal conditions as they were granted on their recent Australian tour. The party would travel saloon (class).'

Whether he had the NZRL authority to do so or not, Mair had revealed just how supportive rugby league authorities in England had been to the cash-strapped NZRL, which otherwise would not have had the means to bankroll the venture. President James Carlaw and his officials were convinced the generous terms would more than compensate the NZRL for the costs of staging trials, assembling the touring team and paying the players' allowances, while still leaving a hefty surplus for ground developments.

New Zealand's princely share of the profits was confirmed in an English newspaper, which added…'but this sum (75 per cent) is to be devoted to the furtherance of the game in the Dominion, and must not be used as a bonus to players. The New Zealand players are to have a weekly allowance of £1 when travelling and £2 during their stay in England.'

Such terms, and the lack of a bonus, would not have been attractive to those 1924-25 All Blacks that English commentators had hoped would return as rugby league players. The privately-organised All Golds included eight All Blacks who liked the prospect of stumping up £50 towards tour expenses in return for a share of the eventual profits. But this time the NZRL was offering little more than the 'amateur' All Blacks received on their own tours and the Maori All Blacks would earn on their 1926-27 trip to Britain and France. Any code jumpers faced mandatory life suspensions from the New Zealand Rugby Union for very little, if any, financial gain.

(The only 1924-25 'Invincibles' to subsequently play rugby league were iconic backs Bert Cooke and George Nepia. Revered as the 'prince of centres', Cooke joined Auckland club Richmond in 1932 and represented New Zealand against England that year and against Australia in 1935. The most famous of all fullbacks, Nepia spent two years in British rugby league before returning to play for Manukau in Auckland and for New Zealand Maori and New Zealand in one Test against the 1937 Kangaroos.)

The English Rugby League, as was the custom, called for clubs to request fixtures against the tourists, saying it would arrange the itinerary to produce the best results but was not able to guarantee all clubs the more lucrative Saturday dates. The division of gates was to follow the system of previous tours, with seventy per cent to the visitors after the deduction of tax and the home clubs to pay all match expenses out of their thirty per cent share. In county and Test matches the division would be 65-35 because the national and county bodies would have to pay ten per cent for ground rental.

It is likely English officials revealed the financial conditions, particularly the meagre player payments, at the NZRL's request. The Otago Rugby League had expressed concern that some newspaper reports had stated the New Zealand touring team would be comprised of professional players. NZRL president James Carlaw ridiculed the suggestion and his council asked its British counterpart 'to have the conditions of the tour published in all the leading English newspapers making clear the status of all players chosen'.

Some Australian officials had still not reconciled themselves to missing the tour invitation. In April, little more than three months before the team would be chosen, the English *Athletic News* told the story of a 'mysterious cablegram' from the New South Wales Rugby League claiming that New Zealand was too weak to muster a competitive team.

An *Athletic News* correspondent wrote that he 'cannot reconcile the recent cable from New South Wales which, in advance, attempted to belittle the skill of the New Zealand League team due to visit England next September with the comments which appeared in the *Rugby League News*, the official organ of the NSWRL' after the 1925 New Zealand tour of Australia. The writer pointed out there had been no football since the league's own publication had paid tribute to the skill of the New Zealanders.

'I am wondering, as will others, why the New South Wales League sent the much-discussed cablegram. I can say, however, that the Australian interference was not altogether a surprise, for we received advice four months ago that the New South Wales League was very sore at the invitation

Trials and Tribulations

being given to New Zealand and not to them. But by their own actions the whole business is exposed.

'If the New Zealand representatives of 1925 were as satisfactory as the New South Wales report suggests, it stands to reason that 1926 will show more improvement. In any case, the matter is finally settled and it is to be New Zealand next September and not a combination from Australia and New Zealand. The findings, however, of the *Rugby League News* should give confidence to the Council that their guests for next season will not be so impotent as the last Australian cablegram implied.'

In hindsight, the Australian attempts to undermine New Zealand's sole tour rights were extraordinary. They appeared to come not from the national board of control, which was still in its infancy, but from New South Wales administrators and some Queensland sources.

It is possible that there were some in England who were having second thoughts about the strength of a New Zealand team which had lost all four games in Queensland during its 1925 tour and were keen to see some of the champion Queenslanders in action. Mair gave the impression that he fully supported a pure New Zealand selection but he had never hidden his admiration for the leading players from his home state and might have been in touch with some of his media contacts about bolstering his touring team.

What business it was of the New South Wales Rugby League was anybody's guess. Sydney had ruled the game in Australia from its inauguration, organised the 1911-12 and 1921-22 Australasian tours to Britain and was apparently not content to hand that responsibility to a new national organisation which included Queenslanders. Its officials might have believed that the Australian board of control, because of its newness and inexperience at international affairs, was not showing enough clout with the British.

From 1910 the British Lions had travelled to Australia

Strike! The Tour That Died of Shame

and New Zealand on a four-yearly cycle, one which was interrupted only by two world wars until a five-year period spanned the 1974 and 1979 tours. The Australians realised that having been turned down in 1925 and shut out by New Zealand in 1926, their ambition to reciprocate the Lions' tours every four years had been foiled. The fourth Kangaroos did not make it to Britain until 1929, after which they settled into a four-yearly cycle interrupted only by the Second World War.

Another sporting organisation closer to home was also viewing the upcoming tour with a jaundiced eye. The New Zealand Rugby Union complained the NZRL had no right to call its representative players All Blacks and threatened legal action. While the NZRL stubbornly resisted, New Zealand newspapers never referred to the 1926-27 team as the All Blacks while overseas. When a sub-heading was needed they usually preferred 'New Zealand League team'. But they were the All Blacks as far as the media was concerned in the north of England, where 'rugby' generally meant the thirteen-a-side code.

Although New Zealand teams had worn the emblem of the kiwi over the silver fern from 1911, the NZRL long ignored the obvious when it came to naming its Test and touring teams. That attitude left the media to its own devices and in 1919 the caption atop a *New Zealand Free Lance* photograph of the Australian and New Zealand teams lined up at the Basin Reserve proclaimed: 'The Kangaroo defeats the Moa at rugby league football by 44 to 21'. In 1921 an *Auckland Star* journalist took it upon himself to name the national team the Kiwis. NZRL secretary Owie Carlaw was instructed by his indignant council to send the newspaper's editor a strongly-worded letter stating the team was to be known as the All Blacks and nothing else. It was not until 1938 that a different NZRL council adopted the title Kiwis - and then insisted that any reluctant newspapers use it.

Chairman of the Auckland Rugby League Bill Hammill

added to the unsettled lead-in to the 1926 season when, at a meeting in late April, he stated his board of control 'disagreed with the method of appointing Mr Mair, of Toowoomba, as manager of the League team to tour England'. There was no suggestion the country's biggest league wanted Mair replaced, only voicing a criticism that he had been given the job without the NZRL asking for nominations or considering other candidates. It had taken Auckland six months to raise the matter and it went no further.

When the season finally kicked off there was relief that at last the search could begin to find the players who would put New Zealand on the international rugby league map in the game's heartland. A series of trials was planned, starting in June at provincial and regional levels throughout the country and culminating with an intensive week at Carlaw Park. The second annual North Island v South Island fixture and curtain-raiser trial were planned for 3 July, Auckland was to play a Combined XIII on 7 July and a Probables v Possibles match and curtain-raiser would be the final trials on 10 July. Mair wanted two inter-island games but did not get his way.

The men charged with selecting the tourists, in addition to Mair, were Dick Stirling, Ces Hardingham and Thomas 'Scotty' McClymont. Stirling had been the Canterbury delegate on the NZRL from October 1918, having moved from Christchurch to Auckland. He had been a pioneer administrator in his home province. It was Stirling who moved the motion to form the Sydenham club in Christchurch in 1913, and he was a selector for the club when it won the inaugural Canterbury championship. He also managed the 1921 New Zealand team in Australia.

Hardingham had been a prominent rugby union player who attended the inaugural meeting to establish the Canterbury Rugby League in Christchurch in 1912. A strong-running centre, he played for Canterbury in its first three games that September, at home against Wellington and New South Wales - when he scored two tries in a 28-15 loss - and against Hawkes Bay at Napier. Hardingham was on the original Addington club committee and scored the Magpies' first three tries in a 17-12 loss to St Albans on the opening day of club football in 1913. He was later a foundation member of the Hornby club and in 1916 captained the Panthers to their first competition victory in any grade. Coincidentally, both Stirling and Hardingham were made life members at the same NZRL meeting in 1920 as recognition of the spadework they had done in Christchurch.

McClymont was the new man on the panel, having retired from international football as recently as 1924. He had been chosen as captain for the series against the Lions but suffered a broken arm in the first Test match at Carlaw Park. His career thus ended as it had started, for injury had caused his withdrawal from the sole Test against the 1914 Lions. But between these setbacks McClymont fashioned a distinguished record as a slightly-built man who could slot into any backline position to the benefit of his teams.

Originally from Karangahake in the goldfields district, McClymont had joined up with Ponsonby in 1913. He made his belated New Zealand debut on tour to Australia in 1919, appeared in all three 1920 Tests against England and toured Australia again in 1921. But it was as a selector and coach that McClymont is revered in his sport's folklore. He became coach for the 1928 Lions series, guided Richmond club teams to outstanding success in the 1930s, and selected and coached the Kiwis again in 1938 and from 1947 until 1952.

Before the trials began, the NZRL cleared up a matter involving West Coast forward Neil Mouat, who had made such an indelible impression on the 1925 Australian tour but was missing from the home matches against Queensland. The meeting of 10 June decided to forward the following resolution to Mouat: 'The Council considered that Mr

Trials and Tribulations

Mouatt's (sic) action in refusing to stay in Auckland and play against Queensland was disloyal, especially as far as the Council knew it was only a question of monetary consideration. Mr Mouatt (sic) has had an opportunity of appearing before the selectors and must do as he thinks best. As far as the Council is concerned the matter is now closed.'

There had been no publicity about Mouat's actions, either at the time he slipped out of Auckland or when the resolution was passed by the NZRL. Only one month after accusing Mouat of being 'disloyal' the NZRL was to appoint the West Coaster as vice-captain of the touring team. Having nominated him for the role, Mair and the other selectors must have had no misgivings about Mouat's commitment to the cause.

Whether Mair bothered himself with the regional trials is unlikely. *The Press* in Christchurch reported on 15 June that Stirling and McClymont had attended the weekly Canterbury board of control meeting as a lead-up to the final South Island trial between Canterbury and an Otago-West Coast combined team. Hardingham, of course, already lived in Christchurch. But there was no mention of Mair. Stirling told the Canterbury officials of hopes the New Zealand team would play in Canada on its return journey, but only if such a match was guaranteed to be a financial success. He did not say whether it would be against Canadian opponents or an in-house demonstration game.

It was inevitable players from the 1925 tour to Australia and home matches against Queensland would form the nucleus of the 1926-27 All Blacks. They had been drilled in Ernest Mair's radical 'tactics' and had satisfied him with their improvement, if not always the results they had achieved. They must have also been of the all-important 'right type' considering Mair's many references to the 1925 New Zealand squad being akin to a happy family. Furthermore, Mair would not have known much about unproven contenders from outside Auckland.

Strike! The Tour That Died of Shame

Maurice Wetherill, the skilled Auckland stand-off half who had made his debut against the 1924 Lions, was a shock withdrawal from tour contention after the announcement of the inter-island teams. His place in the North line-up was taken by Jack Kirwan. Newspapers of that era did not probe into players' circumstances and no reason was given for Wetherill's decision. Missing the tour left a gap in an impeccable rugby league record for a man who came back to captain his country against the 1928 Lions and tour Australia in 1930 before serving as a Test referee.

Auckland centre Hec Brisbane, ever-present in the New Zealand backline during the Test series triumph over the Lions two years earlier and an impressive performer in Australia, had broken his collarbone playing for Marist against Grafton in early May. However, Brisbane recovered in time for trials week.

But time was up for the two most senior members of the 1925 New Zealand touring team, captain and stand-off half Bert Laing and hooker Sam Lowrie, who had returned home with deposed coach Charles Pearce before the tour was completed. Their international careers extended back to 1919, they were well into their thirties and their positions of honour within the game's history were secure.

That left twenty of the twenty-three 1925 tourists vying for berths on the boat to Britain. Ten of them were backs and they all had strong prospects of re-selection, along with centre Ben Davidson, who had debuted in the second Queensland match at Carlaw Park, and young Ponsonby inside back Hector Cole, who was a reserve against Queensland. If all were chosen only two vacancies remained in the rearguard.

Of the eleven forwards who toured Australia, only Lowrie was a pre-trial scratching. Canterbury second-rower Jack Ellis and hooker Tony Green were eliminated when they did not make the final South Island trial. Auckland second-rower Horace Dixon and prop Jim O'Brien (Marist) advanced as far as the curtain-raiser on final trials day. (It is necessary to list O'Brien's club, for namesake Jim O'Brien, from Devonport, was also in the Auckland front-row.) The O'Briens, hooker Neville St George and fellow Aucklander Arthur Singe had packed down together in the second Queensland home game. But none were tour certainties, considering the formidable challenges expected from southern forwards.

Otago's sudden rugby league prominence catapulted fullback Bert Eckhoff, centre Bill Vorrath and wing Percy Hickey into the South Island backline. They were an interesting group. Eckhoff went on to earn New Zealand honours as a forward in 1928 and 1930. The versatile Vorrath scored an unbeaten century for Otago in a Plunket Shield cricket match against Wellington in 1927-28 before dying in 1934 at the age of twenty-nine. Hickey had played rugby union for Taranaki and Wellington and toured Australia with the 1922 All Blacks. Ironically, the only Otago man to tour Britain was to be forward Harry Thomas, who started the week as a reserve for South Island.

There were two other All Blacks on trial. Loose forward Lou Petersen wore the black jersey against New South Wales in 1921, on the 1922 Australian tour and against the 1923 New South Welshmen before switching codes with his Christchurch Marist club in 1924. Hooker Phonse Carroll had been a team-mate of Petersen in 1921, having already toured New South Wales in 1920. He had been a stalwart of Manawatu packs for five years before turning to rugby league in 1925. Both players gained New Zealand honours in their first rugby league seasons and were very much in the selectors' thinking.

From the start of the week a pattern emerged which was long a feature of New Zealand rugby league. Auckland supplied a great majority of the most proficient backs, while South Island provinces - which, for the only time, included South Canterbury - had sent a plentiful supply of tough, mobile forwards to Carlaw Park. South Canterbury was represented by 1924 Test forward Bill Devine, a policeman whose most recent transfer had been from Christchurch to Timaru. The heaviest trialist at 103kg, Devine was considered a strong tour candidate even if he was short on match fitness.

The North Island side consisted of twelve Aucklanders and centre Wally Desmond, who had moved from Canterbury to Wellington earlier that year. Although North won 31-22 and finished with eleven men after halves Hector Cole and William 'Tim' Peckham were injured with the scoreboard showing 31-12, only eight of its players made the touring team. Seven South Island representatives, plus reserve Thomas, were to join them. As the week advanced several 'possibles' included in the curtain-raiser on that first Saturday became 'probables' by the second weekend.

Desmond and Davidson swapped between centre and wing during the inter-island clash, were among the try-scorers and both advanced their tour claims. Cole was another big mover, touching down twice before injury sidelined him. But he had made an indelible impression.

'The South Island fielded a great team of forwards. But the majority of the backs were not up to North Island's standard,' reported the Press Association. For North, fullback Dufty was the outstanding player, being brilliant in all departments. Of the other backs, Desmond, Davidson, Cole, Kirwan and Peckham all showed excellent form. For the South, the best backs were Hall, Vorrath and Sanders, and the best forwards Mouat, Mason, Petersen and Henry. North's other try-scorers were Kirwan, Littlewood and Avery and Dufty kicked five goals. Mouat's five goals for South complemented tries by Brittenden, Mason, Tallentire and Wright.

'The A and B trial provided good football. For the A team, Gregory, Brown, Brisbane and Delgrosso were the most promising backs, and Payne and O'Brien the most

Trials and Tribulations

prominent forwards. For the B team, Parkes, Webb and Mansill were the best backs, with Thomas, Dixon and Bass showing out in the forwards.' Crowd estimates ranged from 'more than 15,000' to 'between 18,000 and 20,000', emphasising the wide public interest.

That night West Coast forward Jack Wright and Canterbury forwards Lou Petersen and Frank Henry were released from further trials. No reason was given in *The Press*, but in the light of their subsequent selection they must have done enough in eighty minutes to convince the selectors of their worth. Heading in the opposite direction via Cook Strait ferry from Lyttelton to Wellington and by rail to Auckland was Hornby and Canterbury forward Henry 'Punch' Vivian, who had been summoned to the later trials.

Vivian was a big man for his era. Described in one newspaper as 'the strongest of a strong family' of football-playing brothers, he was also sufficiently nimble to switch to the backs when required. No-one doubted his courage after *The Star* in Christchurch told its readers that prior to a match with arch rival Marist two weeks earlier Vivian had 'split his thumb with an axe, cutting right through the nail and showing up the bone. This, however, did not keep Vivian off the field and he played his usual dashing game in the forwards.'

On the Wednesday a Combined XIII, with Vivian at stand-off half outside Wilson Hall, beat Auckland 28-21. Canterbury three-quarters Jim Sanders must have clinched his tour spot with a try-scoring treble. Mouat contributed a try and five goals and Desmond and Hall added tries. Auckland chose to give fringe candidates an opportunity to shine and did not field all of its regular players. Delgrosso scored twice, Lewis, Littlewood and Webb once apiece and Mansill kicked three goals.

'The outstanding player on the field was undoubtedly Mouat (West Coast). He worked in splendidly with the forwards and backs alike, and made innumerable openings.

Strike! The Tour That Died of Shame

He seemed to be always where the ball was,' reported the Press Association. 'Menzies (South Auckland) was another to show first-class form, and in the Auckland vanguard Clarke, Townsend and O'Brien were the best. Hall, Desmond, Sanders and Hickey were the king-pins of the southern rearguard. Eckhoff, when moved from fullback to five-eighths in the second spell, also played well. (For Auckland) Webb was good, and Mansill and Littlewood on the wings made some splendid runs.'

The *Auckland Star* named scrum-half Hall and loose forward Mouat as the outstanding individuals, waxing lyrical about Hall's opening try - he dummied past the defence, short punted over the cover, regathered and scored. Sanders was said to have 'provided himself with a ticket to England by rattling on two tries reminiscent of (former All Blacks and All Golds wing) Duncan McGregor.' Desmond's try was rated 'a beauty' in an impressive second spell. Carroll, Menzies and Thomas were stand-out Combined XIII forwards. Auckland scrum-half Delgrosso was rated a 'must go' on his form and known ability to play at stand-off and wing. Hutt and Herring were ranked the best Auckland forwards.

Remembering that southern forwards Frank Henry, Lou Petersen and Jack Wright had been released and presumably pencilled in for the tour, and that Auckland inside back Hector Cole was injured but probably in the selectors' notebooks, it was inevitable several final trialists would miss the boat. And there was always the possibility of a bolter having a blinder in the early game to dazzle the selectors. The curtain-raiser teams comprised Auckland hopefuls plus Otago backs Bill Vorrath and Bert Eckhoff on opposing sides.

The final trial teams were (from Auckland unless otherwise stated, and giving the backline positions then in vogue):

Trials and Tribulations

Probables: fullback Craddock Dufty; three-quarters Jim Sanders (Canterbury), Wally Desmond (Wellington), Ivan Littlewood; five-eighths Jack Kirwan, Stan Webb; halfback Wilson Hall (Canterbury); forwards Ernie Herring, Phonse Carroll (Wellington), Henry Vivian (Canterbury), Arthur Singe, Len Mason (Canterbury), Bert Avery (captain).

Possibles: fullback Charles Gregory; three-quarters Percy Hickey (Otago), Ben Davidson, Jim Parkes; five-eighths Hec Brisbane, Lawrence Riley; halfback Frank Delgrosso; forwards Jim O'Brien (Devonport), Jim Tallentire (West Coast), Joe Menzies (South Auckland), Bill Devine (South Canterbury), Harry Thomas (Otago), Neil Mouat (West Coast, captain).

To add to the intrigue there was no same-day announcement of the team to the 12,000 fans who attended on that showery, howling north-easterly Saturday, nor even to the players and officials under the Carlaw Park grandstand at the after-match function. Instead, selectors Ernest Mair, Dick Stirling, Ces Hardingham and Scotty McClymont deliberated for another twenty-four hours before the team was released to the newspapers on Monday, 14 July.

'The selectors will have a hard job to pick a good set of backs to tour England, but they will have no difficulty in choosing a rattling good forward combination,' reported the Press Association after the Possibles had beaten the Probables 32-15. 'The (Possibles) forwards especially were par excellence, every man playing ideal football. While each one of the six played up to form, both Mouat (West Coast) and Devine (South Canterbury) played superbly. It was a treat to watch Devine, with all his weight, score two beautiful tries. Tallentire hooked consistently and scored once.

'Delgrosso at half proved himself a versatile back, one breakaway on his part electrifying the crowd. He is certain to be the second halfback chosen. Of the three-quarters, both Hickey and Davidson shone out. Both have plenty of pace and are gifted with an ability to side step and cut in. Both are certainties for the trip. Of the five-eighths, Riley (Ponsonby) played brilliantly and has a rare chance of getting his cap. Brisbane has pace and runs very straight but did not impress as much as Riley. Gregory, as usual, was safe, not a ball being missed, nor did he fail to get his man.

'On the Probables side the forwards played well, but were not nearly so good as their opponents. Avery was everywhere the ball was, while Mason, Singe and Vivian played well. Wilson Hall at halfback is assured of a trip, his play today losing none of its dash. Kirwan and Webb were not over-brilliant, although the former will most likely be chosen in the three-quarter line. Sanders and Littlewood on the wings repeatedly showed their pace. Sanders is certain to be selected and Littlewood is a possibility. Dufty, although not as sure as last week, will still be number one fullback.'

Devine (two), Brisbane (two), Tallentire, Mouat, Hickey and Menzies scored tries for the winners and Mouat kicked four goals. Probables points came from two Desmond tries, a penalty try and three Dufty goals.

According to the *Weekly Press* and *N.Z. Referee* the most significant feature of the early game was the goalkicking of big Ponsonby three-quarters George Gardiner which, it said, bordered on the sensational. Gardiner converted all six tries as his team just held on to win 30-28 after scoring the first twenty-five points. Four years earlier Gardiner had toured Australia as a forward with the New Zealand Maori team. He was to be the 'bolter' for Britain.

The team, published first in Monday afternoon newspapers, was announced as:

> Fullbacks: Craddock Dufty (Auckland), Charles Gregory (Auckland).

Trials and Tribulations

Wing three-quarters: Lou Brown (Auckland), George Gardiner (Auckland), Jim Parkes (Auckland), Jim Sanders (Canterbury).

Centre three-quarters: Ben Davidson (Auckland), Wally Desmond (Wellington).

Five-eighths: Hec Brisbane (Auckland), Hector Cole (Auckland), Jack Kirwan (Auckland), Stan Webb (Auckland).

Halfbacks: Frank Delgrosso (Auckland), Wilson Hall (Canterbury).

Forwards (in alphabetical order): Bert Avery (Auckland), Phonse Carroll (Wellington), Bill Devine (South Canterbury), Frank Henry (Canterbury), Ernie Herring (Auckland), Len Mason (Canterbury), Neil Mouat (West Coast), Lou Petersen (Canterbury), Arthur Singe (Auckland), Harry Thomas (Otago), Henry Vivian (Canterbury), Jack Wright (West Coast).

Avery was appointed captain and Mouat vice-captain.

But that was not the end of it. Almost two weeks later Vivian withdrew because of a family bereavement (the reason was not given at the time). His place was taken by South Auckland front-rower Joe Menzies, who had been listed as the first forward reserve.

The unlucky Vivian was never to wear the New Zealand jersey, although he continued giving great service for Hornby into the 1930s. Incredibly, this remarkable character reappeared on the field in 1946 to play a full forty-minute half for the Prebbleton team he was coaching. 'Punch' Vivian was then about forty-five years old.

4

THE 1926-27 ALL BLACKS

Auckland's daily newspapers agreed on most aspects of the team selection. Both the *New Zealand Herald* and *Auckland Star* writers were of the opinion the strength lay with the forwards and the backs might struggle to compete against their British opponents. Because of the depth and excellence of the forward trialists it was inevitable some worthy candidates would miss out. That was not the case with all backline positions.

'Followers of the code will have no misgivings in regard to the play of the forwards while on tour, but the backs will need to improve considerably to hold their own with the best of the English League teams,' commented the *Star*. 'In this respect they will fortunately be in the hands of a very capable coach in Mr E H Mair, who has quite a way of getting the best collective results out of a team.'

The *Star* described George Gardiner as 'the surprise selection in the three-quarter line. The massive Ponsonby three-quarter made a late run in the trial games on Saturday, when his determined attacking work and a run of wonderful goalkicking turned the scale in his favour.' Of course, the *Star* scribe was probably somewhat red-faced after labelling Otago's former All Blacks wing Percy Hickey as a 'certainty for the trip' after the final trial.

But the *Herald* critic was just as much caught off-guard by Gardiner's inclusion, saying his club form had been 'very poor'. He did, however, have 'all the qualifications essential to a great player. He is fast, and he can use his weight to good advantage. Coaching should develop his ability in which case the Ponsonby player should be the most successful of the wings, but only in that position.'

Hooker Alf Townsend, from the City club in Auckland, was regarded as the unluckiest player by both newspapers. In modern times selectors would be grilled by the media if they chose only one specialist hooker in a team facing thirty-four matches against British professionals who would undoubtedly use every trick in the book, and every trick not in the book, to wrest possession from what were then writhing, combative scrums. But in 1926 the panel simply gave its team list to the NZRL and withdrew from public scrutiny.

'The forwards chosen will make a fast, clever and formidable spearhead, and should be capable of standing up to any opposing vanguard that they will meet. Carroll, the ex-rugby union All Black, is the only hooking specialist that has been chosen and evidently it is the intention to play one of the others - possibly Herring - as the reserve hooker,' reported the *Star*. 'Possession of the ball from the set scrums will be a very important matter on the tour, and the exclusion of Townsend, the City hooker, who did so well in the trial games, has caused general comment.'

The *Herald* commented that 'New Zealand can be justly proud of the forwards chosen to wear the black jersey, for they are all up to international standard. The forwards are fast and all are good at handling the ball. They are of two different types. Those from the South are clever scrummagers, and the Auckland men fine players in the open.

'It will be recognised that in Menzies and O'Brien two very good forwards were omitted, and both are a little unlucky. Menzies (who was to belatedly make the tour when Henry Vivian withdrew) showed first-class form in the trial games. He and Mouat were the best seen in action. O'Brien (the Devonport club prop) was always conspicuous by his dashing play and he is equal to any of the front-row forwards chosen. However, the selectors must have experienced considerable difficulty in arriving at a final decision as there are at least sixteen forwards of practically equal merit.

'The surprise of the selection is the omission of Townsend, whose hooking has been most consistent throughout. Several reasons have been advanced why the Auckland man was overlooked and rumour is current that his style of hooking would be questioned in England. This seems incredible, seeing that Townsend has been allowed to play in every trial match arranged, and it must be a keen disappointment to be told at the eleventh hour that his methods would be questioned on the tour.

'Carroll may be a useful hooker but whether he is better than Townsend was never proved in a game. To include both would have been a wiser plan and the team's strength would not have been in any way weakened. As no second hooker has been mentioned, it is evidently intended to school one of the other forwards selected,' said the *Herald*.

(Alf Townsend's only appearance in a New Zealand jersey was to be in the deciding third 1928 Test against England at English Park in Christchurch. He was then representing Otago, having transferred from Auckland in 1927. Even then Townsend had to wait his turn after Auckland veteran Wally Somers was preferred for the first two Tests).

Possession was indeed nine-tenths of rugby league law before the introduction of the first limited-tackle rule in

The 1926-27 All Blacks

1967. The scrummaging rivalry was invariably fierce and often brutal for once it had the ball a team could retain it indefinitely. Specialist hookers were worth their weight in winning pay bonuses in the Australian and British professional competitions, and their team-mates would happily 'carry' them if they lacked agility in open play. Most old-time hookers took more interest in their scrum figures at fulltime than the actual match result.

While the Auckland media sympathised with local man Townsend, West Coaster Jim Tallintire, from the Runanga club, had also caught the eyes of the pundits during the trials. Neville St George, the first choice in 1925, was also overlooked as the selectors decided that Herring had the versatility to switch from prop to hooker when required and would develop sufficient striking skills to understudy Carroll.

As it transpired, the inclusion of big wing George Gardiner was to bring unexpected benefits when the All Blacks found themselves with only five regular forwards in mid-tour. Gardiner reverted to the forward role he had filled earlier in his career. But Carroll, the sole specialist hooker, was one of the seven players who cut themselves adrift, and were later sent packing altogether. Herring was fated to play in more matches - an exhausting thirty of the thirty-four - than any other player, starting the tour with an eleven-game sequence, mostly at prop, and finishing it with another eleven-game sequence, mostly at hooker.

Townsend's absence apart, the *Herald* and *Star* writers did not dwell on the individual forward selections. They had no complaints that only three Auckland representatives, Bert Avery, Arthur Singe and Herring, were named among the twelve. It had been regularly acknowledged throughout the trials that those from south of the Bombay Hills had very compelling claims for selection. A possible exception had been beefy Bill Devine, the South Canterbury policeman who arrived in Auckland obviously short of a gallop.

Strike! The Tour That Died of Shame

'Up to Saturday there was a doubt in regard to Devine's selection. Through no fault of his own he has not been able to get much practice this season, but although obviously much over-weight, he fairly and squarely won his place by his display last Saturday,' said the *Star* of Devine's rampaging two-try performance in the final trial. Because they were more exposed to the critics than the forwards, the backs were individually analysed by both newspapers.

'It was generally expected that Dufty and Gregory would be the chosen fullbacks, and no fault can be found with their inclusion,' said the *Herald*. 'Dufty usually performs best in big football but his form is not consistent and he is liable to give patchy exhibitions. His reputation will, no doubt, precede him, as many (British) writers, after the 1924 English tour of New Zealand, claimed that Dufty was one of the greatest fullbacks in the world. In Sydney last season Dufty was classed with J Sullivan, England's brilliant player.

'Gregory, on this season's club form, is the more consistent fullback and his ability to rise to the occasion has often been demonstrated. Gregory is a brilliant defensive player. Moreover, he possesses the faculty of turning defence into attack.'

Both scribes were critical of the standard of wing play during the trials, the *Herald* describing the position as 'the weakness of the team'. However, they had faith in Lou Brown, who had sprung to prominence as a teenaged Auckland representative and also had experience of British conditions after spending an amateur season at Wigan. 'He is possibly the fastest League player in the Dominion at the moment, and in Auckland club games has certainly been the most brilliant scoring wing this season,' praised the *Star*. But Brown had not reached such heights in the trials.

'Sanders and Parkes are experienced players who did solid and heavy work, but they did not disclose any better standard than some of the others who were given a trial,' reported the *Star*. The *Herald* man approved of Sanders, who

The 1926-27 All Blacks

'has had much football experience, and is the best of the South Island backs', but went so far as to say Parkes was fortunate to be named ahead of fellow Aucklander Claude List.

'The selection of Davidson as centre three-quarter was a foregone conclusion as he has been the outstanding player in that position,' said the *Star*. 'Davidson has pace, handling ability and finesse, and is an ideal centre to cater for the men outside of him. Desmond, the young Wellington player, has been picked as the understudy. In the trials he revealed promise and particularly cleverness in attack.'

Teams in New Zealand in 1926 traditionally fielded backline formations consisting of a fullback, three three-quarters, two five-eighths and a halfback, rather than the British preference of a fullback, four three-quarters and two halves. Kirwan and Brisbane would be regarded as centres in more modern times, with Cole and Webb stand-off halves. Back then Kirwan and Brisbane were second five-eighths and Cole and Webb first five-eighths.

Surprisingly, neither the *Herald* nor the *Star* made mention of the non-availability of the incumbent New Zealand and Auckland first five-eighths Maurice Wetherill when criticising the standard of inside back performances during the trials.

'The five-eighths play in the code has not been impressive, and the trials did not disclose a pair of the class necessary to give the men behind them the chances that they should have had,' lamented the *Star*. 'Cole showed meteoric dash and was outstanding, while Kirwan and Webb played themselves into the team by consistent good work of a solo nature.

'The surprise selection is Brisbane, although there will be many glad that he has won a place. On the last tour in Australia Brisbane showed up as a brilliant three-quarter, and in club matches this season he has given some fine displays. Of late his form has been patchy, but in fairness it might he said that he has been on the casualty list.

Strike! The Tour That Died of Shame

'The selection of Hall and Delgrosso as the halfbacks will be admitted as the best choice. Hall in the trial games revealed real class, while Delgrosso made good when shifted from wing three-quarter, where obviously he did not have the necessary speed,' said the *Star*. The *Herald* concurred, while also giving Auckland's 'Tiny Tim' Peckham a mention before conceding 'it will be generally recognised that the better players have been chosen'.

Both newspapers mentioned that English authorities had not yet forwarded the itinerary, but expected them to arrange at least two matches in France at the end of the itinerary.

Brief biographies of the 1926-27
New Zealand rugby league All Blacks:

Calvin Thomas Craddock Dufty (*Grafton club, Auckland*), fullback, aged 26 years, weight 14st (90kg), height 6ft (183cm). As a 19-year-old in 1919 Craddock Dufty had signalled his arrival with a try and eight goals while playing centre for Auckland against Hawkes Bay in a Northern Union Cup defence at Eden Park. He played all four home Tests against Australia at fullback later that season, kicking five goals and a field goal on debut at the Basin Reserve. Dufty was an imposing figure, as big and strong as most forwards, in the decade after the First World War. He toured Australia with the New Zealand Maori team in 1922 and New Zealand in 1925 and shared in the 1924 Test series victory over the Lions.

Charles Edward Gregory (*Marist club, Auckland*), fullback, aged 25 years, weight 10st 13lb (70kg), height 5ft 7in (170cm). Invariably known as 'Pope' Gregory, he was renowned for the sturdiness of his defence despite being of slight build. Gregory rose to prominence with the champion Marist club team in 1924 and represented Auckland against

The 1926-27 All Blacks

England that season. For the rest of the 1920s he and Craddock Dufty were rivals and sometimes team-mates. In 1925 they toured Australia together, sharing the fullback and goalkicking duties in the big games. Gregory then played twice for New Zealand and for Auckland in a busy eight days against the Queensland tourists at Carlaw Park. He could also play at centre.

Louie Ernest Brown (*City club, Auckland*), wing, aged 22 years, weight 10st 6lb (66kg), height 5ft 8in (173cm). This dashing wing made a sensational debut for Auckland as a seventeen-year-old replacement against New South Wales in 1922. He scored three tries and was immediately stamped for greatness. After spending 1923 with the Newton club in Auckland, he went to England and played as an amateur in the Wigan reserve team. The international transfer ban prevented him from doing more than that. Brown toured Australia with the 1925 New Zealand team. The prospect of renewing acquaintances with Brown might have been the catalyst for Wigan campaigning to have the transfer ban lifted.

James Parkes (*Richmond club, Auckland*), wing, aged 28 years, weight 13st (83kg), height 5ft 10in (178cm). Jim Parkes, a strongly built outside back, became the first of forty-one internationals from the Richmond club through to 1985, after which the Kiwis were mostly chosen from professional clubs. But Parkes was actually an import from Canterbury. He was with the Hornby club in 1925 when he played for South Island in the inaugural inter-island match, toured Australia with the New Zealand team and played in the thrilling 25-24 first 'Test' victory against Queensland at Carlaw Park. Parkes transferred to Richmond for the 1926 season and showed enough in the trials to earn selection for another tour.

Strike! The Tour That Died of Shame

George Gardiner (*Ponsonby club, Auckland*), wing, aged 28 years, weight 13st 9lb (87kg), height 6ft 2in (188cm). Blockbusting runs and booming goal kicks propelled Gardiner from the early trial into the touring team. But he was far from being an unknown. Gardiner was already one of the personalities of the code in Auckland. He had toured Australia as a forward with New Zealand Maori in 1922, when he also played for Australasia in a special match against the Kangaroos at Sydney. Gardiner was a second-rower for Auckland against the 1924 Lions and at centre when Auckland Province met Queensland in 1925. He was with Marist when it won the 1924 club championship before linking up with Ponsonby.

James Sanders (*Addington club, Canterbury*), wing or centre, aged 26 years, weight 11st 9lb (75kg), height 5ft 10in (178cm). Canterbury's most capped international between the wars. Jim Sanders was first selected for the province while still a junior player, only to be ruled out because he lacked senior experience. A twinkle-toed utility back for his club and province, Sanders could direct play from stand-off half, penetrate in midfield, or finish off scoring moves on the wing. Sanders made his Test debut in the 26-10 defeat of Australia at Sydenham Park in 1919, played all three Tests against the 1920 Lions, toured Australia in 1921 and 1925 and appeared in both games against the Queenslanders at Carlaw Park.

Walter Leslie Desmond (*Wellington*), centre, aged 20 years, weight 11st 10lb (75kg), height 5ft 8in (173cm). The youngest member of the touring team, Wally Desmond had transferred from Canterbury to Wellington, where the code was struggling for its existence, before the start of the 1926 season. But his reputation as a highly promising three-quarters was such that he was the only non-Aucklander included in the North Island team on the opening trials

The 1926-27 All Blacks

weekend. Given that opportunity, he made every post a winner. Desmond had represented Canterbury in 1925 and was so highly respected by his former Linwood club that he went back to Christchurch to be officially farewelled by his old team-mates.

Benjamin Alfred Davidson (*City club, Auckland*), centre, aged 28 years, weight 11st 9lb (75kg), height 5ft 8in (173cm). Ben Davidson was a member of a premier sporting family, with three over-achieving brothers. Bill was the New Zealand fullback and goalkicker from 1919 to 1921, George finished fifth in the 200 metres final at the 1920 Olympic Games at Antwerp in addition to playing rugby league for Auckland and Ben completed a treble of national representation for New Zealand against the 1925 Queensland tourists. Ben was blessed with a fair share of the family speed but he was also a clever and skilful footballer who had debuted for Auckland in 1921 and was the country's leading centre in 1926.

John Patrick Kirwan (*Marist club, Auckland*), second five-eighth, aged 30 years, weight 12st 2lb (77kg), height 5ft 10in (178cm). The most recent convert from rugby union among the backs. Marist shocked Devonport late in the 1924 season when it not only signed Jack Kirwan, a Wairarapa, Hawkes Bay and Auckland representative, but also fielded him alongside Hec Brisbane in the Monteith Shield play-off. Kirwan relished the change of codes and won selection for New Zealand's tour of Australia and two-match home series against Queensland in 1925. There was never any doubt he would make a belated tour of Britain, having been considered among the unlucky ones to miss the 1924-25 All Blacks.

Hector William Brisbane (*Marist club, Auckland*), second five-eighth, aged 23 years, weight 11st 9lb (75kg), height 5ft

Strike! The Tour That Died of Shame

9in (175cm). This classy midfield back had enjoyed a stellar 1924 season, appearing in all three Tests against England and scoring the spectacular last-minute try which clinched the series for New Zealand at Wellington. Hec Brisbane also played for Auckland City and Auckland Province against the Lions and finished the year off by sharing in Marist's club championship triumph. Brisbane was a star of the 1925 tour to Australia and, though a certainty to tour Britain, faced an anxious recovery from a broken collarbone to prove his form and fitness were up to his usual high standards.

Hector Stanley Esmond Cole (*Ponsonby club, Auckland*), first five-eighth, aged 23 years, weight 11st 5lb (72kg), height 5ft 10in (178cm). Caught the eye with his incisive displays in the Ponsonby team which won the Roope Rooster and Stormont Shield competitions in 1925, when he was a reserve for the first home 'Test' against Queensland and went on Auckland's trip to Christchurch and Greymouth. Cole assisted Ponsonby to win the 1926 club championship but fate would have it that he received just one chance to stake his tour claims. After scoring two tries for North Island and setting up another, Cole was forced out of the trials with an injury. The men who mattered most decided he had done enough.

Stanley George Webb (*Devonport club, Auckland*), first five-eighth and halfback, aged 25 years, weight 11st 7lb (73kg), height 5ft 9in (175cm). Better known as a halfback, Webb had toured Australia in that position with Wilson Hall and then replaced an injured Hall for the second home game against Queensland in 1925. He also played there for Auckland against Queensland and in the City club team which won the 1925 championship. New Zealand coach Ernest Mair had experimented with Webb at centre in Australia and was keen for him to play there regularly. But with Hector Cole out injured, Webb was tried at first five-eighth in the final trial and was chosen for the tour with a utility role in mind.

Frank August Delgrosso (*Ponsonby club, Auckland*), halfback, aged 26 years, weight 11st 7lb (73kg), height 5ft 9in (175cm). The son of an Italian immigrant, Delgrosso played in every backline position during his representative career but was pitted against Wilson Hall at halfback in the final trial and impressed enough to be selected as Hall's understudy. One of the most experienced internationals, he had toured Australia in 1921 as a fullback, played at first five-eighth in the 1924 Tests against the Lions and was regularly on the wing in Australia and at home in 1925. Delgrosso kicked the goal for the famous first 'Test' win over Queensland at Carlaw Park. His versatility and varied skills were invaluable.

Wilson Hall (*Hornby club, Canterbury*), halfback, aged 21 years, weight 11st 2lb (71kg), height 5ft 6in (168cm). Curiously, most contemporary publications hyphenated his name as Wilson-Hall and often added the initial A, but it has since been confirmed that Wilson was his only Christian name and Hall his surname. Toured Australia and played the first 'Test' match against Queensland from Waikato in 1925 before moving south to work at the Islington freezing works, near Hornby, in early 1926. Had the distinction of playing in the first (1925) inter-island match for North and the second (1926) for South. An outstanding performer during the trials, Hall was always destined to be the first-choice halfback.

Herbert Avery (*Grafton club, Auckland*), loose forward and captain, aged 30 years, weight 13st 4lb (84kg), height 5ft 11in (180cm). The finest player of his era, Bert Avery had shown promise for Ponsonby before serving with the Army in the First World War. On his return he joined Maritime (later

Strike! The Tour That Died of Shame

Grafton Athletic) and made his Test debut against the 1919 Australians. From then on he was an automatic selection for his province and country and shared in milestones such as Auckland's 1920 defeat of England and New Zealand's 1924 series victory over England. Avery toured Australia in 1921 and 1925, the second time as vice-captain and was promoted to the captaincy for the home games against Queensland.

Thomas Neil Mouat (*Marist club, West Coast*), loose forward and vice-captain, aged 26 years, weight 13st 6lb (85kg), height 6ft 2in (188cm). Neil Mouat played rugby union for West Coast and in Wellington before his club changed codes in 1924. The rangy backrower and prolific goalkicker made such an impact that he played in the first and third Tests against England a few months later. Australian critics were so impressed with his displays on the 1925 tour that one compared him with the great All Blacks flanker Charlie Seeling. Mouat's leadership qualities were undeniable as captain of his province and island. He was destined to be Avery's deputy even before showing out as the best forward in the trials.

Louis Charles Petersen (*Marist club, Canterbury*), second-rower, aged 29 years, weight 13st 7lb (86kg), height 6ft 2in (188cm). Lou Petersen was a fast and forceful flanker who played rugby union for Canterbury from 1919 to 1923, including a 6-4 victory over the 1921 Springboks. He was an All Blacks reserve against South Africa before playing against New South Wales at home in 1921 and 1923, and on tour in 1922. Petersen adopted rugby league with enthusiasm in 1924, appearing in the second and third Tests against England. He did not tour Australia in 1925 but was recalled for the first match against Queensland at Auckland in 1925 and captained Canterbury to its first victory over Auckland.

The 1926-27 All Blacks

Leonard Tasman Mason (*Hornby club, Canterbury*), second-rower, aged 23 years, weight 15st 2lb (96kg), height 6ft (183cm). Len Mason displayed sufficient early promise to represent Waikato as a teenager. He was briefly with Grafton Athletic in 1925, gaining further honours for Auckland against Canterbury at Christchurch. At the start of the 1926 season employment at the Islington freezing works took him south, along with Wilson Hall, to a grateful Hornby club which won the Canterbury championship. Mason was extremely mobile for a big man and capable of filling in as a centre when required. He also had remarkable resilience, thriving on the intensity of the trials week to earn tour selection.

Henry Edward Thomas (*Athletic club, Otago*), second-rower, aged 26 years, weight 12st 4lb (78kg), height 6ft (183cm). 'Harry' Thomas was among many prominent rugby union players who adopted rugby league in the wake of Dunedin staging the third Test of the 1924 Lions tour. In 1925 he had the distinction of being the first rugby league international chosen after the formation of the Otago Rugby League. Thomas had played in the inaugural inter-island fixture in 1925 before touring Australia and it was no disgrace he had to settle with being South's forward reserve in 1926, for those ahead of him were Mouat, Petersen, Mason, Henry and Wright. His wholehearted efforts in the trials clinched his re-selection.

Arthur Percy Singe (*Marist club, Auckland*), second-rower, aged 29 years, weight 13st 7lb (86kg), height 6ft (183cm). After war service, Singe was in the 1919 New Zealand Army rugby union side which beat Wales and won the King's Cup against Commonwealth and French opponents. By 1921 he was thriving in the hurly-burly of rugby league forward play and represented Auckland against New Zealand. Singe appeared in all three of Auckland's games against

Strike! The Tour That Died of Shame

Australian Universities and also against the New South Wales tourists in 1922. Regarded by his club as unlucky not to tour Australia in 1925, he was subsequently elevated into the New Zealand pack for the two post-tour games against Queensland.

Alphonsus John Carroll (*Wellington*), hooker, aged 31 years, weight 13st 7lb (86kg), height 5ft 8in (173cm). His pen picture published after selection gave his age as 27, but 'Phonse' Carroll was born in 1895. Originally a horse trainer, he did not follow his brothers into rugby union until 1917. Within two years he was representing Manawatu and North Island on the way to All Black selection in 1920 and 1921. Some blamed Carroll's exclusion from the 1924-25 All Blacks on his having been a conscientious objector during the war. In 1925 he joined the Foxton rugby league club and made the Australian tour, playing at prop and hooker. Carroll was given arguably the toughest assignment as the only specialist hooker.

Ernest Herring (*Grafton club, Auckland*), prop and hooker, aged 28 years, weight 14st 2lb (91kg), height 5ft 10in (178cm). It might have surprised Ernie Herring that he was to be Carroll's understudy as hooker on tour, for his international career extended back to the 1919 New Zealand tour of Australia and was devoid of any previous experience in that role. Herring made his Test debut in the second-row against the 1920 Lions and was a prop in all three 1924 Lions Tests, on tour to Australia in 1925 and against Queensland at home. The selectors apparently decided Herring must have seen enough of front-row techniques to make the adjustment, even when opposed by the hardened British professional hookers.

William Walter Devine (*South Canterbury*), prop, aged 28 years, weight 16st 2lb (103kg), height 5ft 11in (180cm). One

The 1926-27 All Blacks

of the two players at the centre of the Payne Trophy controversy which eventually led to himself, Mouat, Petersen and Wright being available for this team. Bill Devine had debuted in the series-winning second Test against England at Wellington in his first (1924) season of rugby league. But just as a police work transfer to Christchurch had helped spark the Payne Trophy affair so another transfer to Timaru left him without regular club football. Devine was out of shape at the start of the trials but the intense training and playing primed him for a tour-clinching performance in the final game.

Francis Henry (*Hornby club, Christchurch*), prop, aged 25 years, weight 13st 2lb (83kg), height 6ft 2in (188cm). English-born, Frank Henry had represented Durham and North of England at rugby union before signing to play rugby league. His tour pen picture said he had been a trialist for the 1924 Lions until his prospects of selection were spoiled by illness. Henry was with the York club when he decided to try his luck in New Zealand during 1924, becoming the first of three imports - Hall and Mason were the others - who helped Hornby win the 1926 Canterbury title. Henry represented Canterbury and South Island from 1925. It was logical that his knowledge of English conditions and opponents would be an asset.

John Herbert James Wright (*Marist club, West Coast*), prop, aged 24 years, weight 13st 3lb (84kg), height 6ft (183cm). Jack Wright hailed from the sawmilling town of Ngahere and was the only boy in a family of eight. He represented West Coast at rugby union before his Greymouth Marist club followed its Christchurch counterpart to rugby league in the Payne Trophy furore. Wright had been a team-mate of Neil Mouat at club and provincial levels and in 1926 was to join him in the South Island and New Zealand teams. He must have made a very favourable impression in the inter-

Strike! The Tour That Died of Shame

island match for, along with Henry and Petersen, he was released from further trials and subsequently chosen for the touring team.

Arthur Britton Menzies (*Ngaruawahia club, South Auckland*), prop, aged 28, weight 13st (83kg), height 6ft (183cm). Born on Norfolk Island, 'Joe' Menzies served in the First World War and was highly regarded as an all-round sportsman. He was prominent in Waikato wood chopping, cricket and tennis as well as being a mainstay of the rugby league pack. Menzies played for Auckland Province against the 1925 Queensland tourists. During trials week Menzies advanced from the curtain-raiser on the first day, to the Combined XIII which beat Auckland in midweek, then into the final trial. Originally the first forward reserve, he replaced Henry Vivian when that Canterbury forward withdrew from the tour.

The co-manager in charge of finances was George Henry Ponder, an accountant who was the South Auckland delegate on the NZRL council. He first became involved with the game in 1921 as the Newtown club delegate to the Wellington Rugby League, was vice-chairman of the League for a short period and a referee. After being transferred to Auckland by the Vacuum Oil Company, Ponder was firstly the Wellington delegate to the NZRL before taking over the South Auckland portfolio in 1925. He was also heavily involved in social work in Auckland. Ponder had served his tour apprenticeship while financial manager of the New Zealand team for the 1924 home series against England. In 1926-27 he was responsible for the overall running of the touring team and liaising with the English Rugby League.

    Queenslander Ernest Mair held the dual titles of NZRL representative on the Australian Rugby League board of control and official coach to the NZRL when it was confirmed he would be the tour co-manager and coach. His

The 1926-27 All Blacks

duties predominantly involved the selecting and preparation of the teams to take on the British clubs and counties and the England and Wales Test teams. But Mair was not travelling alone, for his wife, Mildred, was also a member of the touring party.

That was not quite a unique situation, for Dr Henry Thacker's wife, Monica, travelled to Australia with the 1913 New Zealand team that her husband co-managed. Monica Thacker appears in the official team photograph wearing what looked to be her finest, feathery Cup Day hat. But that was a short trans-Tasman jaunt compared to the seven-month tour faced by the 1926-27 All Blacks. Nor was Mildred Mair content to remain in the background. On occasions she led the team onto the field, carrying a New Zealand flag in one hand and a stuffed kiwi mascot in the other. She also held those accessories when photographed with the players and managers before the opening game at Dewsbury and even on the playing field at Central Park, Wigan, shortly before kick-off in the first Test match.

The thirty-strong group was completed by Joseph Russell Patrick O'Shaughnessy, the official press agent. Aged in his early twenties, Joe O'Shaughnessy was yet another to find his way to rugby league via the Payne Trophy upheaval. While at St Bede's College in Christchurch, O'Shaughnessy captained the first XV, played for the top teams at both cricket and soccer and was the school's heavyweight boxing champion.

In 1925, the second season after the Marist club turned to rugby league, O'Shaughnessy was appointed secretary and delegate to the Canterbury Rugby League. Not only did this young man wield considerable influence within his club's administration, he also played for the Marist B team in the Canterbury senior competition. O'Shaughnessy was therefore closely aligned to club-mates Bill Devine and Lou Petersen and probably also Greymouth Marist men Neil Mouat and Jack Wright.

Strike! The Tour That Died of Shame

O'Shaughnessy had applied to the NZRL for the position, but it was not confirmed until 22 July, less than two weeks before departure. On 9 July O'Shaughnessy asked that his boat ticket to England be paid as he was 'having certain difficulties in arranging finance'. He subsequently accepted an offer of £25 as an immediate advance, and a promise that if the tour was a financial success he would be granted £75 on his return to New Zealand.

Although a Press Association message from Auckland on 26 July reported 'there are one or two other players who have not yet completed arrangements for their passports', Vivian was to remain the only withdrawal and Menzies the sole replacement. The next forward reserves were Auckland pair Jim O'Brien (the Devonport one) and Lou Hutt, while Otago's Bert Eckhoff and Aucklanders Ivan Littlewood, Stan Prentice and Lawrence Riley were the unrequired stand-by backs.

5

MUTINY ON THE HIGH SEAS

The *Auckland Star* published a photographic montage of the twenty-six selected players on the day the team was announced, along with the rather vague information that 'in the event of the team making good in its games against the elect of the English League footballers, it may be sent to France also, and may play matches in America on the way home in an apostolic capacity'. There seemed to be more definite news that the team would play Auckland before leaving on board the *Tainui* on 7 August. They would arrive in England on 14 September, six days before the opening match against a Welsh club.

However, those travel arrangements were to be changed twice. The departure date was initially put back a week and a second game at Wellington was added to the preparations. But when the English Rugby League sent its final itinerary the opening match was listed for Dewsbury on 11 September. Long-suffering NZRL secretary Owie Carlaw rebooked the team on the *Aorangi* from Auckland on 3 August.

Strike! The Tour That Died of Shame

'Arrangements have been made with the Canadian National Railways for the team to travel in a special tourist car from Vancouver to Montreal. It was stated that the extra cost of travelling via Canada would be about £1,000. The alteration of plans means the abandonment of the proposed match in Wellington,' reported the Press Association.

Carlaw referred fullback Charles Gregory's plea for financial assistance to the NZRL council. Gregory wrote that he had a widowed mother to support and asked to be placed in the same category as married men with respect to out-of-pocket allowances. But the unsympathetic councillors 'declined the application on the grounds that, firstly, it was against the constitution and, secondly, an undesirable precedent would be established'.

Two weeks before departure the Canterbury Rugby League forwarded a similar application from Jim Sanders, its most experienced international between the wars, 'on account of his domestic position'. That was also declined. It is possible that other players made similar enquiries. Clearly, there was no pot of gold luring the players to Britain.

Occupations of the players were not given with their pen pictures. The great majority would have conformed to the working class foundations of what was still a very young sport in New Zealand. Fifty years after the 1926-27 tour there were still complaints that government departments discriminated between sports. Cricket and rugby union representatives would be paid all or part of their wages while on tour, but their rugby league counterparts were not accorded similar recognition.

John A Lee, the Member for Auckland East, raised the matter in Parliament in September. He asked Prime Minister Gordon Coates whether it was true that the 1924-25 rugby union All Blacks who were civil servants received half-pay from the Government while those in the New Zealand rugby league touring team were not treated alike.

Mutiny on the High Seas

Lee wished to know whether the fact the league players received ten shillings a day out-of-pocket expenses as against the four shillings and six pence paid to the All Blacks was used as an avenue of unfair discrimination. This was causing a great deal of dissatisfaction in Auckland, where the league game was well established, said Lee, who ten years later was to become president of the Auckland Rugby League.

The Prime Minister stated that only one name of a civil servant in the league team had been brought to his notice (presumably policeman Bill Devine). That man would receive £4.10s a week plus expenses while on tour and he (Coates) was advised that the department would not be wise to pay him half-pay in these circumstances.

The Press Association reported a short, sharp exchange which followed Coates being cut off in mid-sentence:

Lee: 'I am informed that he receives only ten shillings.'

J S Dickson (Parnell): 'Yes, ten shillings a day.'

Coates: 'It is a question whether the department should grant him half-pay, whereas in an amateur game...'

H E Holland (Christchurch North) interjected: 'Is league not an amateur game?'

H M Campbell (Hawkes Bay): 'That is the difference. It is not. One is a professional, and the other is an amateur.'

Lee: 'It is not professional. It is only a matter of paying ten shillings a day expenses.'

Coates ended the discussion with his reply: 'Well, that is the position.'

NZRL secretary Owie Carlaw wrote to the Prime Minister disputing his statement that players were paid £4 10s a week, plus out-of-pocket expenses. Carlaw said tourists were receiving ten shillings per day, except Sundays, and no other allowances. He told Coates that league players 'resented very much' the statement by H M Campbell MP

Strike! The Tour That Died of Shame

that they were professionals. Coates replied he very much regretted if any remarks of his had led to misunderstanding of the actual position.

Those employed in the private sector were at the mercy of their bosses, but the prestige of having a rugby union All Black on one's staff, usually in a position where he was visible to the spending public, generally counted for much more consideration than a rugby league player who might be labouring on the wharves, in a workshop or a factory.

It was customary for clubs in both sports to take up monetary collections among members and presenting their touring players with wallets containing the proceeds. Rugby union wallets, garnished by affluent sponsors, tended to be somewhat fatter than rugby league ones.

Despite the contributions from both the English and New Zealand leagues, the 1926-27 players and their dependents had to exist for seven months on modest incomes, with considerable sacrifices being made by the mothers, wives and children who depended on their menfolk for the family's income.

But the changing travel and itinerary arrangements, and players' private requests for financial assistance, all happened out of the public view. Naturally, there was considerable excitement and optimism within rugby league circles that the first official New Zealand team was bound for Britain.

An *Auckland Star* correspondent signing himself 'League Official' was moved to claim New Zealand and England would be meeting to decide the best team in the world: 'It is an open question as to who holds the world's championship honours in the game. New South Wales held for years the pride of place in Australia, until Queensland administered defeat to them three years ago. The formidable English team visited Australia in 1924 and won the Ashes from an all-Australia team. Fresh from their victories the same English team came to New Zealand to lose the Ashes to the Dominion in a series of three Test games.

Mutiny on the High Seas

'The New Zealand team followed this up by journeying to Australia, defeating the New South Wales side, but to meet defeat at the hands of the Queenslanders. This defeat was subsequently avenged in New Zealand. The authorities in England, recognising the advancement of the Dominion side, invited the team to visit England and engage in a series of matches. It is in defence of the Ashes won against the Englishmen that the team is visiting England.'

It was in that general air of euphoria that nationwide farewells were held by clubs and provincial bodies to honour their representatives. In Christchurch, Marist club president Rev Brother Phelan spoke glowingly of dual international Lou Petersen, who 'had a fine football record - he had played in the Army (rugby union) team and in England, and as a soldier had fought on the same ground as the battle of Waterloo was decided'. Official press agent Joe O'Shaughnessy was also given a hearty send-off. Bill Devine, a former club-mate of Petersen and O'Shaughnessy, was given a public farewell by Mayor of Timaru G J Wallace as South Canterbury's only New Zealand rugby league international.

The southern contingent travelled to Auckland in two groups, depending whether the players were required for the pre-tour match against Auckland at Carlaw Park. Len Mason and Wilson Hall performed a farewell haka on the deck of the ferry steamer before it left Lyttelton for Wellington to connect with the train to Auckland. English-born Frank Henry was with them, but his haka lessons were still to be learned. Five days later, Jim Sanders, Petersen and O'Shaughnessy were showered with confetti by enthusiastic well-wishes at Christchurch railway station as they boarded the 5.05pm train for Lyttelton, where a band and more streamers awaited them.

While that trio was crossing Cook Strait another function was being held by the Auckland Rugby League Glee Club. Bill Hammill, chairman of the league's management committee, expressed hopes the team would at least equal the record of the triumphant 1907-08 All Golds. In reply, New Zealand coach Ernest Mair said the standard in England was higher than ever. Notwithstanding that, he believed the New Zealanders would return with a proud record. They were the best equipped team to leave the country and Mair predicted his team would achieve unexpected success.

There was also a function arranged at Carlaw Park for the presentation of blazers. The Wellington *Evening Post* scribe could not resist a dig at the NZRL: 'It is interesting to note that after the recent objection to the Press use of the term "Kiwis" instead of "All Blacks," the monogram consists of a fern leaf and a kiwi.' Nor was that the end of the socialising, for on the day before departure there was to be a mayoral function at noon and an NZRL dinner in the evening. Not to mention the dockside festivities, attended by 'some couple of thousand' supporters, before the *Aorangi* pulled away from the wharf.

But there was one send-off Mair and his team did not enjoy - the 52-32 drubbing handed out by Auckland at Carlaw Park three days before their departure. Mair had plumped for a strong, if not quite full strength, line-up of Craddock Dufty at fullback, George Gardiner, Wally Desmond and Lou Brown in the three-quarters, Hector Cole and Wilson Hall at five-eighths, Frank Delgrosso as halfback, a front-row of Frank Henry, Phonse Carroll and Ernie Herring, second-rowers Len Mason and Harry Thomas and captain Bert Avery at the back.

Ominously, Maurice Wetherill led the rout with three tries, underlining just how sorely he would be missed on the tour. The unrelated Jim O'Briens were devastating in the Auckland front-row, the Marist version scoring two tries and the Devonport man one. Horace Dixon, who had been discarded by Mair after the 1925 season, also touched down twice as the New Zealand team conceded twelve tries and

Mutiny on the High Seas

eight goals. New Zealand's points came from tries to Hall (two), Brown, Desmond, Avery, Mason, Henry and Carroll, and goals from Gardiner (three) and Dufty.

'The fact of the matter was the Blacks were a dismal failure,' reported the *Weekly Press*. 'Viewed as a final try out for a team that is about to represent New Zealand overseas the game was disappointing in the extreme. No doubt most of the touring team had one eye on the *Aorangi*, which leaves here on Tuesday, but for all that, not one, excepting Carroll, enhanced his reputation as a footballer.

'From fullback to hooker they were outplayed. The team had undergone a course of "tactics" at the hands of their coach, Mr Mair, but no sign of them was visible to the spectators. As previous touring teams have come a crash before leaving New Zealand and made good abroad, the supporters at home here can only hope that history will repeat itself.' Most of the 15,000 spectators echoed those thoughts as they trooped out of the park.

Down in Christchurch, the *Star* posed the question, 'Did N.Z. League Team Forget Its Signal Code?' above a subheading of 'Anyway, its Display Against Auckland Was Shocking, And Critics Are Scornful'. After such descriptive headlines, the several hundred words which followed were not entirely necessary to explain the writer's opinion of the departing tourists.

'It was understood that the team had been in training for a week, had undergone a course on tactics, had a code of signals; but apparently they forgot the tactics and lost the reference book explaining the signals,' smirked the *Star*. The only consolation had been a similar happening to the 1924-25 rugby union All Blacks. They were beaten 14-3 by Auckland as a prelude to an unbeaten tour of Britain.

'On the other hand, the very many critics who did not agree with the selection when announced hotly declared it was only what they expected on a fine day; that the big southerners were rugby union forwards bound to be nonplussed by the nippy passing characteristic of league play,' said the *Star* in dismissing any argument the tourists were saving themselves. Such a result would be the worst advertisement imaginable for the team on the eve of its departure, especially after a week of special training and tactical coaching.

'The one object of the week's training at Victoria Park (some of the members being paid by the N.Z. Council) was to enable the team to take the field in the best possible condition. And after being put through a course of "tactics" by Mr Mair, the players were taught a code of signals to be broadcast by Delgrosso. Are we to believe that all this was camouflage, and that they were not trying?'

Match reports of the debacle, by coincidence, appeared in the *Auckland Star*'s eight o'clock edition alongside a three-column article by Ernest Mair outlining 'The Task Ahead'. In that Mair had the temerity to laud the high standards of league in northern England by saying a sixty percent success rate by his team would be the equal of the unbeaten record of the 1924-25 All Blacks against, in his obvious opinion, softer southern opposition.

'How is Mr Mair feeling now, in view of the fact he was also one of the New Zealanders' selectors?' asked the *Star* scribe, an unabashed admirer of that All Black squad. 'Nobody minds (Mair) trying to gloss over generally recognised weaknesses, but even good Leaguers take exception to a "Bananalander" making odious, even libellous comparisons with the best fifteen that ever trod a field.'

Meanwhile, deposed 1925 coach-turned-poet Charles Pearce was putting his own dire predictions to paper in Christchurch. In part they read:

> In the Year nineteen hundred and twenty-six
> Ernest Mair was declaring he could fix
> Said Widnes, You'll see

Mutiny on the High Seas

You'll be beaten by me
A long way more than nineteen to six

In the year nineteen hundred and twenty-six
The New Zealand team will then be in a fix
Says Bert Avery, You're right
We shall put up a fight
Even though we are beaten 50 to six

In the Year nineteen hundred and twenty-six
When Wigan will show you some tricks
Some good folks will declare
Pack up Mr Mair
You're a long way from those Baskerville tricks

Pearce, who had been a member of Albert Baskerville's pioneering 1907-08 All Golds and shared in the inaugural Test series victories over the Northern Union and Australia, was obviously convinced that Mair's much publicised 'methods' would not overcome the uncompromising approach of the British professionals.

As previously mentioned, Pearce wrote that 'those in the know' were aware Mair was 'all heifer dust'. He also penned a warning that financial manager George Ponder would be 'a moral cot case in April next' with 'a woeful tale to tell of the Kiwis' financial failure - your troubles are ahead of you Boy'. Even a bitter Pearce might have regretted just how accurate his predictions were to prove.

It is not known whether any newspapers which published the harsh comments about the team and coach in the wake of the heavy loss to Auckland reached the *Aorangi* before it steamed out of the harbour on 3 August. What is certain is the relief which must have been felt all around, among the team members lining the ship's railing and the NZRL officials waving from the docks, that the ambitious venture was finally under way.

Strike! The Tour That Died of Shame

But the first problem was already brewing. It had cost £53 10s 5d to transport the players from their homes to the port of embarkation, an amount which the NZRL believed would be paid by the English Rugby League. The ERL council, in turn, was adamant it was not its responsibility. The wrangle dragged on for fifteen months. In December 1927, having received a letter from agents Thomas Cook and Son complaining the NZRL had 'finally' refused to pay, the English, while still convinced it had not been their responsibility, agreed to foot the bill 'to avoid further friction'.

The *Aorangi* was a 17,491 gross tonnage Canadian Australasian Royal Mail Line vessel operated by the Union Steam Ship Company of New Zealand. Launched as recently as 1924, she could be expected to provide comfortable passage to Vancouver via Suva, Honolulu and Victoria. The players were then to travel overland by rail to Montreal in their private car. Their second sea voyage would be aboard the *Minnedosa*, a nine-year-old Canadian Pacific steamship refitted in 1925 to a gross tonnage of 15,186 and catering for cabin (206), tourist (545) and third class (590) passengers. It was to stop at Cherbourg on the way to Southampton.

Any prospect of an idyllic crossing of the Pacific lasted no more than a couple of days, until the first players attempted to charge their laundry bills to the team account. Mair wrote to the NZRL from Suva on 6 August and Ponder sent a cable from the ship three days later that the players 'wished their laundry bill to be paid'. NZRL secretary Owie Carlaw reported to the next meeting that after consulting members he had replied 'that the council were of the opinion that laundry came under the appellation of personal expenses and as such could not be paid as per players' agreement'. His actions were approved.

The Honolulu stopover merited a paragraph in the *Brisbane Courier*, which told its readers that team members

Mutiny on the High Seas

had been entertained by the Chamber of Commerce and the British War Veterans. It quoted Mair as saying he 'hoped to return via Honolulu and to play a game here'. It was again not mentioned whether there were any rugby league players in Hawaii to provide opposition or whether Mair had an internal exhibition game in mind.

Even before the team arrived in England, information began to filter through to Auckland that disharmony between some players and management had not only flared again but had reached serious proportions, as the NZRL council minutes of 2 September disclosed.

'The meeting opened in committee to consider a cable received from the managers of the touring team advising that four players were desirous of returning to New Zealand and requesting that two forwards should be sent to England to replace them. The secretary advised that after consultation with the president he had forwarded the following cable to (English Rugby League secretary) Mr (John) Wilson: "This is very urgent. Instruct Ponder cable immediately particular reason men wish to return".

'Eighteen hours after the original cable had been received the managers again cabled desiring the cancellation of their previous cable. The members recognised the seriousness of the position seeing that before the team had reached England dissension had broken out amongst the players. It was recognised, however, that until a reply had been received to the secretary's cable it would be injudicious to take any drastic action.'

Because the NZRL retreated into committee when dealing with the split between an increasing number of forwards and managers Mair and Ponder, the only detailed information of what went wrong on two oceans was related by official press agent Joe O'Shaughnessy after the team's return in early March 1927. O'Shaughnessy's comments were made in Auckland and circulated to every major newspaper in the country.

Strike! The Tour That Died of Shame

'Almost immediately after leaving Auckland on the *Aorangi* the players discovered they had to pay their own laundry bills,' he said. 'Most of them thought that the laundry bills would be paid for them and they got a nasty jar when they found they had to pay their own bills, which on board ship are rather high.' They were travelling through the tropics and O'Shaughnessy said the hot weather was a catalyst for the second in-camp eruption.

'Orders were issued by both managers, Mr Mair and Mr Ponder, that collars and ties must be worn at meals in the saloon. On the night prior to the arrival of the team in Suva a meeting of the team and the managers was held in the saloon. Mr Ponder had ordered Avery, Carroll and others to wear collars and ties when at meals, as the steward had ordered this to be done. Mr Ponder told Carroll that he would take drastic action if he were not obeyed. Many of the team objected to wearing collars and ties owing to the great heat.'

Trust between the increasingly unsettled players and the management was undermined when vice-captain Neil Mouat approached the *Aorangi*'s head steward to ask for a relaxation in the dress code at meals. The head steward claimed to know nothing about any instruction that collars and ties were compulsory. It did not help that the more often the players were required to dress formally for meals the more their laundry accounts ate into their modest allowances.

An incident at Vancouver, concerning two players who refused to perform a haka at the railway station prior to the departure of the 10.15pm train for Montreal, was next mentioned by O'Shaughnessy. He named the players as Neil Mouat and Arthur Singe.

'There were on the platform three negro guards and five officials of the Canadian National Railways,' said O'Shaughnessy. 'Mouat defended himself by saying he had refused because he thought they were cheapening the haka,

Mutiny on the High Seas

and the team was not a theatrical troupe. He would do the haka at the proper place and at the proper time.

'After leaving Montreal (on board the *Minnedosa*), training was commenced. From this training on several occasions several players were missing but nothing was said to them. On the fourth morning out, three players, Singe, Wright and Mouat, were absent from training. At 2pm that day they were arraigned before a full meeting of the team and charged by the managers with "wilfully absenting themselves from training".

'Here it should be noted that at no time did the two managers issue a general warning to the team that penalties would be imposed if they did not attend. Instead of the managers approaching the three men concerned for an explanation of their absence they took the very drastic step of taking the three men before a full meeting of the team immediately.

'At the meeting the three men were asked for an explanation and they said they had slept in. This explanation was not accepted and they were fined ten shillings each. They objected to this penalty in view of the fact that others, on previous occasions, had not been so penalised. At the meeting the three players asked for their tickets back to New Zealand. Three others, Petersen, Carroll and Henry, objecting to the alleged unjust treatment to the three men charged at the meeting, also asked for their tickets back. But, prior to arriving at Southampton, the matter was amicably settled, the fines being lifted and the men concerned agreeing to carry on in England.'

O'Shaughnessy's sympathy for the players might have stemmed from his being secretary of the Christchurch Marist club, for which Petersen was a star player and Bill Devine (who was not mentioned in this part of the press agent's narration) a former member. Mouat and Wright were from O'Shaughnessy's sister Marist club in Greymouth and Singe from the Auckland Marist club.

There was no mention by O'Shannessey that the

99

disaffected players had been defiantly singing The Red Flag, the anthem of the more volatile working classes. Red flags had been hoisted by revolutionaries for decades and as recently as 1923 communist Russia had adopted a predominantly red flag. Sources other than O'Shaughnessy claimed it was sung by the 1926-27 All Black 'malcontents', as they came to be known in numerous references.

That peace appeared to have been restored before the players landed at Southampton confirms the cable from the managers informing the NZRL of four (unnamed) players wanting to return home by the first available boat, and asking for two replacement forwards, was sent from the *Minnedosa*. So, too, was the second message, effectively cancelling the first. But the NZRL replied directly to English Rugby League secretary John Wilson. It must have been a puzzled and perhaps nervous group of ERL officials assembled on the wharf to meet these curious Colonials.

Not that the numbers added up between the managers' cables and O'Shaughnessy's story. He named Singe, Wright and Mouat as having been fined and wanting to return home by the first available ship, and Petersen, Carroll and Henry as supporting them with a similar request. Yet Ponder and Mair told the NZRL of only four players, not six, wanting to withdraw from the tour.

When the NZRL council reconvened on 9 September it was in receipt of another cable from the managers reopening the laundry issue. Sent two days earlier, Ponder and Mair now strongly recommended the players' laundry bills be paid in addition to their weekly allowances. President James Carlaw moved the motion that the council's previous decision be rescinded and Ponder be instructed to pay the laundry accounts, while 'at the same time using economy in connection with this item of expenditure'. It was carried, but only after secretary Owie Carlaw's amendment that no player's laundry account should exceed three shillings per week was defeated by seven votes to five.

Mutiny on the High Seas

The councillors did not need any reminders of how parlous the code's finances were, for the next item on the agenda dealt with the terms of the loan the NZRL had obtained from the Otago Rugby League.

Another touchy subject - whether the international transfer regulations should be altered to remove the two-year residential qualification for Australasian players from either code wanting to join British clubs - was raised by an English Rugby League letter. In this instance the British clubs wanted free access to New Zealand rugby union players. But the NZRL councillors were unanimous the existing agreement must remain in place.

The two Leagues, when negotiating the financial terms of the tour, would have taken into account that rugby league's north of England heartland had suffered terribly from the General Strike which lasted for ten days from 3 May, 1926. They were presumably confident that once the national strike had ended the situation would rapidly improve and life would be back to near-normal by the time the New Zealanders arrived in September.

The General Strike had been called by the Trades Union Congress in an unsuccessful attempt to force the British government to act to prevent wage reductions and worsening conditions for coal miners. Several international factors had caused productivity in British mines to fall dramatically after the First World War, yet mine owners wanted to normalise inflated wartime profits even during times of economic instability. That took the form of wage reductions of up to twenty-five per cent and longer working hours for miners.

From 1 May one million miners were locked out and the General Strike was reportedly staged in defence of miners' wages and hours. Railway men, transport workers, printers, dock workers, iron workers and steel workers were also called out. Armed forces and volunteers maintained basic services. On 12 May the Trades Union Congress called off the strike on the proviso there was no victimisation of strikers. The Government stated it did not have that power, so the General Strike ended without any such agreement.

The miners continued to maintain resistance and stayed above ground. However, by October - a month after the New Zealand tour began - many of them had been forced back to work, especially those with young families. They had endured extreme hardship, even extreme hunger. By the end of November most miners were again down the pits. Those in work were forced to accept longer hours, lower wages and regional wage settlements. Most of those who were not permitted back became permanently unemployed. To a man, the strikers felt they had achieved nothing. Morale was low throughout the traditionally proud north.

Rugby league had since its inception been associated with the coal mining industry. The breakaway from the London-based, upper-class Rugby Football Union in 1895 was driven by the belief in Lancashire and Yorkshire that working men should receive 'broken time' payments for missing Saturday shifts when they were playing football.

Although it was not one of the 1895 originals, no club more typified the intertwining of rugby league and mining than Featherstone Rovers in west Yorkshire. Founded to provide sport for coal miners, its fixtures before the First World War were held at the Featherstone Main Colliery Welfare Ground. When the Rovers joined the semi-professional leagues in 1921 it was playing at Post Office Road, on a compact ground within sight of mine shafts and coal heaps.

Featherstone was a mid-table club in the mid-1920s. It finished fifteenth of twenty-seven teams in 1925-26 and eleventh of twenty-nine during the winter of the New Zealand tour. The club asked to be granted the first tour match to coincide with the opening of a new grandstand, but the RFL declined its request. Featherstone was instead offered a midweek game, but turned it down in the belief its

Mutiny on the High Seas

share of the receipts would not cover the match fee and other expenses. Those fears were confirmed when Bramley played New Zealand on the date originally allocated to Featherstone and suffered a sizeable loss.

Featherstone's withdrawal was an omen of what was to come. Newspaper headlines and articles had highlighted strikes and lockouts on their general news pages for months and would continue to do so while the New Zealanders were in Britain. That was inevitable. No-one knew then that the touring team would introduce stories about strikes and lockouts to the sports pages as well.

Another Yorkshire club, Castleford, also forfeited its place on the itinerary. Castleford was situated just a few collieries down the road from Featherstone and had been formed as recently as June 1926. It already faced a huge task establishing itself in a professional league during a time of unemployment which, according to one report, had reached '99 per cent' in Castleford. As it happened, Castleford was destined to finish last in its debut season with just five wins and a draw from thirty-six fixtures.

The New Zealanders had their headquarters at the West Park Hotel in Harrogate, where the 1921-22 Kangaroos had also been based. Harrogate was renowned as Yorkshire's spa town, a far cry from the grimy mining villages and sprawling cities which surrounded it. The first mineral spring had been found in 1571 and during the early twentieth century it was extremely popular among the English elite and European nobility. Situated on the edge of the Yorkshire Dales, Harrogate has since developed into a dormitory town for commuters working in the big cities and rugby league strongholds of Leeds and Bradford.

Thirty-four matches made up the revised itinerary. New Zealand was to play all of the twenty-nine professional clubs except Featherstone Rovers and Castleford. There were to be three Tests against England (effectively Great Britain because Welsh players were eligible), a match against Wales

Strike! The Tour That Died of Shame

(given Test status by the NZRL) and games against Yorkshire, Lancashire and Cumberland counties.

The final itinerary was:

September 11 v Dewsbury
September 16 v Leigh
September 18 v Halifax
September 21 v Rochdale Hornets
September 25 v Barrow
September 28 v Widnes
October 2 v England, First Test *at Wigan*
October 6 v York
October 9 v Warrington
October 13 v Bramley
October 16 v Hull
October 20 v Bradford Northern
October 23 v Oldham
October 27 v Leeds
October 30 v St Helens Recreation
November 3 v Salford
November 6 v Huddersfield
November 13 v England, Second Test *at Hull*
November 17 v Wigan Highfield
November 20 v Batley
November 23 v Keighley
November 27 v Swinton
December 4 v Wales *at Pontypridd*
December 9 v St Helens
December 11 v Wigan
December 15 v Yorkshire *at Huddersfield*
December 18 v Hunslet
December 25 v Pontypridd
December 27 v Broughton Rangers
December 28 v Wakefield Trinity
January 1 v Hull Kingston Rovers

Mutiny on the High Seas

January 3 v Lancashire *at Leigh*
January 8 v Cumberland *at Workington*
January 15 v England, Third Test *at Leeds*

An earlier version was extended by two weeks with a fixture against Wakefield Trinity on 22 January and what would have been the first rugby league match on French soil, between New Zealand and England at Paris on 29 January. But the Wakefield encounter was later shuffled into the Christmas crush and plans to take the game across the English Channel were to sit on a shelf at English Rugby League headquarters for a few more years.

There was little provision for Christmas festivities. Beginning at Pontypridd in Wales on Christmas Day, the New Zealanders faced the daunting prospect of five games in ten days, culminating with a representative fixture against Lancashire county, and all of them separated by mind-numbing rail journeys. In the midst of a harsh English winter, that would have been a tortuous assignment for a fully fit complement of twenty-six players, let alone a squad which was to be drastically reduced in numbers. Such a schedule would never be permitted in modern times, but in pre-floodlighting days it was not uncommon for touring teams to play three times a week. The 1926-27 players were fortunate that Sunday sport had not yet become acceptable, for many of their successors were committed to numerous double-header weekends while on tour.

6

'SMOOTH AS A BILLIARD TABLE'

It was to be 29 October before the general public in England or New Zealand learned there were disciplinary problems within the New Zealand camp. Until then only a few prominent officials in both countries, and the players themselves, were aware the tour was lurching from one crisis to another and threatening to implode altogether.

Official press agent Joe O'Shaughnessy restricted himself to covering the on-field action for the agency supplying New Zealand newspapers. His reports were sent by cable and were printed in the next day's publications. Presumably because of the costs of dispatching cables, his stories were comparatively brief, containing little more than descriptions of scoring movements and a New Zealand team list.

However, extensive background articles were written by co-manager and coach Ernest Mair, the man at the centre of the storm which swirled around the West Park Hotel in Harrogate. Mair had made a pre-tour arrangement to correspond for the *Auckland Star* and *The Star* in Christchurch. He was prolific in his output but his

'Smooth as a Billiard Table'

observations were sent by sea and took between four and six weeks to appear in print.

Mair had obvious motives for giving the impression the 1926-27 All Blacks were a 'happy family', one of his favourite descriptions for the 1925 New Zealand tourists to Australia. After all, he was in charge of the team and the running of a successful campaign. Anything controversial would reflect on him as much as the players.

So when Mair provided details of the outward trip from Auckland to Harrogate there was no hint of dirty laundry being aired, players getting hot under the collar over dinner on sultry tropical nights, refusals to perform impromptu native dances on near-deserted Canadian railway stations or fines being imposed and then withdrawn for non-attendance at shipboard work-outs. Nor of requests for, or threats to issue, return boat tickets from Southampton.

Yet Mair's writings were invaluable in fleshing out the despatches from O'Shaughnessy. The complications in transporting a sports team from New Zealand to Britain in the era before international air travel were immense. But those involved experienced much more adventure than their modern counterparts. The voyages across two oceans and the Canadian rail journey would have been an unforgettable experience.

The trip via Suva, Honolulu, Victoria, Vancouver, Winnepeg and Montreal took twenty-eight days, eleven fewer than if the team had travelled via the Panama Canal as originally intended. Mair welcomed the change because it also provided three opportunities for on-land training en route to Britain and a much more extensive build-up to the opening match after arrival.

'The team will never forget the magnificent send-off accorded them from the wharf at Auckland. They have never ceased talking about it,' wrote Mair when painting a picture of idyllic life on the Pacific wave. 'Joe Menzies has been unanimously appointed pianist for the team, and even up to the present stage has played a very big part in bringing the best out of the players in the many sing-songs held on the *Aorangi*.'

Writing just before the team arrived in Montreal on 25 August (in an *Auckland Star* article published thirty-four days later), Mair thanked the ship's captain for his generosity. 'The use of the top deck and the appliances in the *Aorangi*'s up-to-date gymnasium were placed at our disposal, the boys taking full advantage of the privileges. The bosun made a rubbing down table and trestles, which enabled the boys to be massaged. A separate room was also provided for this purpose. The boys were so pleased with their treatment that every available photo of the team was autographed by the boys and presented to the officers and crew.

'Realising that one hour on land is more beneficial than six on board ship, I was naturally anxious to secure ground practice for the team on the way over. Suva was cabled, and the Mayor handed the cable over to the football people, who not only granted us the use of their beautiful (but hard) level ground, but requested that we include four of their players in the exhibition game that we intended staging.

'This fitted in nicely as four of our players were not quite up to concert pitch, and their four players filled the breaches. They promised to secure a half holiday for the two schools there if we delayed our practice until the afternoon, which we did. The biggest crowd to date at a football match was the result. The four Fiji players showed exceptional form, and two of them, were they playing in Auckland, would cause the selectors worry when choosing an Auckland thirteen.'

Jack Kirwan was a victim of the hard playing surface, losing 'bark' from his wrist and elbow which required daily treatment and had still not fully healed when the team reached Montreal. Wally Desmond was sidelined in Suva, having seriously cut himself in a collision with a goal post in

'Smooth as a Billiard Table'

the pre-tour match in Auckland. Ernie Herring and Charles Gregory were also excused after suffering from seasickness. Mair revealed the players used a portion of their allowances to purchase bunches of bananas and dozens of pineapples and pawpaw. Phonse Carroll scored a fine souvenir when a native policeman presented him with his cane.

Between Suva and Honolulu, the New Zealanders showed their competitiveness in various contests staged for the passengers. George Gardiner, Lou Brown and Craddock Dufty dressed as a 'Maori family' to be acclaimed as the stars of the ship's fancy dress ball. Neil Mouat won the men's bucket quoits, men's deck quoits, and swept the men's singles, men's doubles and mixed doubles deck tennis competitions. On arrival in the Hawaiian islands, Mair made use of his swimming contacts to secure another training ground at Punahou College.

'It was my pleasure to swim against Honolulu's champions when they held the world's honours, during their various visits to Australia. How they reciprocated! It was unanimously voted by the boys to be the greatest day they had ever had. After they had decorated us with their wreaths of flowers, which must be worn during one's stay, they rushed us through a hurriedly arranged but wonderful programme.

'The sights of the island were quickly motored over, a real Hawaiian lunch of nine courses (hosted by the British War Veterans' Association), a trip to their splendid aquarium, and then last, but not least, practice at riding the surf at their famous Waikiki Beach in canoes and surf boards. Paul Kealona and Sam Kananomoku, two of the world's most famous swimmers, put in the afternoon giving instruction. Everyone had a heavy heart when the gangway of the *Aorangi* went up.

'Should we come back this way, games at Suva and Honolulu can be arranged. The college ground at Honolulu was a trifle softer than the ground at Suva, but both are ideal for games should we play at these places. The trip from Auckland to Vancouver was very calm, quite unexpected for a 6000-mile journey. The only fly in the ointment was the heat between Suva and Honolulu. Fortunately, a nice breeze blew, otherwise there would have been many cot cases.'

The *Aorangi* arrived at Victoria late in the afternoon of 19 August and berthed at Vancouver the next morning. Canadian National Railway officials boarded the boat to not only finalise onward travel arrangements but also to confirm a ground was available for another practice. Mair reported it was the same field used by the 'Union All Blacks' on their most recent stopover. He then made the remarkable statement that 'arrangements were made here for a game should we be returning this way, and the same at Victoria, Edmonton, Saskatoon, Calgary and possibly Montreal'.

What the players thought about the prospect of staging a six-match exhibition tour of Canada after a five-month trek through Britain and France was not recorded by their coach. Perhaps he had not told them in fear of another revolt. In the evening the New Zealanders were guests of the Vancouver Lacrosse Association. They were in awe that the long twilight permitted play to continue until 8.30pm. The lacrosse fans appreciated the haka which culminated an enjoyable stay. Once again, Mair said there were 'sad hearts' when the 600-ton engine pulled their train out of Vancouver railway station.

'The only drawback to this long, but very interesting and educational trip across Canada is the lack of opportunity to continue the exercises practiced on the *Aorangi*. Not that there was no walking to do, for to go to lunch from your carriage was long enough. The team certainly miss the exercise in physical culture, scrum practice etc, done daily on board ship from Auckland to Vancouver,' he wrote.

'On arrival in Winnepeg we were shown over the city, which was one of the old forts of note in the early Indian days. At Edmonton the officials met us on arrival, and did

'Smooth as a Billiard Table'

the honours. A further demonstration was made at Saskatoon, where we were welcomed by the Mayor. The (five-day) journey across Canada, with no practice, good food, nippy atmosphere, has caused the weight of several players to increase, but hard work for the next six days on the *Minnedosa* will off-set that.'

Mair was already planning for the opening match against Dewsbury, then seventeen days ahead: 'The selectors realise the great call on the players in such a big tour, and are concentrating on the first five matches and the Tests.' He even listed his probable line-up. Clearly, Mair was planning to give prospective Test players plenty of match practice before the first Test at Wigan, the seventh fixture on the itinerary. The implication was that quite a number of players would receive little game time during their first month in Britain.

'The boys are confident. They are realising the big hurdles in front of them, and intend tackling their job in the right way. New Zealanders can rest assured that we will all do our best to keep the Dominion's colours flying, that we shall all act off, as well as on, the field in a manner that will reflect great credit on God's Own Country, and that we shall be just as modest in victory as we shall be congratulatory to our opponents in defeat should the fates decree that way.'

Mair was to resume his travelogue by sea mail from Harrogate on 5 September, though he overlooked two happenings which occurred during the few hours the team spent in Montreal. Another correspondent filled in the gap for the *Auckland Star* in an article printed on 30 September.

This writer included a description of the visitors: 'The twenty-eight bronzed and husky New Zealanders forming the famous All Black League team en route to England were accorded a warm welcome when they stepped off the trans-continental train at Bonaventure Station. But their stay in Montreal was regrettably necessarily brief, for they had to sail for England later in the morning on the *Minnedosa*. The

Strike! The Tour That Died of Shame

Canadian populance rubbed their eyes with extreme surprise when they beheld the All Blacks, virtually all of whom were men of big and sturdy physique, bearing unmistakable signs of the excellent football condition they were in despite their long journey half-way across the world from the Antipodes.'

On a cool morning the players were well rugged up in heavy overcoats and many of them wore thick black and white scarves around their necks. The team uniform included a hat which bore a black and white band with a badge in front bearing the initials N.Z. Each piece of luggage bore stickers proclaiming it belonged to the 'New Zealand Football League All Blacks, 1926-27 Tour', with a kiwi emblem also prominent.

'Immediately after leaving the train the team climbed into a big char-a-banc (motor coach) and departed for the steamship sheds singing a rollicking song, the truck groaning under their weight. W Devine, a member of the team, the heaviest back (sic) in all New Zealand with his 247 pounds, astounded Canadian sportsmen by his wondrous agility on his feet. After bestowing their hand luggage aboard the boat and posing for local photographers, the team indulged in a stroll along Common Street to take a casual look at Montreal's harbour-front before sailing time.'

The writer told how the New Zealanders were highly amused when a heavily laden baggage truck, with a youth clad in overalls sitting atop the load, was rammed by a wayward motor vehicle, dumping the bags and boy onto the street. But their grins vanished when they approached the wreckage and found the familiar black and white kiwi stickers on the spilled trunks and suitcases. With only forty-five minutes to departure time, a Canadian National Railways official hurried to the rescue and commandeered another truck to relay the players' possessions to the *Minnedosa*.

While the local media was amused by that episode,

'Smooth as a Billiard Table'

newspaper reporters were serious when querying Mair whether his team had the right to be called All Blacks. That right had been challenged by an expatriate New Zealander, Lieutenant H Gladstone Hill, in a letter to the editor of the Montreal *Daily Star*. Hill's complaint was published under a sub-heading of 'How About the All Blacks?'

'If the professional Rugby football element want to go to England and play Northern Union football, that is their business, but I am not going to see them use the name and work on the reputation of the two famous All Black teams without making a protest and letting the public know the exact position,' he wrote. Hill went on to explain to the newspaper's readers that the All Black title had been bestowed upon the Dave Gallaher-captained 1905-06 New Zealand rugby union side during its tour of Britain.

'Northern Union football was unknown in New Zealand at that time and for many years afterwards (sic). The professional code became popular in England, and in the past ten years has made a great deal of headway in New Zealand. Although the name "All Blacks" is not the registered property of the New Zealand Rugby Union, the amateur body, it has been recognised for many years as designating the amateur touring team and it is ungentlemanly for the professionals to use the name.

'Nearly all of the men in the All Blacks professional team that passed through Montreal on August 25 on the way to Europe played the amateur code in New Zealand and then turned professional. I know several of them personally, and have seen them play both codes. Devine, the heaviest back (sic) in New Zealand, played for my home town and was a policeman in private life.'

Hill went on to say that Gallaher had died at Flanders during the First World War, and the unbeaten 1924-25 All Blacks had made a special pilgrimage to his graveside. He concluded his letter with: 'In regard to the professionals calling themselves the All Blacks, let them play the game and establish a reputation of their own deeds. Then good luck to them. Otherwise, I strongly object. Yours sincerely (signed) Lieut. H Gladstone Hill.'

'We are every one of us entitled to bear the All Black colours and insignia, despite any statements to the contrary,' Mair told journalists. 'As a matter of fact, anything in the way of a football aggravation coming from New Zealand can call themselves All Blacks with full rights.' No doubt Mair was relieved the *Minnedosa* was steaming towards Southampton before Lieutenant H Gladstone Hill had the opportunity to pen a rebuttal of his own.

'Our voyage across the Atlantic in the *Minnedosa* was as smooth as that from Auckland to Vancouver - like a billiard table,' wrote Mair in opening his second *Auckland Star* article after arriving in Harrogate. 'Naturally everyone longed to reach Southampton, and the only disappointment was to meet one of the worst fogs in the history of the English Channel, which delayed our berthing, the fog signals going every two minutes all one day and night.'

Mair was impressed that a powerful delegation from the English Rugby League council had travelled 300 miles from the north to meet his team at the wharf. It included chairman Ted Osborne and his co-manager from the 1924 Lions touring team Harry Dannatt, secretary John Wilson, who had been one of the managers with the 1920 Lions in New Zealand, and a bevy of founders and representatives of the sport, which had only changed its name from Northern Union four years earlier.

Because the ship had berthed too late for a proper customs inspection, the English officials stayed on board overnight. A planned welcoming banquet at the First Avenue Hotel in London had to be postponed and was transferred to a venue in Leeds three weeks later. Once the formalities had been completed it would have been surprising if Osborne and Wilson had not asked Mair and co-manager George Ponder about the worrying

'Smooth as a Billiard Table'

communication from the NZRL alerting them to problems within the touring party. But Mair was not about to let any scandals out of the bag for the reading public back home.

'Both Messrs Wilson and Osborne have been untiring in their efforts to make the All Blacks feel quite at home,' he wrote. 'They acceded to a request to appoint Harold Wagstaff (who skippered the 1914 and 1920 England teams to Australia and New Zealand) to point out the various differences in the English rule interpretations to those in vogue in the two countries on each side of the Tasman. At the present time England's greatest captain and centre three-quarter is coaching Halifax, having forsaken his old but wonderful club of years gone by, Huddersfield. Harold is the proprietor of a thriving hotel business in Halifax.

'There were many pretty scenes from the train from Southampton to London, to Leeds, and thence to Harrogate by motor, where we arrived at eight in the evening. We received a royal Yorkshire welcome in Leeds when we broke our journey there. Our residence at Harrogate is the West Park Hotel, the same as occupied by the Australians in 1921-22. We have the hotel entirely to ourselves and Harrogate is ideal as a headquarters, being conveniently situated for travelling, (with) healthy surroundings and an invigorating atmosphere.'

On their first Saturday in England the tourists were invited by directors of the Leeds club to be their guests at a match against St Helens Recreation at Headingley. Mair wrote at length about the different rule interpretations between England and New Zealand. The list included rules relating to forward passes, knock-ons, play-the-balls, the packing of scrums, hooking methods, positioning of referees for goal kicks and even the number of balls issued for a match - virtually every basic fundamental of the rugby league game.

Mair must have been greatly concerned when he discovered the scrummaging techniques to be nothing like

Strike! The Tour That Died of Shame

he imagined. Instead of striking for the ball cleanly, he wrote that the Leeds and St Helens hookers 'raked every way but the right way, and should have been penalised in eighty per cent of the scrums. The scrums resembled a dozen schoolboys scrambling for a penny, for (with) the rakes going down on the ground the scrums continually caved in the centre.' Mair was relieved to be told by Wagstaff that the referee in that particular match had erred in his rulings. But scrums, and hookers who trapped the ball with their knees, were to haunt Mair and his dwindling band of followers throughout the itinerary.

At that stage Mair wrote of a thirty-seven match tour, perhaps having been informed by ERL officials that they were considering proposals to play one match each in Paris, London and Belfast. He repeated previous statements that the All Blacks were keen to show their hosts that they had improved since their 1924 home series victory over England, that they would display sportsmanship on and off the field and would help 'to knit closer those bonds of Empire that are so dear to everyone'.

7

THE GAMES BEGIN

The start of a faraway international sports campaign, whether it be the opening ball in a cricket Test series or the kick-off to a rugby league tour, inevitably brings with it anxieties for the fans back home. They tend to approach such occasions with a mixture of faith, hope and charity - faith in the chosen players, hope they will live up to their best form, and, if they initially stumble, charity that they will get better as they adjust to foreign conditions.

Dewsbury was given the honour of being the first club to host the first New Zealand rugby league team to play on English soil for eighteen years. It had finished sixteenth in the 1925-26 championship and was to improve four places in the current season. Dewsbury had beaten the Kangaroos five years earlier and at Crown Flatt it had a distinctive sloping ground that confounded many visiting sides.

In the week leading up to the game, the New Zealanders trained diligently on a Harrogate soccer field after rugby union authorities predictably refused to allow the 'professionals' use of their facilities. Yet much was made in

Strike! The Tour That Died of Shame

the English media that the tourists were amateurs receiving nothing more than weekly allowances. Comparisons with the 1924-25 rugby union All Blacks were inevitable and actually encouraged by coach Ernest Mair.

The *Sporting Life* and *Sportsman* conducted an extensive interview with Mair, who explained all profits from the tour would be channelled back to the NZRL to promote the game and not into the players' pockets. 'Not a single member of the side has ever received a penny for playing football, and never will, but we play the game under the laws of the Rugby League and hence are debarred from participating in the rugby union game.'

Asked to compare his team with their unbeaten 15-a-side predecessors, Mair replied: 'I am glad you asked me that question. I am not exaggerating when I say it is superior to the team that won all its games over here in 1925. There is no question that our forwards comprise the best pack that New Zealand has ever produced.' Mair rated fullback Craddock Dufty as a better player than All Blacks fullback George Nepia, and said other backs would prove at least the equal of Bert Cooke and Mark Nicholls, whose success he attributed to unorthodox methods that were unknown to their opponents. His team would be similarly difficult to contain because of new tactics they had devised and practiced.

Mair told the *Daily Telegraph* that physical training had been conducted under the 'Swedish system' for an hour every morning while on board ship, followed by scrum practice for three-quarters of an hour, and massage. 'We are quite sure that we have the best side that has ever left New Zealand, either Union or League, and no better pack of forwards has ever come to England. The weight of our forwards ranges from thirteen stone to seventeen stone and our heaviest man, Devine, curiously enough, is one of our fastest.'

But there was widespread frustration in New Zealand when no match reports appeared in the morning newspapers of Monday, 13 September, despite the

The Games Begin

Dewsbury game having been played early Sunday morning New Zealand time. Readers of *The Press* in Christchurch learned from another source that New Zealand had won 13-9 in front of 16,000 spectators. A solitary paragraph relayed information provided by Canterbury Rugby League president Dr Henry Thacker, who had arranged for results to be telegraphed direct to him.

But the formidable Dr Thacker, at various times Mayor of Christchurch and a Member of Parliament, was not content to let the matter lie. He announced next day that he intended communicating with the Prime Minister, the High Commissioner and the Minister of Internal Affairs asking for explanations why the telegraph system had broken down.

'There is a member of that party empowered to send press messages, and yet the afternoon papers did not receive their message until midday (Monday). When the All Blacks were in England the messages were in New Zealand by 10 o'clock or 10.30 on Sunday morning and Monday's morning papers had full accounts. We've done nothing criminal and yet we are denied this privilege.' Transmission times were to improve after that.

Press agent Joe O'Shaughnessy reported the New Zealanders recovered from a 2-0 halftime deficit after playing into a strong wind, and trailed twice during the second half, before tries to Ben Davidson, Bert Avery and Neil Mouat and two Craddock Dufty goals completed the 13-9 scoreline. Dewsbury's points came from one try and three goals.

Financial manager George Ponder would have been content with the game receipts of £960, a considerable increase on the £720 returned by the 1921-22 Australians. It had not taken long for the tourists to realise the extent of the crippling miners' strike in England's north and they were worried that patrons would be deterred by the charges of five shillings and nine pence for a reserved grandstand seat, three shillings and sixpence for other seats, and one shilling and sixpence for the terraces.

Strike! The Tour That Died of Shame

'Enthusiasts were present from all over England, some coming from as far south as London; others came from Wales and from Scotland,' wrote O'Shaughnessy in a rare background article. 'We arrived from Harrogate, our headquarters, by motor coach and were driven to the Man and Saddle Hotel, where we lunched. The team to play that afternoon retired to bed and slept until it was time to leave for the ground. The departure from the hotel was taken amid a scene of great enthusiasm. The market square was one dense mass of cheering people and the boys received a great ovation. The town band played us to the ground, heading the crowd.

'Dewsbury is a town of over 20,000 inhabitants, and it is safe to say that the large majority, men, women and children, attended the match. The League code has an astounding hold in the north of England, especially in Lancashire and Yorkshire. Our team was necessarily an experimental one and several matches will be necessary before we can be satisfied that the players have individually struck form.'

If the tourists did not know what to expect in their tour opener, then the local supporters were in for a surprise too. The New Zealand team was not led onto the Crown Flatt pitch by captain Bert Avery but by Mildred Mair, the coach's wife, who was clutching a New Zealand flag in one hand and a stuffed kiwi mascot in the other. George Gardiner led a rousing haka before the Mayor of Dewsbury, Alderman James Kilburn, ceremoniously kicked off. Having local dignitaries kicking off was to become a trend, as was the need for referees to change out of their regulation black sport coats because they clashed with the visitors' black jerseys.

The reaction of the more nervous supporters back in New Zealand to the first-up victory was summed up by an ecstatic, though anonymous, *Auckland Star* scribe the following Saturday: 'If we had received word that a rich uncle had died and left us his fortune we would not have been better pleased than we were to read that our tourists

The Games Begin

won their first match at Home.' Perhaps not all of his readers would have been in total agreement.

When Mair's analytical assessment appeared in the same newspaper six weeks later it stretched for a column and a half. He noted the Dewsbury backs made a point of standing right up on their opponents, favoured spot-tackling and were not reluctant to use grubber kicks behind the defensive line and short punts over their rivals' heads. In contrast, the New Zealand backs positioned themselves too deep, 'which is not good for attack or defence'. He said there was much to be learned about halfback play around the scrum base, in packing more tightly into the scrums, and in not tackling opponents who had cleared the ball.

'The selectors experimented with their team in this game,' wrote Mair. 'Dufty filled the fullback position and Sanders and Gardiner the wing positions. In pioneering with Gardiner New Zealand fans may express surprise, but the selectors felt that his height, weight and fend would be valuable. Their judgement was vindicated by his display, the only real mistake he made being when he crossed the goal line and touched down behind the dead ball line, which is very short at Dewsbury.

'Cole and Kirwan were the five-eighths and, although strange (as were the other backs) to the opposition's spotting tactics, short punting and grubbering, did their work well. Davidson was the centre and was the best back on the ground. Wilson Hall played behind the pack, and played magnificently. He certainly set a seal on the halfback position for the first test, which takes place in three weeks' time. Singe, Carroll, Herring, Petersen, Mouat and Avery were the forwards. They were not too successful in getting the ball from the scrums, a very important factor, but they rose to the occasion in offsetting the opposition when they had possession.'

The *Yorkshire Observer* reduced the crowd to an 'official' 12,237 but agreed with the gate receipts quoted in New

Strike! The Tour That Died of Shame

Zealand reports. The tourists were given a pass mark, with the expectation there would be improvement as combinations were formed. The All Blacks were 'man for man, much more powerful than their opponents' and the smaller and lighter home side was lauded for a gritty display.

'No player made a deeper impression than Hall, the halfback who combined a keen sense of anticipation with brilliant speed and finish. Gardiner, a powerfully built wing three-quarter, also showed fine pace; and at fullback Dufty proved cool under pressure. While the forwards were a strong, lusty lot in the open, they were usually beaten for possession in the scrums and there was a tendency to offside play when the packs were formed. These defects will doubtless disappear, however, with a greater familiarity with the scrum rules. Avery, the captain, gave a fine exhibition as loose forward,' said the *Observer*.

An after-match function, hosted by the Dewsbury club, was held at the Town Hall. Ted Osborne and John Wilson, respectively chairman and secretary of the English Rugby League, had attended the match and Osborne praised the New Zealanders for their performance, while also taking into account they were still acclimatising. Once they were fully fit it would take a strong side to beat them, he said. But all of that good work and good will was undermined when forward Arthur Singe and fullback Craddock Dufty came to blows after the team returned to their Harrogate hotel. It was not a case of a forward bullying a smaller back. Both were big men and Dufty actually out-weighed Singe by half a stone.

The incident was not reported at the time and even when it came to light nearly six months later no explanation was given as to what caused the fight between two Auckland men who only a few hours earlier had been team-mates against Dewsbury. What happened next was not revealed until the Manchester *Daily Dispatch* published a review of the 'troubles' in March 1927, quoting an anonymous informant from among the tourists.

The Games Begin

'After the first match at Dewsbury, on returning to Harrogate, two of them had a stand-up fight of about one minute outside the hotel,' said the *Dispatch*. 'They shook hands immediately afterwards. Next morning, one of them, Singe, was ordered to pack up and return to New Zealand. To the other man, Dufty, nothing was said at all. Petersen also had, in the opinion of the manager, not conducted himself as he should have done, and he also was ordered home.

'A football team is not made up of saints. This was the first offence of the tour, and many thought the sentence too drastic. Thus when Singe and Petersen were ordered home, the other five again stated that they wanted to return as things were not to their satisfaction and they desired to cancel their agreements. Things were in a ghastly mess.

'Then Mr Mair told Petersen, Devine, Wright and Henry that they could stay, but he must send home Mouat and Singe. This they declined, saying they must stay with their friends. There the matter rested for a time, but all harmony had been shattered. The rest of the business is public property. The seven players refused to play so long as Mr Mair was in control.'

Alarm bells began ringing at English Rugby League headquarters, where 'Messrs Preston and Fillan (two members of the ERL council) reported on certain happenings at Harrogate in which there appeared to be serious differences amongst the touring party. They said that the conduct of certain members of the team had been bad and that there had been extreme difficulty in getting the management of the hotel to agree to the party remaining. Even now there was the possibility of two men being sent home and three or four others declining to stay in that event.'

The report was supplemented by chairman Ted Osborne's personal observations after the Dewsbury match. After a long discussion it was eventually decided that a full ERL council meeting would be held at Harrogate on 23 September to investigate the matter. In the meantime, secretary John Wilson was instructed to contact shipping agents Thomas Cook and Son that no action was to be taken by them if the New Zealand managers attempted to book passages.

After just one game, there was already a three-way stand-off. Ernest Mair had singled out vice-captain Mouat and Singe as the chief trouble makers and wanted rid of them; fellow forwards Carroll, Devine, Henry, Petersen and Wright were standing with their mates and would accompany them to the boat if Mair carried out his threat; and the ERL was adamant that no-one was going anywhere until the matter was investigated. Trapped in the middle were co-manager George Ponder and the other nineteen players. It was a shocking situation, with a match against Leigh looming on the following Wednesday and two other games scheduled before the 23 September meeting with the ERL councillors.

Singe did not play another game while Mair was in charge of selection and coaching, and Petersen played only twice in those nineteen fixtures. But Mair selected Carroll and Mouat to make their second appearances of the tour against Leigh, and Devine came into the pack for his tour debut. The instruction that Mouat was 'for the boat' quickly took on a hollow ring.

The team left Harrogate at 9.30 on the morning of their match with Leigh. But it was necessary to change trains three times (there were to be four changes on the return journey) and they did not arrive until 1.30pm, hardly ideal preparation for an international game. At the Leigh railway station they were met by the mayor and councillors, several members of the 1924 Lions touring team to Australasia and thousands of curious spectators. The New Zealanders also looked curiously upon some of the citizens of Leigh -- what Mair described as 'a Darktown jazz band, with weird kinds of gowns and instruments' marched in front of their motor coach en route to the pre-match mayoral reception at the Rope and Anchor Hotel.

The Games Begin

Blissfully unaware of the off-field drama, followers of the game in New Zealand read of a 23-16 victory over Leigh, a club which was to finish seventh in the championship, in their newspapers of 17 September. In front of an admirable 12,000 attendance, the All Blacks had capitalised on a strong wind to lead 17-0 at halftime. Dufty opened the scoring with a magnificent field goal from beyond half way, then converted two corner tries to Gardiner and kicked an easier goal when Carroll scored. Lou Brown and Davidson combined in a 70-yards move for the latter to score soon after the re-start. But from 20-0, the New Zealanders conceded sixteen consecutive points before Ernie Herring completed the scoreline with an unconverted try.

'The tourists occasionally showed brilliant combination, the backs supporting each other well, but they have not yet reached the excellence of other Dominion teams,' said the Press Association's cabled match report. 'The forwards are not yet able to get the ball in the scrums, and are often badly beaten in them.' Reading between the lines, the more discerning must have wondered how the New Zealanders were going to obtain enough possession to challenge more powerful clubs such as Wigan, Warrington, Swinton and St Helens Recs, not to mention the county representative sides and mighty England in the three Test matches.

When Mair's sea-mail story arrived weeks later it was learned that many people had gained admission without paying. 'Considering the state of unemployment in Leigh through the strike, the attendance was remarkable,' he wrote. 'The sum of £540 was taken at the gate, 7500 paying for admission. From a financial aspect the position is encouraging, £1500 being now taken in the first two matches. Large numbers of unemployed broke down the fences, forcing their way in.' Among the spectators were Lancashire residents Charlie Seeling, the famous All Blacks and Wigan forward, and former Australian cricket international and Australian Rules first-grade footballer Ted McDonald.

Strike! The Tour That Died of Shame

Early impressions of the tourists inevitably included the qualification that they would improve as combinations were fused with more match practice. Frank Williams, in the *Halifax Courier*, continued this theme after watching the match at Leigh. But there was another disturbing and recurring theme - scrums - in his preview for the third tour match.

'If they secure more possession the backs will provide spectators with good open play, as they handle well and possess speed above the ordinary,' wrote Williams. 'The forwards are well equipped physically, but the decision to leave behind Townsend, reputed to be the best hooker in New Zealand, has apparently not helped them. Townsend's omission, I hear, was brought about through the New Zealand officials fearing that his style of play would not meet with the approval of English referees.

'The failure to secure the ball was the outstanding weakness of the team at Leigh, the home pack gaining possession with monotonous regularity. The penchant to be out in the open is one of the reasons for the inability to secure the ball in the tight packs. When indulging in passing bouts, the handling of the forwards is almost the equal of the men behind. Backs and forwards also pick up cleanly and can teach many home players a lesson in this respect.

'The five-eighths formation will be eagerly watched, as it is an innovation rarely witnessed in the north of England. Halifax followers should be pleased with Davidson. There is not a great deal of this player, but he can be very sprightly. Gardiner, the leader of the "war cry", is another who will appeal, if only for his magnificent physique. Dufty, the fullback, and Avery, the genial captain, are also notable figures. The former is a brilliant kicker and if the Halifax backs ply him with the ball they will have some leather hunting. Well-built punting seems child's play for Dufty. Not only can he kick but his fielding from all angles is capital and he also has a powerful hand-off when closely pressed.'

The Games Begin

If the sagging morale in the divided New Zealand camp needed to be lifted by a long winning sequence, then the tour suffered a serious blow when Halifax, another mid-table club, won 19-13 at the quaintly named Thrum Hall ground. Seven players, Bert Avery, Neil Mouat, Phonse Carroll, Ben Davidson, Craddock Dufty, George Gardiner and Ernie Herring, lined up for a third time. Hector Cole was a last-minute withdrawal because of a knee injury and Frank Delgrosso, Wally Desmond and Joe Menzies played their first games. Receipts amounted to £1030 from a reported 13,000 spectators.

Dominating possession to the extent that it eventually won fifty-six of the seventy-four scrums against an All Blacks pack which wasted its marked weight advantage through loose scrummaging, Halifax scored all eight first-half points and increased the lead to eleven soon after the restart. The staunch Avery was leading from the front. He claimed two tries before the New Zealanders scored a truly sensational third one. Dufty, hemmed in near his own goal-line, inter-passed with Desmond, and seven players handled the ball before Hec Brisbane touched down to complete a movement which had gone from one set of goal-posts to the other. Dufty's conversion lifted the tourists within one point of Halifax at 14-13 before, according to Mair, the referee cost his team victory.

'Bert Avery, right in front of the Halifax goal posts, tried to get up on four occasions, only to be dumped,' recounted the irate coach. 'A free kick was the only decision, so glaring were the infringements, but he ordered a scrum to the amazement of everyone. This was the turning point of the game, and before the New Zealanders could recover Halifax broke away for Townend to be as surprised as the spectators when awarded a try. Young, goaling, made the final score 19-13.

'One thing is certain. Although there are over thirty matches still to play, this referee, Mr W Wood (Oldham), will

Strike! The Tour That Died of Shame

never officiate in our itinerary again. He did not please either team or the spectators. The large attendance was not slow to show their appreciation of the inspiring football played in the second spell by the New Zealanders, who were unlucky to lose. Another feature, which has been broadcast by the press, was the sportsmanlike manner in which they played their game on the field, and that they can be just as modest in victory as they are spontaneous in their congratulations to their opponents in defeat.'

While the tourists had been unfortunate to encounter referee Wood in an unresponsive mood at Halifax, they were decidedly lucky to escape with an 11-9 win over Rochdale Hornets in midweek. The home team, which was in the process of advancing its league-table ranking from twenty-second in 1925-26 to eighth in 1926-27, led 9-2 at halftime and finished the match with three of the four tries. Wing Jim Parkes scored New Zealand's sole try in his tour debut and Mouat and Len Mason kicked two goals each. Charles Gregory replaced Dufty at fullback but Avery, Mouat, Carroll and Herring continued to bear most of the forward burden.

This was the day that the tourists were to have played the new Castleford club, but, with unemployment so rife in the intensive coal mining town, a swap had been arranged with Rochdale for 3 January. As it eventuated, Castleford pulled out of that date too. Mair was upbeat about the 'better than anticipated' Rochdale gate - 7,600 spectators paid £586, to bring the four-match total to £3120. The locals certainly enjoyed the first half as the Hornets recovered from an early Mason penalty goal to race away for three tries.

Parkes' try was a spectacular effort, being initiated from the scrum-base by Hall, who found Avery in support. Davidson also handled before Parkes touched down. Mouat had earlier kicked a penalty goal and when Mason converted Parkes' try from the sideline it was 9-9. Parkes should have been awarded a second try but he had been pulled back from the goal-line before the referee arrived on

Above: Ernest Mair, sitting front right, in the St Paul's A rugby league team

Above: Ernest Mair with the trophies won over two seasons, 1915 to 1917. Seated is his coach, Fred Larter Jr

Below: Neil Mouat lifts North Island scrum-half Tim Peckham away from the ball as fellow South forward Frank Henry towers over them. At far right is North forward Ernie Herring

Left: George Gardiner, who played at wing and prop, blended speed with size during the now infamous 1926-27 GB Tour

Right: Bert Avery tackles New South Wales' Micky Waterhouse in a 1925 Tour match in Sydney

Above: Lou Brown races around the NSW defence in 1925

Above: The 1926-27 All Blacks. Back row, Arthur Singe, George Gardiner, Bill Devine, Lou Petersen, Len Mason, Harry Thomas, Joe Menzies, Craddock Dufty. Third row: Frank Delgrosso, Wally Desmond, Hector Cole, Ernie Herring, Charles Gregory, Jack Kirwan, Jack Wright. Second row: Jim Sanders, George Ponder (financial manager), Neil Mouat (vice-captain), Bert Avery (captain), Ernest Mair (manager-coach), Phonse Carroll, Frank Henry. Front row: Jim Parkes, Lou Brown, Ben Davidson, Wilson Hall, Stan Webb, Hec Brisbane.

Left: Scenes from Queens Wharf in Auckland. Players aboard ship (top) and family and friends (below) before the *Aorangi* left for Vancouver

Right: Captain Bert Avery is greeted by English Rugby League president Ted Osborne

Above: The tourists arrive at Southampton, England, aboard the *Minnedosa*

Above: An early training session in Harrogate. Tourist Wilson Hall feeds a scrum. Ernest Mair is to the left of Hall, George Gardiner stands behind him, and former Great Britain captain Harold Wagstaff - offering scrummaging tips - is on the right

Left: Craddock Dufty practices his goalkicking at Harrogate with Neil Mouat and Joe Menzies looking on

Below: Ernest Mair uses chessmen to explain his tactics to, from left, Frank Henry, co-manager George Ponder, Len Mason, Arthur Singe, Hec Brisbane and Joe Menzies

Right: The team for the opening match at Dewsbury.
Back row: Joe O'Shaughnessy (press agent), Jack Kirwan, Arthur Singe, Lou Petersen, George Gardiner, Craddock Dufty, Hector Cole, Ernie Herring, 'Bright' Hayhurst (trainer).
Middle row: Phonse Carroll, Ernest Mair (manager-coach), Neil Mouat (vice-captain), Bert Avery (captain), Mildred Mair (wife of manager-coach), George Ponder (financial manager).
Front row: Wilson Hall, Ben Davidson, Jim Sanders

Left: Mildred Mair, carrying a flag and stuffed toy kiwi, leads out the players for the opening game at Dewsbury. She is followed by Bert Avery, Neil Mouat, George Gardiner, Lou Petersen and Craddock Dufty

Right: Hector Cole looks for support during the Dewsbury match. Bert Avery is inside Cole and Wilson Hall at the back

Left: Hooker Phonse Carroll leads the haka before the first Test against Jonty Parkin's England at Central Park, Wigan. Mildred Mair dutifully holds her New Zealand flag and stuffed kiwi at the right

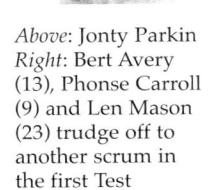

Above: Jonty Parkin
Right: Bert Avery (13), Phonse Carroll (9) and Len Mason (23) trudge off to another scrum in the first Test

Above: Half-time at Hull, from left, George Gardiner, Len Mason, Ernie Herring, Hec Brisbane, Frank Henry, Jim Sanders and Wally Desmond.

Above: Hec Brisbane kicks ahead during the match against Oldham

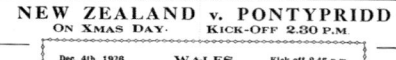

Above & left: Match programme for the Test match against Wales at Pontypridd

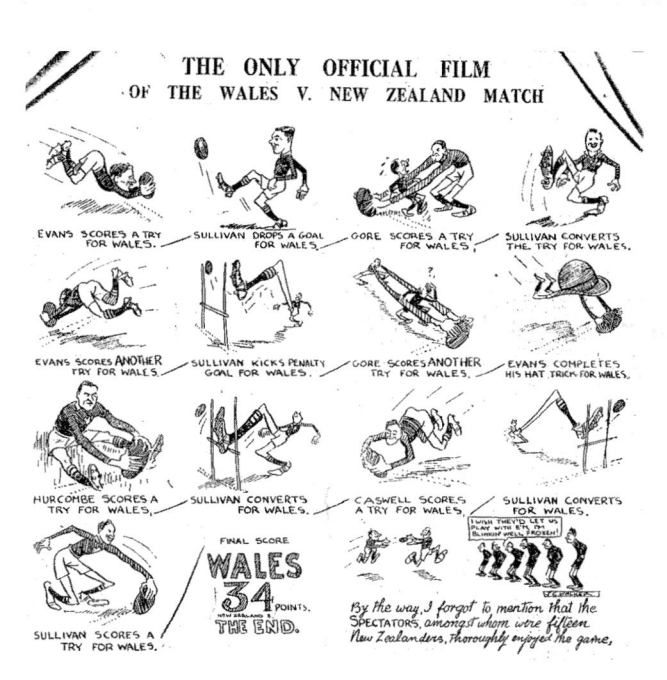

Left: A cartoon from the *Evening Express* celebrates the decisive Welsh victory over the NZ All Blacks

Above: Ernie Herring's 'loyalty medal'

Below: Record try-scorer Bert Avery. There was no better forward in Britain during 1926-27

Below: Wales and Wigan legend Jim Sullivan was to be George Nepia's first opponent when the renowned All Black full-back switched to rugby league

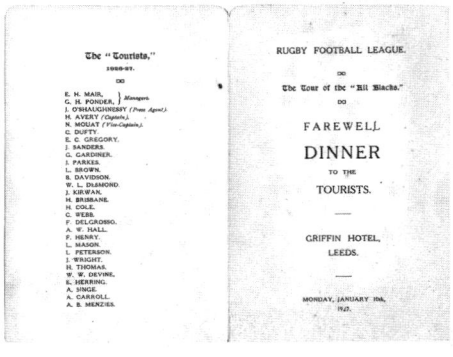

Above: Programme from the 1926-27 Tour farewell dinner, held in Leeds

Above: Lou Brown (standing second from left) and Len Mason (in headgear, standing at right) after Wigan's triumph in the first Challenge Cup final played at Wembley Stadium in 1929

Above: George Gardiner leads the haka at Halifax, in the forward-facing fashion of the day

The Games Begin

the scene. Time was running out when Mouat nudged the New Zealanders ahead with another penalty goal and Rochdale's goalkicking woes continued to the very end when a short-range penalty, and the chance of an honourable draw, went astray.

The *Rochdale Observer* was of the firm opinion that the result was an injustice: 'The Hornets were the better side in their match with the "All Blacks" at the Athletic Grounds yesterday, but the superiority of the visitors in goalkicking and the leniency of the referee (Mr F Peel, of Bradford) in their favour in his interpretation of the rules of the game gave them victory late in the match by a couple of points.'

The *Observer* reported that the haka did not go unchallenged: 'The proceedings at the ground opened with the war cry of the tourists, which was received with much cheering and laughter, and when the Hornets players sprang a surprise on their visitors there was another demonstration from the crowd. They lined up and watched the All Blacks' performance and then, led by Edwards, replied with a defiant shout ending on a high note with something that sounded like "Agorah". This was the first attempt at a response to the New Zealanders' vocal challenge.'

In addition to the loose packing in the scrums, the writer questioned New Zealand's backline formation of one halfback, two five-eighths and three three-quarters. 'It leaves too big a gap down the middle for spry halves, and the Hornets might have made more of this defect than they did.' He predicted the New Zealanders were in for a long, hard winter and would struggle to match up against the better teams.

Next day Mair replied to the criticisms of his team's scrummaging and his selection panel's decision to leave Alf Townsend and other specialist hookers back in New Zealand. The fault, he said, lay with the misinformation provided pre-tour about English methods and the different rule interpretations being applied.

Strike! The Tour That Died of Shame

'We were given to understand that in England "raking" had to be done by the hooker standing up,' Mair told the Manchester *Daily Dispatch*. 'As a result, I instructed hookers generally that the New Zealand method of hookers going down to the ball and thus causing scrums to cave in at the centre was not the method practised in England. We were therefore very much surprised to find, on visiting our first English match between Leeds and St Helens Recs, that the hookers were doing the very thing I had stopped in New Zealand. When I tell you that we left men behind in New Zealand who are extremely clever at this style of hooking you can imagine how very much annoyed we were.'

With regard to other criticisms, Mair admitted the forwards had not scrummaged tightly as a unit, with the second-row breaking off too soon and the front-row not keeping 'under' the opposition. That was because the forwards had been taught a different style of rugby league, in as much as they were expected to take part in movements with their backs and were often positioned all over the field. When they arrived in England they were prepared to play the game entirely as designed by the English Rugby League but found it was very different to that in New Zealand. Mair assured the English people that if his team got an even share of the ball it would win the majority of its matches.

There were pre-tour photographs taken of former British captain Harold Wagstaff working on the All Blacks' scrum formation alongside Mair. But Wagstaff had been the outstanding midfield back of his era and would never have experienced first-hand the writhing monster that was the old-style rugby league scrum. More advice was to be forthcoming from John Higson, an old Hunslet front-rower who played two Tests against the 1908-09 Kangaroos and agreed to assist the New Zealanders. Most of the touring forwards were rugby union converts conceding a vast amount of knowledge to every pack they met.

On 23 September ten members of the English Rugby

The Games Begin

League council, led by chairman Ted Osborne and secretary John Wilson, assembled at the West Park Hotel in Harrogate to meet with the entire touring party. According to Wilson's meticulously penned minutes, only Bill Devine was missing. No reason was given for the absence of the big Timaru policeman. Osborne, who had been empowered by the NZRL to sort the problems out, asked for 'full and frank statements' from all parties.

'Subsequent discussion showed that there existed considerable differences in the party and that a number of players did not see eye to eye with the team manager and coach Mr Mair on matters of discipline and tactics on the field,' recorded Wilson. 'The speakers all agreed that those differences arose either before the team left New Zealand or on the way across. The differences were fully ventilated. Any criticism was fully and fairly met by the managers, (with) Mr Mair offering to forgo any question of tactics or coaching on the field for the next few matches and if this proved successful to allow it to continue.'

Then came the bombshell which the New Zealanders and probably some ERL officials had been covering up from the media in both countries - two of the players, Lou Petersen and Arthur Singe, had removed themselves from the camp. Neither of them had played since the first game twelve days earlier and it was not disclosed when they left the team hotel. But Devine had featured in the second and fourth matches and there was almost certainly a more innocent explanation for his absence. The obvious assumption is that the rift between the coach and two players had escalated after Mair's initial order that they go home, with the upshot that Petersen and Singe took it upon themselves to call his bluff and move out.

'Messrs Petersen and Singe expressed their regret if any action of theirs had caused unrest in the party,' continued Wilson's minutes. 'They expressed themselves as willing and anxious to do all they could to assist the team, on the

Strike! The Tour That Died of Shame

field and off. They shook hands with their managers and later on the same morning brought their baggage from Leeds and settled down in the hotel with their colleagues.'

Osborne thanked the tourists for the frank way in which they had confronted their problems head-on, and said he felt sure harmony would now reign. For their part, managers Mair and Ponder expressed their appreciation to the council members for their help.

In the new spirit of co-operation, the New Zealanders - only thirteen of them, for it was another gripe that non-playing members were left behind at Harrogate - set off next day on one of their longer journeys to play the Barrow club in Cumbria. It was one of six games when they expected to stay away from Harrogate because of distance and travel schedules. After leaving on the Friday morning, they changed trains three times before getting to Barrow at 5.15pm.

On match morning they visited the Vickers ship-building yard and attended the inevitable civic reception. Barrow had been unfortunate to lose its ground during wartime and was playing out of Little Park at Roose. Local knowledge was invaluable, for the playing field featured a distinct slope along one side and players had the unusual experience of running either up or down hill. Rain affected the attendance but Mair felt the gate of £477 was 'remarkable for Barrow at the present time, where there is so much unemployment and thousands are on the dole.'

Avery, Mouat, Carroll and Herring made their fifth consecutive appearances, and fellow forward Mason his fourth. Barrow was not one of Britain's premier clubs but engaged in the most entertaining encounter of the tour to date. Although New Zealand won by only 19-16, it had the result in safe-keeping throughout until a late rush from the home side reduced the winning margin. Avery (two), Desmond, Delgrosso and Herring scored tries and Dufty and Mouat kicked one goal each.

The Games Begin

The win came at a severe cost. First choice fullback and goalkicker Dufty suffered bruised ribs and pluckily played on until the finish. However, he was to be sidelined for the next six games, including the looming first Test match. The Press Association praised Davidson, Dufty, Devine, Avery and Mouat as being 'brilliant' against Barrow, while adding 'the whole team showed better spirit and understanding than in any previous game.'

On the Tuesday of Test week the tourists, plus members of the English Rugby League council and York club officials, were guests of Rountree and Company, a firm of cocoa manufacturers based in York. About eighty people assembled for lunch at the cocoa works before the New Zealanders were guided around sights of the ancient city. All twenty-six players, the two managers, press agent Joe O'Shaughnessy and Mildred Mair were listed in the *Yorkshire Herald* as being present.

What must surely go down in NZRL history as Black September was completed next day with the fixture against modestly performed Widnes at Lowerhouse Lane. Avery was given a break, English-born Frank Henry and Jack Wright came into the pack for the first time, but there was no respite for Mouat, Carroll or Herring. This was their sixth game in nineteen days and Mason's fifth in sixteen days - an assignment made even the more exhausting because of the strenuous travel involved - yet all were to be required to front up again against England three days later. So were Gregory, Brown, Delgrosso, Brisbane, Davidson and Hall among the backs. The New Zealanders were in full dress rehearsal mode.

They won 15-5, keeping Widnes try-less until the closing stages. Cole, who alone was not to back up in the test match, scored a first-half try, and Brown and Mouat went over after the break. Mouat converted them all. Press Association coverage suggested a solution might have been found for New Zealand's scrum hassles. In the first half, at least, they

Strike! The Tour That Died of Shame

had more of the ball than their opponents. Hall and Davidson continued to impress among the backs. But the *Widnes Weekly News* said the virtual New Zealand Test team did not compare in quality with the 1921-22 Kangaroos.

The crowd of about 5000 and a £460 gate disappointed Mair. He was, however, impressed with the refereeing of the Rev. Frank Chambers, who was 'as big in temperament as he is in physique'. Mair approved of his firmness in insisting the halves retire behind the scrums, and in dealing with players who questioned his decisions or 'used adjectives'. He said 'the All Blacks will welcome this reverend gentleman at any time.' Not so the Widnes fans, however, for local newspaper reports told of how the Rev. Chambers' rulings drew regular complaints from the terraces.

Mair provided details of just how difficult it was to travel around the north of England on a railways system disrupted by the coal miners' strike and the increased cost of fuel, which led to some less popular lines having their services seriously disrupted. It was not even practical for the tourists to return to their Yorkshire base between the match at Widnes and the first Test at Wigan three days later.

'To give you an idea of the changing of trains that the All Blacks had to do on the day of the Widnes match, they left Harrogate at noon, changed at Leeds, again at Manchester and at Farnsworth, then (after the game) to Liverpool Central, across to Liverpool Exchange, thence to Southport, where we spent four days concentrating for the first Test. It was useless going back to Harrogate from Widnes, there being no connection on the Wednesday. Thursday was the earliest, and it meant leaving the next morning for Wigan, so the team was taken straight to Southport and were quartered at the Prince of Wales Hotel,' wrote Mair.

8

ROLLER-COASTER RIDE

Even without knowing about the internal strife that had not yet come to public attention, only the most optimistic supporters back home would have given New Zealand much chance of competing with England in the first Test match at Wigan's Central Park on 2 October. While the tourists had won five of their six lead-up matches, they had been stretched to the limit by teams which featured in mid-to-lower positions on the club championship table, were beaten by Halifax and continued to concede huge advantages in scrum possession.

England (which was to field seven adopted Welshmen during the series) had named a truly formidable team, with two of the sport's legends, fullback and goalkicker Jim Sullivan and scrum-half and captain Jonty Parkin, in strategic positions and with pivotal responsibilities. It would be remembered that Sullivan and Parkin were indisposed when New Zealand won the first two Tests at home in 1924 and returned to prevent a whitewash in the third match.

Nine of the thirteen England Test players had toured

Strike! The Tour That Died of Shame

Down Under two years earlier and shared in the coveted Ashes triumph over Australia. Their tour had been declared a success on that score but they clearly had a score to settle with New Zealand. This time the contest was to be held in English conditions and with English referees interpreting the rules in the manner to which they were accustomed. What is more, Craddock Dufty, who the All Blacks would have relied upon to counter the great Sullivan as both goalkicker and last line of defence, was out injured.

In addition to the nine 1924 Lions, England recalled Hull forward Bob Taylor, who had played one Test against the 1921-22 Kangaroos, and debuted Swinton centre Jack Evans, Swinton stand-off half Billo Rees and Batley forward Dai Rees.

New Zealand fielded only four survivors from the losing third 1924 Test in Dunedin - centre Hec Brisbane, wing Frank Delgrosso and forwards Ernie Herring and Neil Mouat. Inspiring captain Bert Avery, who had missed the Dunedin Test through injury, was back at loose forward. Because no Tests had been held on the 1925 Australian tour, fullback Charles Gregory, wing Lou Brown, centre Ben Davidson, halves Wally Desmond and Wilson Hall, forwards Frank Henry and Len Mason and hooker Phonse Carroll were making their debuts at the highest level.

On a summer-like afternoon, the All Blacks surprisingly adopted the British formation of a fullback (Gregory), four three-quarters (Brown, Davidson, Brisbane, Delgrosso) and two halves (Desmond and Hall) for the first time. After half-time Desmond switched to the wing, Hall to stand-off and Delgrosso to scrum-half. The backline then functioned more smoothly. The overworked Mouat, Mason, Avery, Herring and Carroll were joined by Henry in the forward pack. Mouat, Herring and Carroll were making their seventh appearances in three weeks and Avery and Mason had missed just one game each.

Press Association reports credited New Zealand with putting up 'a fine struggle' against the odds before losing 28-

20. English critics found aspects of the tourists' performance deserving of praise but generally agreed the home team was always in command and might have eased up, consciously or otherwise, before conceding points towards the finish.

'The match was only lost by the visitors after a fine struggle and they were by no means disgraced,' New Zealanders read in Monday morning newspapers. 'They do not yet seem accustomed to English methods, and though they lacked the home team's pace, they did not get the ball away from the scrums as quickly as they might. In the loose they showed rare bustling football. Most of their tries followed good work in the open. Mason, Avery and Mouat were the best forwards. Hall was excellent at half, and Brown and Brisbane were the best three-quarters. Gregory played a grand game at fullback.' Parkin was described as being 'the brains of England' who 'initiated nearly every scoring movement'.

Sullivan, who had signed for Wigan in 1921 as a Welsh rugby union prodigy and was to extend his incredible and prolific-scoring career for the club through to 1946, took his chance to dent the New Zealanders' confidence with an early penalty goal from near halfway. The score blew out to 15-0 through tries to Rix, Carr and Taylor before Avery briefly turned the one-way traffic by carrying several opponents across the England goal-line. Mouat converted. But big England loose forward Frank Gallagher got across for the try which made it 20-5 at halftime.

The *Wigan Observer* noted increased energy in New Zealand's second half display. Hall had a try disallowed by referee Bob Robinson for a forward pass and Mason was astray with a goal kick before Avery and Hall conspired to lay on Brisbane's try. Mouat converted again for 20-10. England, however, scored the next eight points and it took late tries to Mason and Davidson, plus two more Mouat goals, to produce the respectable final scoreline of 28-20. A recent book by British rugby league historian Robert Gate claimed Robinson 'unaccountably let the second half run for

Strike! The Tour That Died of Shame

forty-five minutes and New Zealand scored ten points after the whistle should have blown.'

Not all of the drama was on the pitch. A tense situation had developed outside Central Park as thousands of unemployed men gathered, drawn to the venue by their love of the game but with no money to pay the minimum admission fee of two shillings. The *Observer* reported an official attendance of 15,009, comprising 14,709 who paid at the turnstiles and 300 with complimentary tickets. 'The receipts were officially returned at £1643,' it said. 'Under normal conditions this would have been much greater, for a shilling entrance fee at the present time, let along two shillings, was out of the reach of Wigan enthusiasts. Several thousand assembled round the enclosure, but the extra police assistance kept the crowd in order and there was no attempt to rush the gates as was anticipated.'

New Zealand coach Ernest Mair sea-mailed his thoughts on 5 October, though they were not printed in the *Auckland Star* until 10 November. 'Seeing that Wigan's unemployed approaches the 40,000 mark owing to the strike, it is generally admitted that it would have been better to have held the first Test at Leeds and the second or third Test at Wigan in the hope that the coal trouble would have finished. But for the strike the gate takings at Wigan would have passed £3000 comfortably,' he wrote.

'Fortunately for the tour the end of the strike seems in sight, one-seventh of the total strikers having already returned to the mines. The income tax is now four shillings in the pound, and most of them in business would prefer to be out of it all. For the eight (sic) matches to date £5707 has been taken - an average of £815. As a further result of the present trouble our match with Featherstone tomorrow week (13 October) has been cancelled and we play Bramley on that date as there is less unemployment there.'

Mair misrepresented the attendance at 18,000 by kick-off, with 'thousands being wedged everywhere outside and at twenty minutes to full-time 4000-odd had to be let in.' Perhaps referee Robinson felt those admitted late deserved an extra five minutes added on to normal time; or perhaps he was nervous they might riot if deprived of some additional entertainment. Mair claimed Parkin's success at the toss gave England first-half advantages of a strong wind and 'glaring' sun, both of which 'weakened' in the second spell.

But Mair found some positives in defeat: 'The margin was a surprise to every pressman in England, who did not give the All Blacks any hope of victory. Had the game lasted another ten minutes victory would have been with the New Zealanders. At the conclusion of the first spell a 30-points victory for England was the opinion of eighty per cent of the spectators, so easily were the tries scored and so much did England dominate the play.' He predicted 'the personnel of both teams in the second Test will be different', without explaining why.

Ten more games were scheduled against club teams before the second Test at Hull. On the face of it, that provided plenty of time to regroup. In what might have been a spirit of reconciliation, Lou Petersen was restored to the line-up for the midweek match at nearby York, though fellow stay-away Arthur Singe would continue to be ignored. Mouat was rested for the first time but front-rowers Carroll and Herring were again pressed into service. Second-row forward Harry Thomas and stand-off half Stan Webb were to finally make their tour debuts. Frank Henry undoubtedly enjoyed the opportunity to line up against the club he had left to try his luck in New Zealand two years earlier.

Regional newspapers argued over the merits of a 3000 attendance at the Clarence Street ground. 'It was below the average for the club's home games,' said the *Yorkshire Post*. That was contradicted by the *Yorkshire Herald*, which labelled it 'a splendid crowd for a midweek match'. Mair later decreed it to be 'satisfactory under the existing circumstances'. The coach would not have agreed, but English officials were by now probably including the frequently unconvincing form of the visitors among their own 'existing circumstances'.

It was important the New Zealanders regained their winning ways, and they did that by 19-11 thanks largely to wing George Gardiner's contribution of a try and five goals from as many attempts. 'York proved a stubborn side. It was the visitors' superior staying powers, rather than superior football, which gave them the upper hand,' reported the Press Association. 'York had the advantage in the scrummages but the visitors were superior in loose work. They failed to throw the ball about sufficiently, though they tackled well.' Petersen celebrated his return with a try and Kirwan scored the other.

According to Mair, Henry 'demonstrated to his old pals that he had improved out of sight on the form he had displayed when at York. Frank had only one regret - that he did not score a try - though he certainly tried hard enough. Moreover, at the banquet at night, when asked to give a speech he neatly informed his distinguished audience that although he had had a good time in York, and that it was a fine city, he had had a better time in New Zealand, which was the ideal place for all Englishmen.' Ironically, Henry was fated not to return to his adopted country at tour's end.

That same night the NZRL council met in Auckland and rejected an English Rugby League proposal that the two-year qualification period be removed for Australian and New Zealand rugby union players signed by British professional clubs. 'The unanimous decision of the council was that it was strongly opposed to any attempt to alter the existing agreement,' said *The Press*. It was not stated whether the NZRL was worried talented footballers with an eye to attracting offers to play for pay would view rugby union as the only pathway, or if it was suspicious the English clubs were using the other code as a stepping stone towards returning to unrestricted overseas transfers.

Financial manager George Ponder frequently acted as an

Roller-Coaster Ride

ambassador for New Zealand while in England, addressing audiences in various centres about the delights of his homeland and openly touting for immigrants. 'The people of New Zealand did not want England to send her population to America and other places,' the *Warrington Guardian* reported Ponder as telling a football supporters' club gathering at the Warrington Grand Cinema Dance Hall. 'They wanted them to go to New Zealand. If they wished to get out of this country, he advised them to go to their own colonies.' His words were greeted with cries of 'hear, hear' and applause.

Next day, when the All Blacks were due to meet Warrington, Ernest Mair spoke during a pre-match luncheon at Carter's Café. Mair contended his team had not been as 'shrewd' as its opponents in feeding the scrums - virtually accusing opposing scrum-halves of cheating - but even though they had lost the first Test the tourists were still confident of winning the series. Acknowledging that Warrington had finished runner-up to Wigan in the 1925-26 Rugby League Championship, Mair confidently predicted 'you are (also) going to be second in the competition this afternoon'.

The coach is unlikely to have relished the post-match function after Warrington out-classed New Zealand 17-5 at the Wilderspool stadium. An early try to Mason, set up by Brown, and Gardiner's conversion were the only positive returns for the tourists. According to the Press Association, 'the attendance was only 7500 due to heavy rain and a gale of wind, which also hampered the New Zealanders' play'. Warrington's forwards not only dominated the scrums but were also 'exceptionally clever in loose play, consequently the New Zealand backs had few opportunities'. This time the little parade from the pavilion onto the field was led by Mair carrying the kiwi mascot and Ponder carrying an imitation British bulldog.

Both scrum-halves, Delgrosso and Hall, were sidelined with injuries suffered in the Test match, the All Blacks fielding a makeshift halves pairing of Webb and Davidson.

Strike! The Tour That Died of Shame

They were further hampered when Davidson dislocated a thumb in the opening minutes. He did not return to the field until just before halftime and was little more than a passenger thereafter. Avery moved from the pack to stand-off half, leaving only five forwards under siege from six rampant rivals for half an hour. Warrington led 11-5 at halftime despite playing into the elements.

Mair condemned the performance as 'the worst of the tour', criticised the inside backs for falling for the dummy passes of their markers and said the forwards failed to pack tightly in the scrums and tired from their exertions attempting to contain Warrington in the loose. Carroll and Herring must literally have been nearing exhaustion, for both were playing their ninth successive games. On the credit side, Mair wrote that 'Gregory and Brown rose to great heights in attack and defence and saved the side frequently, being easily the best two players in the New Zealand side. On the day we were beaten by a better side and at no stage of the game did we look like mastering the situation.'

There was some relief when the tourists lined up against Bramley, instead of the originally scheduled Featherstone Rovers, at the little Barley Mow ground where the All Golds had opened their pioneering tour. Bramley had finished last in the previous season's championship and was not faring much better in 1926. New Zealand conceded an early try and led 14-5 at the break before racing away to a 35-12 victory. It should have been even more decisive after Avery (two), Brown (two), Parkes (two), Desmond (two) and Sanders shared the nine tries. Gardiner had minimal success as the preferred kicker. Eventually, Gardiner, Mason, Delgrosso and Gregory managed one goal apiece. On a stormy day, only £82 was taken at the gate. Financially, the substituted match did nothing for the tour coffers but it proved to be valuable in other aspects.

The touring selectors had decided to experiment with three of their wings. Gardiner was inserted into the second-row,

Roller-Coaster Ride

Brown slotted into stand-off half, and Parkes played at centre. Mair was delighted with the results. 'It was a pleasure to see both Gardiner and Mason putting every ounce of their thirty-one stone into the scrum from whistle to whistle,' he said. 'As a result it was the best scrummaging to date. We secured the ball from the scrum more often than in any previous game, and it was the first time the New Zealanders used their weight as one man. Frequently they secured the ball after being beaten (to the strike) by pushing Bramley over it.

'Brown was played at five-eighth as an experiment, as this position has been the chief fly in the ointment in our matches. He rose to the occasion and the selectors are wisely persevering with him against our next strong opposition, Hull. Parkes was also brought into centre three-quarter and did all that was asked of him.' Both sides finished with twelve men after their respective scrum-halves were injured. Delgrosso's shoulder problem kept him out of the next four fixtures. Carroll had been given his first rest at Bramley, but the ever-present Herring soldiered on.

Referees and their choice of garb were back in the spotlight. Mair wrote that at one stage, 'Brisbane ran twenty-five yards, sent to Desmond, to Avery, who passed to the referee when tackled. This was a sure try, for two of our men were waiting with no opposition.' A similar incident cost the tourists another probable try. After the game the English Rugby League circularised all referees instructing them not to wear black or blue coats over their jerseys when officiating in matches involving the New Zealanders.

Plans to retain the same thirteen for the encounter with Hull FC were revised with Davidson returning in place of Parkes at centre and a fit-again Hall taking over from the injured Delgrosso at scrum-half. After being met by the mayor, town sheriff and Hull FC officials at the railway station, the official party and players attended the obligatory reception at the Guildhall. Mair assured his audience that the New Zealanders were fielding their best team against

Strike! The Tour That Died of Shame

Hull and promised that they would enhance their reputations. This time he was right.

Hull FC was not only a top-four team but had been unbeaten in thirty-five consecutive games at its Boulevard ground. The Monday afternoon *Auckland Star* banner headlines proclaimed 'N.Z. League Men Gave Best Display At Hull; British Team Lost Unbeaten Record In Last Few Minutes Of Game.' Wilson Hall's return was indeed timely, for it was he who dived across for the equalising try on the blind side of a scrum just before fulltime, giving Gregory the chance to convert and complete a heartening 15-13 result. Brisbane and Desmond were New Zealand's other try-scorers and Gregory's winning goal was his third of the day.

'It was easily the best display the New Zealanders have given in England, and if they had played like that in the first Test England would not now be one-up out of three Tests,' wrote an ecstatic Mair. 'The game see-sawed from start to finish in points, and the spectators were held the whole game. It was anybody's game right up to the last second, for immediately Gregory converted Hall's try the fulltime whistle sounded. It was a game that will live in the memory of all who had the privilege of witnessing it.

'There were many New Zealanders of bygone years in the large audience and how they cheered. How proud they were of the win, of the breaking of the great record, but particularly of the magnificent spirit displayed by the team in its Death or Glory attempt to win if it was at all humanely possible. Every man in the side played as if his life depended upon it, but even then the individual honour went to Gregory, who was not only the best player on the ground, but he gave the best performance of his career with the exception of his game against Queensland at Brisbane last year. His display was wonderful - catching the ball from all angles and heights, tackling his man, placing the ball, extricating himself from all positions, stopping rushes by going down (and) picking the ball from the forwards' toes.

Roller-Coaster Ride

'One will never forget the way the team fought back in the last ten minutes to win back the lead. They fought like terriers, realising that it was a race against time. They deserved their win, and the Hull players and officials were loud in their praise for our play and congratulations for our win.'

He described the scene as 'Pope' Gregory lined up the match-deciding kick: 'Breathless silence reigned when Avery signalled Gregory to come up to have the final shot at goal. As soon as Pope placed the goal many on his side of the grandstand tried to disconcert him in his attempt, which meant so much to New Zealand and to Hull. A draw (would have) saved the record of thirty-five wins in succession, and a win to New Zealand meant much. All eyes were on his attempt and when the ball soared in the air thousands stood up and watched its flight and then all eyes were on the referee. Up went his right hand waving the handkerchief, signalling a goal. Our men jumped up in the air with delight, so happy that they had accomplished something out of the ordinary. This win will considerably help the gate of the second Test at the same ground next month, and help the following gate against Hull Kingston Rovers. The merited win against such a side came at the crossroads of the tour and it has put more spirit into the side.'

Mair continued to keep a running total of the tour finances. At Hull there were 14,000 spectators and the £857 gate took the total receipts to £7,528, lifting the average back up to £684 from the eleven matches. But the New Zealand coach overlooked the fact that two Hull players, Smallwood and Miller, suffered injuries and the home side was left with only eleven defenders as New Zealand salvaged its morale-boosting victory.

The *Hull Evening News*, which did not overlook the local team's injury problems, was nevertheless unstinting in its praise for the tourists. 'Summed up as a whole it was a wonderful game, chock full of excitement until the final whistle went. The oft-repeated statements that the All Blacks cannot scrummage was never confirmed, and if Saturday's game made any flaw in their armoury apparent it was some deficiency in their knowledge of the game. They have no set tactics or methods and appear to take the run of play as it comes. Individualists more than a combination, they have all the physical qualities necessary for the makings of a wonderful team, their strength, speed and stamina being notable.

'They play clean but decidedly robust football, but as they take hard knocks as cheerfully as they give them no fault can be found with their muscular zeal. Except that speed has been sacrificed to bulk in their forward department, they are very fast. They include several players of exceptional ability and under the prevailing circumstances Hull were in no way disgraced in their narrow defeat.' The *Evening News* recalled that Hull FC had not previously lost at the Boulevard since 31 January, 1925, when beaten by Leeds.

Mair recorded that the Hull club retained close links with Albert Baskerville's pioneering 1907-08 New Zealand All Golds. Edgar Wrigley, one of the stars of that team who stayed in Britain to pursue a professional career, was now serving as the Hull trainer. Baskerville's last letter of thanks before departing England had been framed and hung on the clubrooms wall, and an All Golds jersey was a prized memento. It should have been a joyous trip back to Harrogate. But there was again no mention whether all of the players had made the trip across to Hull, or if half of them were left back at base to brood over their situation. Of the seven at loggerheads with Mair, only Henry and Devine played at Hull.

The team management had sent a telegram to New Zealand Prime Minister Gordon Coates and Mrs Coates expressing pleasure at their safe arrival in England, wishing him success at the Imperial Conference he was to attend, and 'expressing our love and loyalty to God's Own Country'. Sir

Roller-Coaster Ride

James Parr, the New Zealand High Commissioner, extended an invitation for the entire touring party to attend an official welcome to the Prime Minister and Mrs Coates in London on the following Monday. However, it was not possible to make the trip south and return in time for the midweek match against Bradford Northern.

Ernie Herring must have wondered if he had gone deaf when his name was not read out in the team to oppose Bradford. The wholehearted front-row forward had toiled away in all of the first eleven games in just thirty-five days, wrestling with some of the toughest men in the north of England. But Herring's respite was to be brief - he was recalled for all of the next six matches. Similarly, after missing the opening fixture, second-rower Len Mason was then in the midst of playing fifteen out of sixteen games, his sole rest having been at York.

New Zealand supporters were delighted to learn of a third successive win when battling Bradford was over-run 38-17 at Birch Lane. Brisbane led the try-scoring spree with a second-half treble, Parkes and Devine both contributed two tries, and Dufty, Davidson and Mason also got on the score sheet. The 18-5 halftime lead consisted of six unconverted tries. Dufty then found his range to convert all four second-half tries and finish with a fifty percent strike-rate. Mason and Desmond missed one goal kick each.

However, the *Yorkshire Observer* was not impressed with the visitors. Instead of using their scant share of scrum possession to launch 'brilliant' attacking moves, the *Observer* accused the New Zealand backs of kicking too often and relying on their speed to chase through and capitalise on a Bradford rearguard which lacked confidence. Rather begrudgingly, the scribe listed Davidson, Cole and Brisbane as being the best backs and Mason and Devine the most impressive of the forwards.

Captain Bert Avery was having only his second day off at Bradford. In Mair's sea-mail report it was revealed that vice-

Strike! The Tour That Died of Shame

captain Neil Mouat was 'still suffering from the effects of an operation' but he did not elaborate. Mouat had not played since the first Test and was to be out of action for six weeks. It was a great shame that captain and vice-captain - arguably New Zealand's two finest forwards - did not team up in any of the last twenty-seven matches. Ben Davidson was acting captain against Bradford Northern.

With Bradford situated only twenty-five miles from Harrogate, travel was, for once, not a problem. In what might be a unique occurrence for any international rugby league team, the New Zealanders visited the Bradford Art Gallery between attending the mayoral welcome at the town hall and the kick-off at Birch Lane. The *Yorkshire Observer* published a photograph of the sightseeing All Blacks, showing fourteen men, including Mair, garbed in hats and overcoats. It was another indication that only players involved in the day's game had made the short trip. Among them would have been unsettled forwards Bill Devine, Frank Henry, Phonse Carroll and, making only his third appearance, Jack Wright.

Ideal weather prevailed and Mair regarded the £275 gate as acceptable. 'The gates have averaged £650, the side winning nine matches out of twelve, scoring 226 points against 172,' he wrote. 'When the history of this tour comes to be written from the inside the performance will be considered very satisfactory.'

The team management had also recently agreed to a proposed match against a Rugby League XIII at the Crystal Palace stadium in London to be added to the itinerary after Christmas and it seemed the roller-coaster ride had taken a decidedly upward turn. But Mair and Ponder could not have known what was awaiting them as they turned their attention towards the next match, against Oldham on Saturday, 23 October, a date that was to go down in rugby league infamy.

9

SEVEN MEN OUT

If a recent Kiwis combination had included blockbusting wing Manu Vatuvei at prop and specialist fullback Brent Webb in the second-row there would have been a media storm. Television, radio, internet and newspaper journalists would have demanded to know the whereabouts of the regular forwards. But on 23 October, 1926, no-one seriously questioned why the New Zealand All Blacks met the powerful Oldham club with wing George Gardiner playing at prop and first-choice fullback Craddock Dufty packing into the second-row.

These days, for tactical purposes, it has become the norm for backs to bow their heads into the depowered huddles which do no more than imitate old-style scrums. Forwards stand out in the backline to spearhead the resulting attack or defence. Referees sometimes tell over-enthusiastic players not to push. Scrum penalties and winning the ball against the put-in are virtually extinct. Veteran front-rowers look on in despair and are almost brought to tears.

But in 1926, four decades before the advent of the

Strike! The Tour That Died of Shame

limited-tackle rule, the scrum was the major source of getting one's hands on the ball. Possession was everything. Teams could retain the heavy leather balls for long periods and grind their opponents into submission. Players would do just about anything to dominate the heaving maelstrom that was the scrum. It was also the All Blacks' weakness. Their scrum-halves, props and hookers were all totally confused by the British rule interpretations, were frequently penalised for adopting New Zealand methods and the backrowers were regularly accused of packing too loosely.

The strapping Gardiner had past experience in the forwards and New Zealand coach Ernest Mair put him in the second-row against Bramley and Hull as he tried desperately to solve the scrummaging riddle. That was an experiment which might not have been appreciated by some of the touring forwards who were denied games. While Dufty was also a big man for the times, he had been selected for the tour purely to kick goals and play fullback. His sudden switch to the forwards should have sparked plenty of inquiries from newspaper journalists.

Instead, the *Oldham Standard* was more intent on informing its readers of who had attended, and what had been said, at the after-match function in the Oldham Town Hall. When the local newspaper did get around to the actual football, it reported that Oldham's 15-10 victory had been achieved against top-notch opposition. If the scribe even asked why there were only four specialist forwards then the smooth-talking Mair must have been too smart for him.

'The tourists played their strongest available side and, as was stated by the manager afterwards, it was the best team they had turned out since the tour began,' said the *Standard*. It was what the Oldham fans wanted to hear. They were already bubbling at having watched the home team extend its proud international record. Oldham had now beaten five of the six teams from Down Under, dating back to the New Zealand Native football team of 1888-89.

Seven Men Out

New Zealand readers were at a loss to understand what was going on when the Press Association cable listed the team without offering any explanation as to its unusual composition. An eagle-eyed *Auckland Star* sub-editor suspected something out of the ordinary had happened in far-off Oldham. The fourth of his four single-column stacked headlines read: 'Dufty In The Forwards'. But pointing out the anomaly, and including a small photograph of Dufty with the otherwise uninformative story, only magnified the puzzlement.

By the time Mair's sea-mail coverage was published on 9 December, the 'troubles' within the New Zealand team were well documented. Mair, as usual, glossed over the situation, no doubt having expected everything to be resolved well before his words reached the home audience. 'Their (Oldham) team was at full strength, and the New Zealanders were not favoured in this contest, particularly as they were playing their fullback and winger in the forwards - Dufty and Gardiner.' Later, he added, 'the thirteen players who represented New Zealand were the finest set of lads put on the field since the tour began'.

The cover-up could have succeeded had Joe Menzies, who had played only once in more than a month because of injury, been available. Provided, of course, that a speedy solution was found to the team's off-field strife. Mair could have passed off Gardiner's presence in the pack as nothing more than further experimentation. But the only specialist forwards Mair could call on were Len Mason, Ernie Herring, Harry Thomas and captain Bert Avery. The other seven had hardened their attitudes that they would not play while Mair was in charge of selection and coaching. They would be labelled 'strikers' by their team managers and fellow players.

English Rugby League council minutes reveal that the latest crisis had its foundation during the previous week. Managers Mair and George Ponder attended a meeting of the ERL tour sub-committee on Wednesday, 20 October, and

Strike! The Tour That Died of Shame

admitted that because of a disturbance by 'one or two members of the party' the West Park Hotel landlady had asked that they all leave by the Friday.

'They further stated that they had decided to send home to New Zealand by the steamship *Athenic* on 12 November four members of the team, Messrs Henry, Petersen, Singe and Mouat,' recorded ERL secretary John Wilson. 'Mr Mair stated that if those four men were got out of the hotel the landlady, in his opinion, would consent to the remainder staying. The managers asked for the support of the committee in the action they proposed to take, and this was accorded. The landlady asked that someone from the (ERL) council stay at Harrogate on Wednesday night and the secretary undertook to see to this.'

No venue or time of day was given for the 20 October meeting but presumably it was held after the match against Bradford Northern, when Frank Henry (and other 'malcontents' Bill Devine, Phonse Carroll and Jack Wright) had played. The matter was referred to the next full meeting of the ERL council to be held in eight days, the homeward bookings were cancelled, and, in the meantime, another uneasy truce prevailed at the West Park Hotel. It lasted less than three days, a later ERL minute revealed, before all seven discontented forwards refused to play under Mair's management against Oldham.

Oldham would have been a stern challenge for a full-strength New Zealand team. It was in the course of making four consecutive Challenge Cup final appearances, losing to Wigan in 1924, beating Hull Kingston Rovers in 1925, losing to Swinton in 1926 and beating the same opponent in 1927. Oldham fielded 1924 Lions Sid Rix, Albert Brough, Ernest Knapman and Bob Sloman. Its Watersheddings ground was a foreboding place for opposing sides, the most elevated and reputedly the coldest venue in the north of England. The biggest club crowd of the entire tour, 16,000, paid £1136 to watch Oldham capture another Australasian scalp.

Seven Men Out

New Zealand trailed by nine points at halftime before staging a strong comeback. Tries to Ben Davidson and Avery, both converted by Dufty, got the tourists as close as 10-12 and the game became very exciting. It remained in the balance until Oldham clinched victory with a last-minute unconverted try. The *Oldham Standard* gave the ball-starved tourists considerable credit, lauding Gardiner and Avery as the most effective forwards, admiring the skills of centres Davidson and Jim Sanders, and describing fullback Charles Gregory as being 'a great opponent' for Oldham international fullback Knapman.

George Smith, who was variously a champion jockey, prolific-scoring All Blacks wing and world-record breaking athlete before assisting Albert Baskerville to assemble the All Golds in 1907, and fellow All Golds outside back Joseph Lavery attended the game and the banquet which followed it. Smith and Lavery had stayed on in England after signing for Oldham and Leeds, respectively. The Oldham club presented Mair with an autographed programme and menu cards from Baskerville's visit.

Despite the upheaval, the tourists honoured a promise to provide nine players for a charity match between England captain Jonty Parkin's XIII and Wakefield Trinity in aid of the Mayor's Distress Fund on the Monday after the Oldham game. Parkin's entire pack was made up of New Zealanders, Gardiner, Jim Parkes, Mason, Herring, Thomas and Avery. Wilson Hall partnered Parkin in the halves and Davidson and Lou Brown continued their centre-wing partnership. Brown scored four tries and Herring one, and Gardiner kicked a goal, in the 17-13 win at the Belle Vue stadium.

Parkes, the Auckland and former Canterbury wing, had put his hand up to not just make up the forward numbers but also to try and solve the hooking problem. At that stage of the tour he had made only four appearances in his regular position, scoring a commendable five tries. His selfless offer was to result in him virtually making a fulltime transition to the front-row but also ensured him of far more game time. The tyro hooker was to prove he had some proficiency in his adopted role.

Leeds loomed as a difficult opponent two days after the charity fixture, and the beleaguered New Zealanders displayed considerable resolve in winning 13-11 at Headingley. Davidson scored two tries before damaging a leg seriously enough to rule him out of the next three fixtures. Herring got the other try and Dufty converted two of them. Parkes was out of his depth in the first-half scrums before enjoying some success. His selflessness enabled Dufty to return to the backline, playing in the centres with Gregory at fullback.

'The New Zealand rugby league tourists played one of the best games of their tour to beat Leeds at Headingley,' reported the *Leeds Mercury*, 'but there was little in it and the last five minutes were as exciting as anything seen Leeds' way lately. Avery and his men were two points up and Leeds tried everything they knew to get the try which would have given the club its first victory over a touring side.

'The strong part of the All Blacks' attack is the close passing in which their forwards take part, and in the second half many times they turned defence into attack very quickly. It was in this half, too, that their backs made the Leeds defence look weak and both Brown and Dufty made dashing runs which should have ended in tries.' Davidson, Hall and Gregory also received most favourable mentions.

Mair later wrote of 'the All Blacks fighting for their lives to keep the two points lead. From six scrums near the close of the game Leeds won the ball and on each occasion their players went in determinedly. Knowing that a try meant defeat, the All Blacks sent in flying tackle after tackle. This went on at top pressure for the last ten minutes and when the final whistle went each side was completely done in. The win gave the All Blacks double figures in wins - ten out of fourteen.'

The next day George Ponder and Ernest Mair attended

the English Rugby League meeting at the Victoria Hotel, Deansgate. According to the minutes, they were there for 'an interview with the council and to ask its advice on the differences that had arisen between certain members of the team and Mr Mair'. It would have been a daunting experience to be confronted by the fifteen men who considered themselves responsible not just for the running of the game in Britain but also to oversee its development in the colonies. For the first time it was admitted that the tour might not run its course.

'Mr Mair recounted what he had already told the council of the origin of the trouble,' wrote ERL secretary John Wilson. 'He felt that a number of players had not been loyal to his management such as he had a right to expect, but had to reluctantly admit that the tour could not be carried on with men standing out as at present. He singled out N Mouat as the leader of the party in opposition to him and the decision to send home this player and Singe had resulted in five others declining to remain. The players were all forwards and to carry on without them was going to be difficult if not impossible.

'Mr Ponder followed. He agreed in the main with the statement by Mr Mair, but said that things had to be taken as they were and there was no gainsaying (denying that) Mr Mair's management had not been successful. He withdrew from the position he took at Bradford a week ago, and was now of the opinion that it was impossible to carry on the tour if the decision to send men home was persisted in. That meant the loss of seven forwards, and with a number of members sick and injured the tour would simply come to a close.

'He had discussed the situation with Mr Mair, who was aware what he was going to say, and his solution to the problem was that Mr Mair should take the holiday his health really required, leave the hotel, and let himself (Ponder) carry on the management alone or with such assistance as he required supplied by the council.'

Strike! The Tour That Died of Shame

Obviously, managers Ponder and Mair were no longer thinking in unison. In the week since the crisis meeting after the Bradford Northern match the previously supportive Ponder had decided Mair - who he believed to be suffering ill health, presumably stress - should leave his post as demanded by the seven players. He had told Mair as much and expected the coach to comply with his recommendation.

The ERL minutes continued: 'In the interests of the tour, the (English) League and New Zealand, Mr Mair at first agreed to this proposal but subsequently rather withdrew. When leaving the room so that the council could discuss the matter (Mair) asked that the "status quo" be maintained as he had thought of another solution. The two managers then retired. After discussion the council decided that their advice to the managers was that the suggestion made by Mr Ponder should be carried out, and that Mr Mair should leave the hotel and take a holiday for a month, leaving Mr Ponder to conduct the business of the tour.

'Mr Mair said that on further consideration outside, he could not now agree to that, and said that he had thought of a plan to get over the trouble which he could put into operation when he returned to Harrogate. He declined, however, to say what the plan was. The chairman thereupon pointed out that it was futile trying to be of any help owing to the continual shifting of ground and stated quite definitely that the opinion of the council was that the suggestion made by Mr Ponder was originally accepted by Mr Mair. He had no more to say on the subject.'

Ted Osborne, the ERL chairman, was obviously exasperated by Mair's initial agreement and subsequent refusal to accept Ponder's proposition that he step down, not just from his duties as coach and selector but from the team altogether. Ponder had been confident he could work in conjunction with captain Bert Avery and vice-captain Neil Mouat to get the tour back on an even keel. As Mair had pointed out in his most recent dispatch to New Zealand, ten

Seven Men Out

of the first fourteen games had been won and the Test series was still to be decided. Instead, the so-called 'strike' was to continue for three more matches before Ponder's proposal was revisited. By then it would be less than five days before the second Test match.

Word was spreading that the touring team was falling apart. A cabled report from London, published in New Zealand newspapers on 29 October, said 'the trouble among the New Zealand rugby league players is said to be due to a half-dozen players insisting there should be a more impartial selection of the team, and objections to what they consider the ultra-economy of the management in, for instance, sending only a bare team to the place of a match and leaving the remainder at headquarters.' It quoted the New Zealand management as denying reports some members of the team had refused to play against St Helens Recreation the following day. Management claimed the team would be at full strength.

That did not happen. Frank Delgrosso returned from injury to partner Wilson Hall in the halves but Parkes and Gardiner again joined the four available forwards as the All Blacks suffered their biggest defeat to date by 28-14. The now defunct St Helens 'Recs' club, which grew out of the massive Pilkington's Glass Works, was then markedly stronger than the neighbouring and enduring St Helens club. 'Recs' was to improve from fifth in 1925-26 to top the Rugby League Championship table in 1926-27.

Mair's comments were bitter-sweet: 'Once again we were unable to field our best side and Gardiner and Mason had to get up from their (sick) beds to take the field. This game with St Helens was one of thrills. Each side threw the leather about and with the exception of the last twenty minutes it was anyone's game. It is a strange thing that half way through the second half in every game the All Blacks put their run in. They never seem to get going generally in the first half.

Strike! The Tour That Died of Shame

'When the scores were 19-14 against them, it was the general opinion they would win, but the playing of the same players in the forwards for so long, through injuries and sickness, and the shoulder injuries of Delgrosso and Cole, took its toll.' Again, Mair avoided revealing why the same few forwards were gallantly carrying so much of the burden. Sanders (two), Avery and Mason were New Zealand's try-scorers and Gregory kicked one goal.

The *St Helens Reporter* told its readers 'the Recs licked the All Blacks hollow on Saturday' and continued in that vein. It calculated that if the New Zealand team was inserted in the Rugby League Championship table its nine wins and five losses against club opposition would place it tenth of the thirty teams, and concluded, 'So really it was not surprising that the Recs should win so comfortably'. While visiting St Helens the All Blacks followed the lead of the All Golds and viewed the house where former New Zealand Prime Minister Richard John Seddon was born.

Front-rower Joe Menzies came back to give Avery a rest in the 18-10 victory over Salford at Weaste on 3 November. Sanders claimed a first-half try with 'a brilliant run in which Brisbane participated,' according to the Press Association. After the break, 'the Blacks again asserted their superiority and gave a magnificent exhibition of combination, forwards and backs alike being prominent. The result was that Delgrosso, Gardiner and Dufty all ran in, Dufty converting two.'

The Manchester *Daily Dispatch* was glowing in its praise of the tourists, singling Dufty out as an 'outstanding genius' among the backs. Individually, Brown, Sanders and Brisbane caught the writer's eye. Stand-off half Delgrosso and scrum-half Hall prospered after they swapped positions at halftime. Thomas and Mason impressed most in the forward exchanges and the ever-willing Parkes continued to have more hooking success that others previously tried in that position.

Seven Men Out

Otago forward Harry Thomas was enjoying his increased game time. Mair wrote that Thomas 'took part in two incidents - tackling the referee by mistake and (being) reprimanded by the linesman for telling him the ball was not out. As in the previous game, Thomas was the best forward on the ground. Jack Kirwan (playing his first game since York four weeks earlier because of a muscle injury) was chosen by the selection committee to lead the side. Gardiner and Mason were still suffering from the effects of influenza but played. It is a strange feature about these Wednesday games that we have never been beaten and have had four different captains - Davidson, Kirwan, Mouat and Avery.'

But Mair was becoming morose over other matters. 'Once again the signs of a wretched November were evident with the rain and fog. Towards the end of the game the fog invaded the ground, screening the view, and later held up the train which was to convey us back to Leeds.' After reporting takings of £230, Mair commented, 'One thing is certain. If the coal strike does not finish within the next month, the position financially for the tour will be anything but rosy.'

The next night, in Auckland, the NZRL went into committee to discuss a cable from the tour managers informing them that three players had mutually gone on strike in support of four others who, owing to misbehaviour, had been ordered home. Those seven players had demanded that Mair be recalled. The managers further advised that the rest of the party remained loyal and that ERL chairman Osborne was mediating. The NZRL decided to take no action pending advice from Osborne, although chairman James Carlaw was authorised to send a personal cable to the players - a plea for all to put their differences behind them.

At the same meeting the NZRL council received a telegram from West Coast Rugby League president Jim Wingham. He recommended that endeavours be made to

Strike! The Tour That Died of Shame

enlist the services of Prime Minister Gordon Coates, who was still in England, to 'fix the present trouble'. It was decided not to bother the premier.

Huddersfield was the third successive Saturday opponent to beat the sagging remnants of the New Zealand team, but only by 10-8. Nothing went right for the visitors. Hall was the best player on the waterlogged Fartown pitch until he staggered off with a suspected broken arm. The home side's first try was conceded unopposed when fullback Dufty did not attempt to tackle the scorer, mistakenly believing he had stepped into touch. And Dufty hit an upright with one penalty attempt and was just short with a long-range shot which would have drawn the match. Avery's return gave Gardiner - the wing who had slogged away as a forward in six of the previous seven games - a much-needed spell. Kirwan and Brown scored tries and Dufty kicked one goal in front of a rain-reduced crowd of 5,000.

'The losing of Hall a quarter of an hour from the finish meant the game for New Zealand,' wrote Mair. 'He was playing splendid football and in the many attempts the All Blacks launched in the last ten minutes his absence was sorely felt, for Huddersfield was not the better side on the day's play.' Mair reported that Hall's agony continued for hours.

'At first it was thought that Hall had broken his arm but on arrival at the Huddersfield Infirmary we found it was a dislocation. Unfortunately, a motor accident at the same time at Huddersfield, in which three young ladies figured, necessitated Wilson waiting his turn until they had been attended to. It was some considerable time before his turn came, and when it did it was necessary to put him under chloroform to put the elbow right. An X-ray examination the next day proved no break or chip, which the doctor feared.' Hall's injury just a week out from the second Test match was yet another severe blow. He was out of the next eight games.

Huddersfield, where the historic meeting to form the

Seven Men Out

Northern Union had been held in 1895, was only thirty-five miles from Harrogate. Mair's solemn mood would not have improved as heavy rain fell overnight and only increased in intensity from noon until just before kick-off. That, combined with Huddersfield's generally poor form, reduced the gate to £370. Mair did his sums and calculated the accumulated tour takings at £10,176, an average of £598. The sun mockingly shone during the game but the players were wading through slush and the remains of the straw which had been spread to protect the playing field from frosts.

On Monday, 8 November, just five days before the all-important second Test at Hull, the tour reached another crossroads. The *Daily Express* reported that Mouat, Henry, Petersen, Wright, Devine, Singe and Carroll had sent an ultimatum threatening to embark for home eleven days later unless their demands were met.

It made depressing reading when reproduced in the Wellington *Evening Post*: 'The English Rugby League council, which guaranteed the expenses of the tour, tried hard to effect peace at a meeting at Manchester on 28 October, but the friction has continued. They declined to train or play under Mr Mair's control. Mr Mair asserts that he retains the New Zealand council's confidence. The New Zealanders are certain to take the field in the second Test. The odds are greatly against them.'

On that Monday night, the NZRL held an urgently-convened special meeting to consider an extraordinary cable message from vice-captain and alleged rebel leader Neil Mouat which read: "Breakdown tour certain failing your recalling Mair. Seven forwards returning immediately, others dissatisfied. Address reply urgent.' Mouat also claimed ERL secretary John Wilson had threatened to call off the tour and send the whole team home.

After earnest deliberation, the NZRL council authorised secretary Owie Carlaw to cable his English counterpart

Strike! The Tour That Died of Shame

expressing full confidence in the English Rugby League and its president to do their best to arrive at an amicable settlement. If necessary, the ERL was authorised to take strong action. ERL chairman Ted Osborne, armed with the power given him by the NZRL, and with Wilson in tow, headed for the West Park Hotel in Harrogate and another meeting with the entire touring party. This time he would tolerate no ducking and diving from Mair or anyone else.

The Manchester *Daily Dispatch* newspaper was on the case: 'Our Leeds representative was authoritatively informed that as a result all matters relating to the trouble had been amicably settled,' said its edition of 9 November. 'The seven forwards who have recently refused to turn out are available for selection for Saturday's Test match. There will be, however, a slight change in the management of the touring team. Mr E H Mair (manager) will not sit on the selection committee, for a period at any rate. The selection committee will comprise Mr G H Ponder, financial manager, Avery, captain, and Mouat, vice-captain.'

It was commonplace for writers to use pen-names in those days, and 'Observer' commented in the *Dispatch*: 'I have heard many sides of the dispute and it is not for me to apportion the blame. The (English) Rugby League council have been in a very delicate position, owing to the fact that they were heavily committed financially. They have guaranteed the expenses of the tour which will amount to at least £10,000. That amount has not yet been secured from the matches so far played. Still, I believe that the position had got so desperate that unless some settlement was reached a section of the council was prepared to disband the tour after this week rather than tolerate any more of the friction.'

Next day the story hit the headlines in New Zealand - 'Mr Mair Withdraws From League Team Selection Committee' blazed the *Star* in Christchurch, above a sub-heading of 'N.Z. Men's Grievances Redressed; Harmony Again Prevailing.' The headlines actually occupied more space than the three-paragraph lead story received from the Press Association: 'Thanks to the mediation of Mr Osborne, chairman of the Rugby League council, a settlement of the New Zealand footballers' grievances has been effected. Mr Wilson, secretary of the League, says: 'Harmony has been completely restored and it is not likely there will be any renewal of the trouble. The manager, Mr E H Mair, says he has withdrawn unconditionally from the selection committee and his interest in the tour for a certain period will be passive.'

A similar article appeared in the *Brisbane Courier* and would have been avidly devoured by readers in Mair's home state. In England, the *Evening News* recounted some of the problems on board ship and after arrival at Harrogate, before adding a trans-Tasman element: 'Some players disliked Mr Mair's training strictness, saying that he was an Australian with ideas of discipline which were unpalatable to New Zealanders, who were accustomed to different methods. The seven rebels have agreed to do their best now that Mr Mair has resigned the selectorship.'

Ted Osborne almost certainly did not stride into the ERL council meeting at the Griffin Hotel, Leeds, on the night of 10 November waving a piece of paper and declaring 'peace in our time'. But he might as well have. The minutes testify that 'he informed the council of what transpired at Harrogate during his visit on Monday and how eventually Mr Mair had offered to withdraw from the selection committee for a month, and during that period to take merely a passive part in the management of the team.'

The use of the word 'eventually' in the writings of John Wilson, who had been at Harrogate, strongly suggests that Mair did not step down without offering some resistance. Whatever his alleged 'other solution' to reunite the team had been, it had not improved the situation. But there was an apparent compromise - an agreement that Mair would be presented in the best possible light, even made out to be a sacrificial hero, in all subsequent public statements.

Strike! The Tour That Died of Shame

Wilson's minutes thus continued: '(Mair) made this sportsmanlike offer in the interests of peace and the welfare of the tour, and having made it managers and mediators retired to enable the players to discuss it. The players unanimously agreed to accept the offer and to all pull together as a united body under the new management. Messrs Ponder, Avery and Mouat were agreed to as a selection committee for one month, the position to be reconsidered and reviewed at the end of that period. The council, by a unanimous vote, confirmed the action of the chairman and ordered its confirmation to be recorded in the minutes.'

One night later the NZRL held its regular weekly meeting in Auckland and councillors were mightily relieved to receive George Ponder's cable assuring them, 'Everything amicably settled. Mair great sacrifice saved tour.' There was a supporting cable from ERL secretary John Wilson stating, 'All differences settled. Details later'.

Remarkably, Ponder and Mair had not provided the NZRL council with detailed information of the internal strife in any of their first six tour reports sent by sea mail from England. When pressed for an explanation, they replied they had wished to place the entire situation before the ERL tour committee before making a definite report. It was not until their seventh report arrived in December that the NZRL councillors were told the managers' version of what had been going on. While expressing disappointment with the behaviour of some players, the councillors decided to defer any action until the return of the team.

The *Press* newspaper in Chrstchurch published an extensive review of the team's 'troubles' in its Christmas Eve edition, one that was penned by an anonymous 'Own Correspondent' and mailed via sea on 11 November. There were two new revelations.

On 27 October, while their team-mates were playing at Leeds, 'five of the most prominent players of the League team' left behind at Harrogate had travelled in the opposite direction to watch the New Zealand Maori rugby union side against Bradford. 'They acknowledged they had "struck" owing to disagreement with the team manager, Mr E H Mair. It is admitted frankly by some of the players that they could not disabuse their minds that Mr Mair is an Australian whose methods of discipline are unpalatable to men accustomed to something very different in New Zealand.'

After listing the shipboard incidents and the tearing down of 11pm curfew notices at their Harrogate hotel, the article continued: 'In the matter of training, Mr Mair introduced methods not to the liking of many of the players. For the last fortnight seven players have been in open revolt. They would neither go into training nor allow themselves to be selected to play. It is not surprising all sorts of rumours have arisen in consequence.'

Then the second revelation, though it was acknowledged to be a rumour: 'It has been said that some of the Roman Catholics in the party have been "up against" the Protestants, and also that favouritism has been shown to Freemason members of the team. These suggestions are denied.'

This was the first mention of religious undertones to the dispute. All seven 'rebels' were either Roman Catholics or played for Marist clubs in Auckland, Christchurch or Greymouth, and both managers were Freemasons. But that does not explain why Auckland Marist backs Charles Gregory, Jack Kirwan and Hec Brisbane stayed loyal to the management rather than side with club-mate Arthur Singe.

The *Press* report then quoted a sub-leader from the English *Sporting Life* publication: 'It may readily be granted that it is no easy matter to control a body of men throughout a long tour, however honest the manager may be in his convictions as to what should or should not be right or permissible. In that respect Mr Mair is deserving of all the help and goodwill he can command. But this team of New

Strike! The Tour That Died of Shame

Zealanders were announced as a purely amateur combination and in such circumstances, the players might reasonably consider that they should have a fair measure of freedom of movement, and not be submissive to a rigid and cast-iron discipline. The episode is to be deplored.'

Back at Harrogate, the now united playing factions among the All Blacks had little time to whip up a combination capable of challenging England in an all-or-nothing showdown at the Boulevard ground in Hull. Ponder was first and foremost a boardroom administrator and as such would have left it to Avery and Mouat to select the Test team and run what training sessions were possible in the short time available.

10

FROM MAIR TO NIGHTMARE

Contrast the respective England and New Zealand selection meetings leading up to the second Test match on 13 November.

One-up in the series, the home panel had the depth of twenty-nine professional teams from which to choose. They had plumped for experience before the victory at Wigan and could afford to be more adventurous in the second international at Hull. Opting for the best of both worlds, they offered debuts to in-form St Helens Recreation wing Jim Wallace and forward Alec Fildes, St Helens stand-off Les Fairclough, Leeds forward Arthur Thomas and Bradford Northern hooker Bert Smith.

At Harrogate, captain Bert Avery and vice-captain Neil Mouat - with financial manager George Ponder as selection convener - were in a no-win situation attempting to apply the glue to a touring team which had been split by dissension and counter-claims of strikes and lockouts. Even before the seven forwards declined to play under coach Ernest Mair, Mouat's appearances had been restricted by injury and illness and he was out of the Test reckoning. Top scrum-half Wilson Hall was sidelined with a dislocated elbow and Ben Davidson, the most impressive midfield back on tour, was hobbling around on a damaged ankle.

Injuries, illness, the refusal by forwards Mouat, Phonse Carroll, Bill Devine, Frank Henry, Lou Petersen, Arthur Singe and Jack Wright to play for Mair in the previous five games, and Mair's own disinclination to select some of those players before they took their extraordinary action, meant there was a gross imbalance in player appearances, and therefore match fitness and current form, from which to select a Test team. In those days there were no replacements, and certainly no interchanges. The thirteen who ran onto the field to kick off were there for the duration, unless they were so badly injured they could not continue.

Ernie Herring had played in sixteen of the seventeen fixtures, Len Mason in fifteen and Avery in fourteen. But Singe had not stepped onto a playing field since the opening match at Dewsbury more than two months earlier, and Petersen's second and most recent game had been five weeks previous. Henry and Devine had made six appearances each before withdrawing from selection contention. Among the backs, Hec Brisbane had been the busiest with fourteen games. Jack Kirwan had only recently returned from a long injury break and there was a hard decision to make between well-credentialed fullbacks Craddock Dufty and Charles Gregory.

They came up with a team consisting of Gregory at fullback, Lou Brown and Dufty on the wings, Kirwan and Brisbane in the centres, Davidson and Frank Delgrosso as the halves, and a forward pack of Henry, Herring, Devine, Singe, Petersen and Avery (captain). Davidson, however, could not pass a fitness test on match morning and was replaced by Hector Cole. There were four 'rebels' among the forwards, two of them very short of a gallop, and a makeshift backline. Gregory had been judged the better

From Mair to Nightmare

specialist option at fullback, but Dufty's goalkicking was sufficiently valuable for him to be included at wing.

It has not been recorded whether Ernest Mair and his wife Mildred actually left the West Park Hotel at any stage during his agreed one-month stand-down from coaching and selecting. Delgrosso told a neighbour many years later that they had holidayed in Europe. If they did so, it must have been in short spurts, for Mair continued as co-manager and to file indepth match reports via sea mail to newspapers in Auckland and Christchurch. The Hull *Evening News* published photographs of both teams before kick-off in the second Test and a smiling Mair was seated between Avery and Lou Brown. Whereas the caption listed the official positions of George Ponder and Avery in brackets as (manager) and (captain), respectively, Mair was not given a title.

The *Auckland Star* previewed the second Test by recalling New Zealand's belated comeback in its 28-20 defeat by England at Wigan. 'All the critics were unanimous that the New Zealanders lost the game in the first half, and went so far as to predict the Englishmen would find the tourists a vastly improved team when the second Test had to be played.' But that was before the tour all but disintegrated because of the internal war which erupted between Mair and the seven forwards. The *Star* then chose to be wise in hindsight.

'From the cables received it is clear that some of the players consider Mr Mair as being too strict in discipline, but he evidently had some queer customers to deal with. The singing of The Red Flag on board the steamer when on route to England perhaps did not possess any real significance but it brought a reprimand from the manager.

'Again, before the team sailed, one prominent player from the south was before the New Zealand council, or some members of that body. The player concerned had, during the playing of the National Anthem at an Auckland theatre, remained sitting in his seat with his hat on. His action was strongly resented by the New Zealand council and the player, when reprimanded, gave his promise not to do anything during the tour to which exception might be taken.

'Again, when the New Zealand team toured Australia last year more than one player gave trouble, but those players were included in the team for England, although a prominent member of the council at a meeting moved that not one of the players concerned should be included in the team for England. Unfortunately, perhaps, he failed to find a seconder.

'From this it will be recognised that the coach, Mr Mair, was always liable to have his authority challenged, particularly if he endeavoured to apply methods which tightened up considerably the latitude players had been enjoying previously. However, all is apparently well again and we in New Zealand can only hope the team will be at full strength tomorrow and in a position to wipe out the defeat received in the first Test.'

The National Anthem referred to would have been 'God Save The King'. It is a fair bet that the 'prominent player from the south' who did not remove his hat and stand for the anthem was Mouat, an Irish sympathiser in its centuries-old dispute with the British. Deposed 1925 New Zealand coach Charles Pearce had written cryptically of the big West Coaster: 'Neil Mouat wears green underclothing and is alleged to train on Sinn Fein literature and the life of De Valera. The preparation is thorough.' Yet the NZRL council, and Mair himself, had so much confidence in Mouat that he was appointed vice-captain to Avery.

Hopes that the tour would be revitalised by news of the New Zealand team's troubles being over, and that a big crowd would be attracted to The Boulevard, were dashed by the English weather. On the field, the All Blacks did their best to rescue the Test series before going down 21-11 after literally draining all reserves of energy. Their spirited performance brought admiration from journalists writing for newspapers in both countries, and also from Mair.

From Mair to Nightmare

'The prevailing conditions combined to make the second Test match between England and the All Blacks a failure, but while allowing that the gate receipts, £592, were poor, the game in itself will stand as a splendid exhibition under the dual handicap of a sodden ground and a greasy ball,' reported the *Hull Evening News*. 'Moreover, it will be placed on mental record as a contest not to be forgotten for the reason that it might just as easily have gone the other way and left the third Test match as the deciding game for the destination of the Ashes.

'While England won in the end rather easily, the impression created by the contest was that the losers had been just too late in setting their house in order to be in a position to display their real qualities. The All Blacks' reconstructed thirteen went far enough to prove that they had sufficient ability in their ranks to make a formidable side, but the settling of their domestic differences came too late for them to field a team sufficiently fit to go all the way against the pick of the English Rugby League. While their stamina remained unimpaired they were quite as good as their ultimate masters, but their falling away in the closing stages was distinctly obvious, and no one can quarrel with the view that physical fitness was the chief factor in deciding the issue.'

England was fortunate to win the toss and had the strong wind and rain at its back when the New Zealanders were still struggling to find their combinations. The *Evening News* also said the home side monopolised the scrums - so much so that its cartoonist drew New Zealand scrum-half Frank Delgrosso 'wearing a look of astonishment when the ball accidentally came out of his side of the pack' - and had other marked advantages in its backline speed and the dominant figure of Jim Sullivan at fullback.

Nevertheless, New Zealand opened the scoring when Brown made a fine run for Petersen to score his second try on tour in just his third appearance. But England struck back

Strike! The Tour That Died of Shame

to lead 13-3 by halftime. The wind dropped away and the sun came out when it was New Zealand's turn to run with the elements. The All Blacks then stunned their rivals with two tries, Singe putting Avery across for the first and Kirwan and Avery setting up Brown for a spectacular sprint to touch down in the corner. Dufty missed both conversions but Gregory had kicked a penalty goal and the New Zealanders were just two points behind.

According to the *Evening News*, New Zealand had lost a 'gift' try when Brisbane and Dufty muffed the final pass. Reprieved, a fitter England team came back with another eight points to clinch the Test at 21-11 and the series at two-nil. The All Blacks had their chance to win and because they were unable to grasp it they paid the penalty. But their display enhanced their reputation considerably. There was praise heaped upon Brown, 'a very dangerous customer' on the wing, Delgrosso and Brisbane for being 'dashing and clever' in the halves, and Petersen, Avery and Singe, 'a trio of magnificent workers who rivalled anything on the winning side, who harried the English backs unceasingly'.

Mair echoed the thoughts of financial manager George Ponder in his coverage of the Test. After bemoaning the adverse weather, the unaffordable two shillings minimum entry charge and the playing of the match at a comparatively isolated venue which meant fans incurred more expense in travel costs, Mair commented that 'such a paltry amount as £592 for a Test match was a colossal shock, for there were only about 7,000 present'. He agreed with local commentators that England won the match because its forwards were stronger over the last twenty minutes.

'This is where we shone in the first Test, and in this one went down,' wrote the estranged coach. 'The selectors were faced with the awkward task of picking a team that would help the position. They selected two forwards who had played fourteen and sixteen matches respectively out of seventeen, and the other four members of the pack had played only one, two, six and six matches, respectively. In a game, particularly a Test, every player must be able to stick it out for the full eighty minutes, he must not be stale and he must have had sufficient match play to see the game through without dying away.

'It was unfortunate that Parkes (who has been the most successful hooker of the side) and Thomas (on his form in recent matches, no superior in the team) had to be eliminated, but when the selectors' position is realised they are to be sympathised with instead of criticised. We did not see much of the ball from the scrums, which gave our backs plenty of chasing to do, and naturally made a difference to them when it came to their turn to attack.

'There was not a slacker in the New Zealand side, and every man gave his best from whistle to whistle. Despite England's ten-point victory there was very little in it, they being slightly the better side on the afternoon's performance. On one occasion when the scores stood 13-11 against us Dufty missed from an easy position. In fact the sodden ball had him puzzled, and he had a day off at goal kicking from positions which are his strong point.'

The Test series was irretrievably lost, the glories of the 1924 home successes over England had faded from memory, and the tourists could only look ahead to a hard slog into the teeth of the northern winter. At that stage they were facing another sixteen matches in the north of England, including clashes with powerful clubs such as Wigan and Swinton, the Lancashire, Yorkshire and Cumberland county teams, and a third Test match, before finishing the tour with proposed fixtures in London and Paris. It was a daunting prospect.

They were not aware of it at the time, but a Queensland Rugby League official named W F Stock gleefully put the boot into the All Blacks via a letter published in the Brisbane *Telegraph* on 16 November and partially reproduced in the *Auckland Star* two weeks later. Apparently Stock had not gotten over the New Zealanders being invited to tour

Strike! The Tour That Died of Shame

England ahead of Australasia, Australia or even Queensland.

'When the New Zealand Rugby League team left for England towards the close of our last football season there were very few people in Queensland who gave them much chance of winning many games. I said over and over again they would not win more than half a dozen matches. And if all the games had been honestly fought, I have no doubt that my prediction would have been correct,' wrote Stock, who from half a world away accused English referees of being lenient on the tourists.

'How they must be wishing that they had invited an Australasian side. The English Rugby League is now paying the penalty of allowing itself to be guided by the opinions of two individuals, and it has only itself to blame. However, although the New Zealand team is so weak, a friend assures me that several players would not return to this part of the world if the two years residential qualification ban were not in force. They would be received with open arms by many of the big clubs.'

Stock made the unsubstantiated claim that 'it was expected there would be serious trouble sooner or later'. Obviously no friend of fellow Queenslander Ernest Mair, he speculated that the 'mutiny' staged by seven forwards was made as a protest against coaching tactics 'which have so far failed'. The *Star* reproduced about 700 of Stock's words before giving up and adding a footnote that 'the (*Telegraph*) article contains much more in the same strain'.

Wigan Highfield, a club formed in 1922 and which played at Tunstall Lane until relocated to London in 1933, was beaten 14-2 on 17 November. Mouat made his first appearance since the first Test forty-six days earlier and kicked a goal to complement tries by George Gardiner (two), Wally Desmond and Phonse Carroll. The entire forward formation - Devine, Carroll, Henry, Petersen, Singe and Mouat - had been involved in the dispute with Mair. Wright

From Mair to Nightmare

was not to return for another week. Gardiner celebrated his relocation to the wing with the first two tries as New Zealand overcame another saturated ground and enthusiastic opposition.

'It was one of the longest journeys of the tour for club games and coupled with the further restriction of trains by the coal strike, it was necessary to have breakfast at 6.15am,' wrote Mair. 'It was naturally a long day by the time we returned to Harrogate at 10.30pm. A four and a half hours journey via Leeds and Manchester brought us at noon to Wigan, which is seventy-seven miles from Harrogate. A civic reception by the Mayor of Wigan at the Town Hall was followed by the usual photograph outside and the signing of the visitors' book. Then came a lunch as the guests of the Wigan Highfield club.' Mair's match report included the remark that 'Mouat is not quite himself yet'.

He made no comment about the 'rebellious' composition of the pack, other than mentioning Herring and Avery were given a well-earned rest. 'Gregory hurt his hand in the second Test and was unable to play, and elbow and ankle injuries were still keeping Wilson Hall and Davidson out of action. Webb, who was playing his third game, was played behind the scrum and was a success, so much so that the selectors will give him a further trial in the game against Batley on Saturday.' Mair was obviously still being kept abreast of the selection panel's thinking, presumably by Ponder and/or Avery.

Mair reviewed the depressed English economy, reporting one-third of the downtrodden, striking miners had resumed work. 'Everything pointed to the strike finishing on Remembrance Day - November 11 - but the vote narrowly turned down the proposals to accept the conditions offered. However, the miners are now going back in such numbers on their own accord that should their executive not recommend an immediate resumption the strike will finish itself shortly.' He again attacked the one shilling and sixpence minimum fee for entry to New Zealand's matches against club teams. New Zealanders at home would not understand that striking miners were, ironically, unable to afford coal to keep their families warm in the harsh climate. Watching sport remained an impossible luxury for the majority.

'Coal is still very dear, and this necessity for English homes at this time of the year has to be done without in thousands of cases. Policemen can only control a certain number of unemployed when they gather together outside the gates. But when they increase to large dimensions it is out of the question to hold them in check, apart from the damage they would do to the fences etc. in getting through them. As a result, it is necessary to let them in for what they have in their pockets at a certain part of the first half, and (to let in) the balance free during the second spell.

'The New Zealand side could not have visited England at a worse time than the present. Moreover, should the strike finish by the end of November the aftermath will be such that it is doubtful whether the lost financial position will be recovered. We are having typical English November weather - wet, cold and foggy days which are interfering with everything,' said Mair. Overnight rain continued until an hour before the Wigan Highfield game, and only £82 was taken at the turnstiles.

George Ponder, meanwhile, was still selling New Zealand as a fine place for enterprising English folk to resettle. He told the Dewsbury supporters' club of his homeland's history and its temperate climate, of its trade within the Empire, of extensive railways development, of the land available to be farmed, and of the opportunities for working men. A labourer could earn £4 2s 6d a week and a young clerk £18 or £20 a month. Clothing might be a little dearer than in England but food was cheaper. The New Zealand Government was prepared to advance money to those desirous of building their own houses to the extent of ninety per cent. Incomes of under £300 were tax free and other tax rates were much lower than in England. How the embattled Ponder must have longed to be returning home as he spoke!

On the morning of the Batley match the English *All Sports Weekly* took its turn to review the problems which had bedevilled the tour, and the agreement brokered by ERL chairman Ted Osborne and secretary John Wilson. 'The Rugby League Council will think twice before they invite another New Zealand team over, for they have been caused many anxious moments,' it said. The writer, who claimed 'members of the council' were his sources, hinted strongly that the ERL might not want Mair to have anything further to do with the tour. 'Mr Mair has relinquished control of the team for one month and even then it is questionable whether he will resume his duties. The council, who are financing the tour, have intimated to Mr Mair that at the end of the month they will review the position.' He signed off by doubting very much whether the tourists' proposed London and Paris fixtures would eventuate.

Expectations that the united All Blacks had ignited a winning spree at Wigan Highfield were dashed immediately when Batley triumphed 19-17 at Mount Pleasant on another rainy day and another saturated pitch. Mair commented that every spectator deserved a Victoria Cross for braving the elements. With the exception of Wilson Hall, the tourists had a full roster of players to choose from and the loss, narrow as it was, to a club destined to finish nineteenth in the 1926-27 championship would have been shattering. Ben Davidson was back in the centres and the impressive-looking forward pack of Henry, Carroll, Singe, Petersen, Mason and Avery should have exerted a major influence on proceedings.

Instead, the two teams indulged in a seesawing tussle, beginning with Henry capitalising on a Gardiner break to open the scoring. Davidson set Brown up for another try, and Gardiner got across just before halftime. But the New Zealanders, with three Dufty goals, led only 15-14 at the break and were vulnerable to a side growing in confidence. Dufty nudged the lead out to three points with a penalty goal, only for Batley to reply with a try midway through the second spell which, when converted, clinched a famous victory for the home team.

'More attractive football than that served in the first half one has never seen played under similar conditions,' said the *Batley Reporter* newspaper. 'Both sides threw the greasy ball about with refreshing freedom and exhilarating movements succeeded each other in thrilling style. No fewer than twenty-nine points were scored during the progress of the first half, first one side leading and then the other.' Batley's Test loose forward Frank Gallagher was prominent in most of Batley's scoring moves, including the match-winner.

'The New Zealanders were very unfortunate,' wrote Mair. 'They should have won by at least ten points and were easily a ten-points better side on the afternoon's display. The hoodoo of Saturday defeats and midweek wins once more prevailed.' Mair expressed amazement that in the twentieth game of the tour yet another referee had to be asked to remove his black coat in mid-match to avoid confusion with the New Zealand jerseys.

The *Batley Reporter* became just the latest local publication to point to scrummaging as the tourists' fundamental weakness. 'In the open their forwards were a fine, virile force, but in the art of securing possession they were woefully deficient. As a consequence, their backs had limited opportunities.' It was a familiar phrase, as was the *Reporter*'s assessment of the backline's tendency to spoil some brilliant handling and team-work with poor finishing when tries should have been registered. The scribe felt they would have thrived on a dry surface.

'Men like Webb, Davidson and Brown invariably made

From Mair to Nightmare

progress in possession, but the man who attracted most attention was Dufty, who played a great game at fullback, and in the absence of whose sterling defensive work the tourists would probably have suffered a heavier defeat. The one and only disappointing feature of the match was the attendance, which was not more than 3,000. The "gate" amounted to only £222, or £186 after the payment of tax.'

Jack Wright was the last of the 'malcontents' to resume playing, when the New Zealanders beat Keighley 21-3 in fine conditions at Lawkholme Lane to maintain their unbeaten march through the midweek games. Tries to Sanders, Singe and Davidson and two Mouat goals provided the visitors with thirteen unanswered first-half points. Though conceding a try soon after the resumption, they responded strongly for Carroll and Mouat to add further tries, with Mouat converting the first of them.

However, the rugby league correspondent of the *Keighley News* condemned the All Blacks as being 'patchy' in combination. But he was highly impressed with the individual work of backs Davidson, Sanders, Brown and Delgrosso. He did not provide an assessment of the forwards, either singly or as a unit, preferring to lambast the Keighley players for lacking confidence. The one shilling and sixpence admission fee was blamed for restricting the crowd to 3,864 and the receipts to £293 - by comparison, the 1907-08 All Golds had attracted 8,000 fans who paid £350. The implication was if the charges had been lowered more people would have attended and therefore boosted the revenue. Mair calculated the average tour gate to have slipped to £541.

Mair obviously enjoyed his day at Keighley: 'This place is noted for the pride it takes in its district in every way, and a different atmosphere prevailed for our visit there. No stone was unturned to make our visit a very happy one. After the game the teams were entertained at a banquet by the Keighley club, where the usual toasts were proposed and responded to. The banquet was certainly the most successful one to date, and the team's visit will be remembered for many a long day. The fog caused our train to misfire and, it being out of the question to catch our connection, the Keighley club kindly arranged a char-a-banc to take us back to Harrogate.'

Managers Ponder and Mair were invited along to another English Rugby League meeting, this time under more convivial circumstances. The ERL had just awarded Australia and New Zealand full membership of its council, although Mair reported they would only have input at annual rather than regular meetings. But the concession allowed Mair, in particular, to discuss rule interpretations. The New Zealand officials left confident that the Lions would tour Down Under in 1928, despite being at loggerheads with the Australians over laws pertaining to the play-the-ball and dropping out from the goal-line.

While further discussion on removing the two-year residential ban for Antipodean rugby union players was held over until the next ERL meeting on 15 December, Mair believed the British clubs would not stop there. 'It is my opinion that the ban on amateur players will be lifted. Moreover, it is apparent that the feeling amongst many of the League clubs is to even raise the ban on rugby league players in Australia and New Zealand. The English clubs are ever on the lookout for classy backs, and now that Wales has been exhausted their field for players must naturally turn towards Australia and New Zealand.'

An arduous series of matches now awaited the All Blacks. In turn, they were to be confronted by Challenge Cup holder and 1926-27 champion-in-waiting Swinton, the Welsh national team at Pontypridd, the much improved St Helens club, reigning champion Wigan, the Yorkshire county representatives at Huddersfield, and top-ten club Hunslet. They were to lose to all six of them. In the midst of this depressing sequence of non-success the tourists were to be split once again, this time not just for the remainder of the itinerary but for the entire lifetimes of most of those involved.

It should have been one of the finest performances of the tour, for New Zealand scored four tries and conceded only two to star-studded Swinton. But a last-minute field goal by fullback Jack Pearson edged Swinton home by 16-14. While Bert Morris kicked two conversions and two penalty goals for the locals, New Zealand's only goal was a penalty by Mouat to reduce the halftime deficit to 7-2.

'New Zealand led nine minutes after the resumption, Desmond, Brown and then Desmond again scoring tries, all of which were the result of remarkable speed and delightful work,' reported the Press Association. Brown was also to touch down a second time, after a thrilling run by Davidson, to give the tourists a 14-9 advantage. But forward Tom Halliwell crashed over for the try which gave Morris the chance to tie the totals and set the scene for Pearson's clincher.

The Swinton *Journal* accused the New Zealanders of indulging in gamesmanship, conceding penalties when their opponents were in the process of scoring tries. 'There were times when the referee allowed the opposition considerable latitude and on two occasions he awarded Swinton free-kicks when players were actually over the line for tries. In the first instance Mouat deliberately ran offside from the scrum practically on the line and Bryn Evans crossed; while in the second half Beswick grounded behind the posts but as Cole was standing offside a penalty was awarded. The latter award certainly brought Swinton two points but it also cost them three.

'The New Zealanders are a well-built set of men and made some dangerous forward rushes. Their handling, too, was a great improvement on some of the previous games, and altogether they played entertaining football. Davidson was a most thrustful centre, and once Brown and Desmond got on the move there was very little chance of catching them. These two wingers each scored a couple of tries, but they were of the snap variety and the result of defensive errors by the home men. Not one of the four tries was converted although the positions were favourable. Gregory missed one easy shot and Mouat four. Delgrosso, who worked the scrum, was outplayed by Bryn Evans and Brisbane never got the measure of "Billo" Rees. Gregory played brilliantly at fullback and Avery, Mouat and Petersen were the best of a set of forwards who were beaten in the scrums.'

Because the Lancashire county fixture had been postponed from the following Wednesday until 3 January, the New Zealanders found themselves with the luxury of a free week to prepare for the Welsh Test match at faraway Pontypridd in south-east Wales. As Mair had written in relation to the international transfer ban, English rugby league clubs had raided Welsh rugby union for talent and there were plenty of seasoned men to choose from. But the inclusion of four players from the first-season Pontypridd professional club suggested that the team was selected partly with match promotion in mind.

Criticisms that the Welshmen were below full strength were silenced when they gave New Zealand a 34-8 thrashing in front of about 10,000 spectators at Taff Vale Park. With Jim Sullivan starring at fullback, Wales scored eight tries to New Zealand's two, by Delgrosso and Thomas. Delgrosso converted his own try to give the tourists an all-too-brief 5-3 lead.

The New Zealand team was not as strong as it might have been. Mouat had succumbed to the illness which spelled the beginning of the end of his tour. Dufty was laid up with a ligament injury suffered at practice. Both Jim Parkes, at wing, and Harry Thomas, in the forwards, were returning after missing the previous five games. The team consisted of Gregory, Brown, Davidson, Kirwan, Parkes,

From Mair to Nightmare

Brisbane Delgrosso, Mason, Carroll, Devine, Wright, Thomas and Avery. Curiously, the team list printed in the match programme included Desmond, Henry and Mouat, whose places were taken by Kirwan, Carroll and Avery on match day.

'Gallant little Wales rose to the great occasion and so thoroughly mastered their opponents that in addition to compiling the highest aggregate of the tour, the margin of points in their favour was exactly double that of any other team against the tourists,' reported the *Athletic News*. 'Feeble scrummaging, inability to make headway by the half-backs, and inaccurate combination by the three-quarter backs revealed the All Blacks in a mood that was a positive invitation for alert opponents to gather points almost at will.

'With the exception of Gregory at fullback, the remaining members of the back division did little to stem the flowing Welsh tide. Davidson is palpably not fit, and long before halftime was practically a passenger. Brown, the one three-quarter who invariably makes an appeal as a player capable of great deeds, never received a pass in the first half. Afterwards, as outside half, he found his opportunities strictly limited by the brilliance of Rees. Little that is creditable can be said of the All Blacks forwards. Avery was an outstanding exception and his determination was worthy of a better cause.'

In midweek, the Wellington *Evening Post*'s Auckland reporter gained access to a letter from an unnamed Auckland member of the team, presumably posted about the time of the 'strike' prior to the Oldham game. The anonymous player described the team as 'a great side ruined'. He deplored the selection error made in leaving specialist hookers at home, criticised the English interpretation of the scrum rules, and lamented the absence of Auckland stand-off half Maurice Wetherill 'as his equal has not been seen at Home.' Without Wetherill, England captain Jonty Parkin dominated the first Test match despite the New Zealanders variously trying Desmond, Delgrosso, Hall and Davidson against him during the game. Davidson had been 'the sheet anchor of the New Zealand backs' and had received an offer of £800 from Halifax to stay over. But the two-year qualification period would prevent him accepting.

Referring to the split, the anonymous All Black said: 'It came at an unfortunate time, and shook the team badly. Just imagine a team picked and six players saying at the very last moment that they were not going to play. Their grievance was with the team manager. You know my views in regard to Mr Mair, but I can say he has done all in his power to help us and to make the tour successful.' Evidence here that the action taken by the 'malcontents' occurred just before the team left Harrogate for Oldham, almost certainly after an ultimatum demanding that Mair step aside was rejected by management.

Another controversy engulfed the New Zealanders during their 22-12 loss to St Helens at Knowsley Road on 9 December. Gardiner was sent from the field for striking a touch judge. Interviewed by journalists after the match, Gardiner claimed he had been racially abused. 'The touch judge signalled a try when Ellaby crossed. I disagreed with him and said so. The judge said: "Keep your eyes open, you dirty Dago." I lost my temper and struck him,' said the big Maori wing. The *Daily Mail* reported Gardiner was reluctant to leave the field, eventually going off arm in arm with the referee to the cheers of the crowd. Gardiner told his story again to an unimpressed judiciary committee which stood him down for three games.

The rugby league correspondent of the *St Helens Reporter* was sympathetic towards the All Blacks, saying as many as eight late changes were forced because of an outbreak of influenza in the camp. 'I am strongly of the opinion that if they could play the same side together for a season or two there would be very few teams who could take any change out of them,' he wrote. It was the tourists' first midweek loss and they had scored as many tries - four - as St Helens only

From Mair to Nightmare

to be let down yet again by poor goalkicking. Brown (two), Avery and Gardiner were the scorers of the unconverted tries.

If New Zealand finished with twelve men at St Helens after Gardiner's dismissal, they were to have only eleven standing and one other hobbling in their 36-15 loss to Wigan at Central Park. Gregory twisted his knee after ten minutes and gamely battled on into the second half before collapsing and being carried off. Three minutes after Gregory was initially hurt, Kirwan was knocked out and suffered a nasty head gash when diving to prevent Jim Sullivan from scoring a try. The stretcher bearers got the concussed Kirwan to the dressing room where the local club doctor inserted several stitches in his head wound.

Bert Avery moved to the three-quarters to cover for Kirwan and when Gregory left the field Arthur Singe substituted at fullback. That left only four forwards in a hopeless contest against a formidable Wigan forward pack which included giant South African George van Rooyen. Meanwhile, scrum-half Stan Webb suffered a severe knee injury when he was tackled on the Wigan goal-line. Although he stayed on the field, Webb was ineffective and also had to be carried off at fulltime. Neither Gregory nor Webb was able to play again on tour.

It was no surprise the champion Wigan team should run in ten tries - the tourists were fortunate Sullivan had a rare off-day with his goalkicking - against five unconverted tries to Herring, Brown, Davidson, Webb and Avery. Despite being without Gregory and Kirwan, the eleven remaining New Zealanders briefly held a 15-14 advantage early in the second spell. A try by Sullivan restored Wigan to the lead and the weight of numbers told for the rest of the game.

'Dufty was still unable to play, his wretched ligament still giving him trouble,' wrote Mair. 'How the team have missed him in recent matches, particularly the last three club games. In those games we have scored thirteen tries and converted only one, not to mention missing many kicks at goal from penalties. It lost us the games against Swinton and St Helens, and would have meant victory against Wigan also if our team had remained at full strength. Dufty's absence has also been felt in the line kicking and up-and-unders. Dufty's long punts would have made Sullivan stand deep instead of being level with his three-quarters all through the second spell after New Zealand had lost players with injury.'

After detailing the injuries suffered by Gregory, Kirwan and Webb at Wigan, Mair said Cole was also among the walking wounded after severely wrenching his thigh against St Helens. Fortunately, Davidson's ankle 'stood the test' of playing against Wigan. Mouat was ill with influenza, but it was expected forward Len Mason and scrum-half Wilson Hall would be declared fit for the midweek clash with Yorkshire at Huddersfield. About 9000 spectators attended the Wigan match, paying £605 at the gate.

Mair had some other observations, including the now familiar debate about ticket prices: 'The followers of the game are still protesting about the one shilling and sixpence charge for admission. The aftermath of the strike is still being felt and the argument is being put forward that a reduction to one shilling minimum will show an improvement in the receipts. Personally I do not think so and moreover it would not be fair to the clubs now that the tour is coming to a close - nine more matches to play - to effect a change.'

And another on the referee: 'The referee was Mr Horsdale. The game was so fast in the first half that he was done to a frazzle by the interval and there were several movements in which tries were scored in which he found it difficult to be "present thereat". The game was the fastest witnessed on Central Park for many years, and in the opinion of the local officials no more spectacular colonial tussle has been put up there.'

On the return train journey Mair would have had plenty

of time to reflect that his one-month stand-down period had expired. He should also have known that the English Rugby League was to review the situation and decide whether the coach should be reinstated. During Mair's 'down time' as a selector and coach the New Zealanders had lost six of their eight matches. He would surely have held the view that his services as a tactician were urgently needed. The significance of the date would not have escaped the players, either, especially those who were adamant they would not play again under their Australian nemesis.

Wednesday, 15 December, was to be yet another defining date on the tour. Not only were the New Zealanders to play Yorkshire county at Huddersfield in the afternoon, but the English Rugby League councillors were to meet before the game. The ERL officials were also making up their minds whether Mair should be invited to take back the reins of his troubled touring team. An irreversible force was about to meet an immovable object.

11

TORN APART FOREVER

Ernest Mair was always going to regard his month-long stand-down as exactly that, and not one day longer. No sooner was he back at Harrogate after the decisive and injury-ridden loss to Wigan than he reverted to full selection and coaching mode, focusing on the match with Yorkshire. With the tacit approval of co-manager George Ponder, Mair sat down with captain Bert Avery to choose the side for the match at Huddersfield. Neil Mouat, the vice-captain, third selector and, in Mair's mind, leader of the rebels had been hospitalised.

It is scarcely conceivable that Mair and Ponder did not know the situation was to be reviewed by the English Rugby League before a decision was made whether the coach should be reinstated. It was recorded in the ERL minutes of a month earlier and had been reported in various English newspapers. But Mair did not wait for the ERL meeting at Huddersfield to be held on the morning of the Yorkshire fixture, and there were inevitable and irrevocable repercussions.

Five of the forwards who had previously rebelled against Mair were selected to take on Yorkshire - Phonse Carroll, Bill Devine, Frank Henry, Lou Petersen and Arthur Singe - and they all again refused to train and play under the coach. One newspaper said a sixth, Jack Wright, was unfit, though he had played at Wigan, and Mouat was off the scene. But Wright and Mouat quickly made it known they were still standing shoulder to shoulder with their team-mates. None of them would pull on a jersey while Mair was involved.

When the ERL meeting was held on match morning the councillors were not aware of the revolt within the New Zealand camp. They handled the matters which were on their agenda, including confirmation of George Gardiner's three-match suspension for striking the touch judge at St Helens and decided not to go ahead with any promotional matches involving the tourists in London, Paris, Belfast or south Wales. The tour would officially end with the third Test at Leeds on 15 January.

But this time there was no hiding the mutiny from the media. The *Daily Dispatch* reviewed the earlier dissension and Mair's one-month hiatus. Significantly, the Manchester newspaper recalled 'the matter (was) to be reviewed at the end of that period'. Its story continued, 'The month having expired, Mr Mair resumed his duties this week as one of the team selectors. This caused trouble to break out afresh, and five of the seven forwards concerned with it previously refused to turn out in the match against Yorkshire. The five players have definitely made up their minds not to have Mr Mair as a team selector.'

But the *Dispatch* and other publications believed there had been a quick fix: 'After the match at Fartown yesterday, a meeting of the ERL tour sub-committee was held at which "peace" was again restored on the lines of the previous agreement. Mr Mair has again consented to remain off the selection committee, which work will now apparently be done by Mr G H Ponder and Avery, the captain. The tour lasts only another month and it is hoped there will be no recurrence of the friction. It has been a very unfortunate business all around.'

With English journalists having been assured that matters had been resolved, they devoted much space to a particularly brave performance by the New Zealanders and, especially, their hastily rearranged pack consisting of transplanted wing Jim Parkes at hooker and the five remaining specialist forwards, Joe Menzies, Ernie Herring, Harry Thomas, Len Mason and Avery. There were only fifteen players available, including Craddock Dufty, Frank Delgrosso and Wilson Hall, who all returned from injuries to bolster the backline. The Fartown pitch was frozen and players took a pounding when crash-tackled onto its concrete-like surface.

'Brilliance In Failure' was the headline atop the *Daily Dispatch*'s coverage of 'Yorkshire's Point Win Over All Blacks'. The writer described the county's first success over an overseas team as undeserved and commented, 'while the Yorkshiremen could derive some satisfaction from the victory it would be very scant'. The New Zealanders lost by a tantalising 17-16 after trailing 15-3 at halftime and 17-3 soon afterwards. They would have won had Dufty, who reportedly 'did not look altogether sound', not kicked so erratically. Inaccurate goalkicking had cost them yet another game.

'When the teams retired at halftime with Yorkshire leading by fifteen points to three, I am told that a well-known Yorkshire player declared he "would not give £50 for the lot of them". That player got a rude awakening in the second half, and I fancy his estimate of the value of the tourists would have risen considerably before the end of the game,' said the *Dispatch*. 'The All Blacks took command of the game and we saw such a wonderful rally that I, for one, regret it just failed to pull the game round in their favour.

'There were only about 3000 spectators – receipts £186 –

but they were thrilled by the speed and brilliant passing of the tourists. The spectators forgot all about pride of county, but spurred on the All Blacks in most generous and sporting fashion. I don't think any among the spectators would have been sorry had Yorkshire been beaten, as they undoubtedly should have been on the second half's display. Thus though the All Blacks failed there was brilliance and merit in their failure.'

Mason had opened the scoring after twenty minutes when he gathered in a Davidson cross-kick. The second-half revival produced tries to Brown, Davidson and Avery and two Dufty conversions. In the final act of the game, when New Zealand was awarded a penalty near the touchline but within his range, the less than fully fit Dufty did not have the confidence to shoot for goal. Instead, an up-and-under was hoisted and Yorkshire regained possession as the last seconds ticked away.

Writing in the *Yorkshire Post*, H H Nicholson said the All Blacks were in a desperate plight thirty minutes from fulltime. 'They had a weakened team, short of six forwards, five of whom had refused to play, and they were fourteen points behind. They tackled the job with a rough courage and an intense concentration of effort. With a succession of hammer blows they battered the Yorkshire defence. It was a frail barrier that separated them from a win. I think they should have won. What seemed a fair try scored by Brown was disallowed. The pass, I thought, was not forward; I saw no knock-on.'

Believing it had restored the status quo, the English Rugby League officially notified the New Zealand managers next day that the tour sub-committee had 'decided that the arrangement which was made at Harrogate six weeks ago should continue until such time as the committee rules otherwise. The decision means Mr Mair will stand out of the tourists' selection committee, leaving the work to be done by those who have been in authority since the last trouble, Mr

Strike! The Tour That Died of Shame

G H Ponder, the financial manager, Avery, the captain, and Mouat, the vice-captain.' The ERL was to be shocked by the reaction from Harrogate.

George Ponder had changed his stance. He had decided to defy the English Rugby League and its tour sub-committee, reinstate Ernest Mair as co-selector and coach, and to suspend the six rebellious players who were in the camp. Ponder even invited the *Yorkshire Post* to the West Park Hotel to make a public statement, one which would have infuriated ERL officials.

'The New Zealand managers are in control of the New Zealand team, and will remain in control until the end of the tour,' said Ponder. 'Arrangements are now being made to suspend the men who have broken discipline and refused to turn out with the side. This is demanded by some of the loyal players who say if those who have refused to stand by the team and New Zealand on the tour are not dealt with they will ask to be allowed to return home.'

Ponder told the *Post* he was not prepared to accept the ERL's extension of Mair's stand-down until the tour managers had been given a chance to state their case. 'In fairness to us (the managers and the nineteen 'loyal' players) we should have been given an opportunity of attending this meeting and expressing our views. We have absolute evidence that in the month in which Mr Mair has been stood down some of the seven men who have been the cause of the trouble have broken discipline. Is it fair that the nineteen loyal players should be made the scapegoats for seven men who right from the outset of the tour have set themselves out to defy law and order in the camp?' Ponder also pointed out the New Zealanders' boasted a far more impressive win-loss record when Mair was in charge.

Both Mair and Avery claimed there had been no provision in the agreement for a review to be conducted once the coach's one-month stand-down had expired. Mair told the *Post* that he had only agreed to withdraw 'to make a sacrifice for New Zealand, not through any weakness in my case. At that stage, with illness and injuries to players, it was not possible to carry on without the seven forwards who had refused to play. They refused to capitulate, so for the game, for New Zealand, and the players who had been loyal to the management I made the sacrifice so that the team would not be sent home.

'Avery's statement is that when Mr Mair agreed to stand down so that the trouble could be bridged, there was no mention then of the matter being reviewed in a month,' said the *Post*. 'The agreement was made between himself, as captain, on behalf of his men, and Mr Mair. Avery went on to say that he was not prepared to carry on with the team unless the men who had been the cause of all the trouble were dealt with. He told of happenings within the last month which he claimed showed that some of the seven players concerned had not been loyal even when Mr Mair was off the selection committee, and said that in the match with Wales one of them refused to play.'

Ponder went further the next day, telling the Post that 'as a first step towards a settlement of the troubles within the touring party, arrangements are being made to book passages for the six players back to New Zealand by the first available ship. I am trying to get berths for them on a boat which leaves for New Zealand on December 31, and as far as can now be seen we shall not have their services any longer.

'As far as the (English) Rugby League order is concerned, we are taking no further notice of it. Of course, if the Rugby League council cares to turn nasty, and says the tour is cancelled, that will be their own look-out. For ourselves, we are prepared to carry on and make the tour a success. But to facilitate that, these six players who are causing all the trouble must be sent home. We, of the management, have had no end of trouble and I personally will have no more of it. I have kept quiet a long time trying to preserve the good name of New Zealand football, but when the Rugby League council tell me to knuckle under to six players who have repeatedly broken discipline I think it is time to raise one's voice in protest.'

Ponder repeated that Mair had withdrawn from the selection panel because 'it was the simplest way of solving a difficult problem' not because he was at fault or the recalcitrant players were in the right. 'I have evidence regarding the indiscipline of those players sufficient to sink a ship,' he said. 'There will be something to open the eyes of the New Zealand Rugby League when we get home.' Ponder also emphasised he should have been consulted before Mair's stand-down period was extended.

New Zealand newspapers of 18 December quoted the *Daily Mail* as speculating the tour might be prematurely ended: 'A deadlock has been reached with the New Zealand League footballers in their relations with the Rugby Football League. Messrs Mair and Ponder have refused to accept the League's decision that Mr Mair must abandon the selectorship. Mr Wilson, the League's secretary, says the decision must stand. A member of the League council expresses the opinion that the council, which is paying the piper regarding the losses, will not stand any nonsense and is prepared to immediately end the tour unless its wishes are met. Mr Mair states that it is the intention to send home forthwith the players refusing to turn out. The League council will meet on 22 December, when developments are expected.'

The *Daily Dispatch*, meanwhile, indulged in some editorialising: 'At different times, since the early days of the tour, the council have had players and managers before them. The players apparently have got on well with Mr Ponder but some have from the outset objected to Mr Mair, both as manager and as a member of the selection committee. From what I have been told there has been a great deal of stubbornness on both sides, and what might have been a most successful tour has been spoiled, if not entirely ruined, by internal dissensions.'

'Personally, I have felt that the council ought to have taken disciplinary action against the malcontents in the early stages of the tour, and sent them back by the first available boat. There were, however, obvious objections to this from many points of view, and it was hoped after the free exchange of views that the party would settle down in peace and harmony. Had the council thought otherwise I have not the slightest doubt they would have ended the tour in the early days of October and cut their losses. But they were anxious to keep faith with New Zealand and give the players a chance.'

While the *Dispatch* doubted there was any desire or intention to make anybody a scapegoat, 'when the inner history of the trouble comes to be made known it will be found, I think, that both parties in the dispute have not been free from criticism. The English Rugby League council have been tolerant to the point of leniency. But there can be no disguising the fact they have been badly let down. By whom is for them to say. A great opportunity has been lost for advancing the game in New Zealand. The effect of all this squabbling cannot fail to have an unpleasant influence for some years to come.'

On 18 December the New Zealanders suffered yet another Saturday loss, by 19-12 at Hunslet. They fielded the same team as against Yorkshire, with the exception that Wally Desmond filled in at fullback in the absence of both specialists. While George Ponder kept telling journalists and officials the tour could continue with nineteen loyal players, they were really down to a bare minimum for this fixture. Of the nineteen, Gardiner was suspended, Charles Gregory and Stan Webb had suffered tour-ending injuries, and Dufty and Jack Kirwan were also laid up. Hector Cole was borderline, at best. The thirteen who played Hunslet were the only men available. Ponder and Mair were sailing close to the wind insisting the itinerary could be completed by the 'loyalists'. To make matters worse, Jim Sanders sustained a knock in this game which kept him out of action until the tour-ending third Test almost a month later.

The strain was obviously getting to some of the survivors. Near the end of the Hunslet match the normally mild-mannered Lou Brown was ordered from the field for alleged insolence to the referee. The subsequent judiciary hearing decided the send-off was sufficient penalty and did not impose a suspension. Whether it had a bearing or not, Brown could not be spared and was to play in all of the last fifteen matches. Once again, the tourists staged a big recovery after trailing 13-2 at halftime. But tries to Menzies and Avery, and Delgrosso's three goals, did not even bring them within range of Hunslet.

Eighty minutes of football at Hunslet was but a brief diversion from the storm raging around the team off the field. The *Leeds Mercury* published a statement from English Rugby League secretary John Wilson that the shipping agents had again been instructed not to accept return bookings from anyone which would involve his council in financial obligations. Ponder told the *Athletic News* the 'strikers' had been guilty of disciplinary breaches since the previous inquiry and threatened 'either they go or I relinquish further control of the team'. The *News* headlined its story with the question, 'Is All Blacks' Tour At An End?'

An emergency meeting of the NZRL was held in Auckland on 20 December to consider the following cable from Ponder and Mair: 'Mouat hospital, dangerously ill. Devine, Carroll, Henry, Singe, Petersen striking. Stopped expenses. Suspended players. Handling position ourselves. Object mediator partial. Carrying on.' The managers obviously felt that the ERL could no longer be regarded as an impartial arbiter in the dispute.

The NZRL councillors had read Press Association reports that the ERL was meeting on 22 December to decide whether the tour should be stopped. Some of them decided it was time to take the matter out of the hands of the English authorities and it took the casting vote of chairman James Carlaw to prevent the tour ending there and then. Six of the twelve NZRL councillors in attendance supported a motion to bring the team home by the first available boat. Carlaw just managed to push through an amendment that no action be taken until the outcome of the ERL meeting was known.

Ponder told English journalists that he had been invited to the ERL meeting but Mair had not been. That, fumed Ponder, was 'a studied insult. Mr Mair will attend and ask to be admitted. If not, he will state his case to the reporters. I will ask for the Press to be admitted, as is the case in New Zealand.' When reminded of the ERL instruction that shipping agents not accept any return bookings from the New Zealanders, Ponder replied it would cost £200 to keep the dissenting players in England and he would not include that item on his tour balance sheet.

As it happened, Mair was allowed into the meeting, but the Press waited outside. Two hours later, ERL chairman Ted Osborne issued a statement: 'The council confirms the action of the sub-committee with regard to Mr Mair ceasing to function until January 10. It supports the suspension of players who have refused to play, and is prepared to continue the tour if Mr Ponder is willing to act as manager. Failing the acceptance of this resolution the whole party must return on December 31. After January 10, Mr Mair can resume his duties as manager if he so desires.' Ponder told the reporters they accepted the statement without prejudice. The 10 January date was the Monday before the third Test, now the final tour match.

The fate of the still-hospitalised Mouat and the other six forwards had been sealed. Ponder had previously announced to the media they were suspended and would not be considered for any of the last seven matches. Now the ERL had confirmed those suspensions, in return for Ponder agreeing that Mair also be effectively suspended from his duties. But the host League had not completely washed its hands of the malcontents. Indeed, they were to offer them a measure of assistance which caused the 'loyalists' to threaten a strike of their own in the Headingley dressing room an hour before the third Test was due to kick off. But that drama was still more than three weeks distant.

Having read the outcome of the ERL meeting in that day's Auckland newspapers, the NZRL council on 23 December contented itself with making the first preparations for the team's return in early March. On the table was a held-over query from the managers whether the party should divide into two at Sydney, with the southern players proceeding to Wellington and the northern members to Auckland. The council decided the entire group should return to Auckland and cabled the managers asking for a full report about the disciplinary problems.

Because matches had been postponed or reshuffled, the New Zealanders were left without a midweek game. But they then faced the incredibly difficult task of playing Pontypridd on Christmas Day, Broughton Rangers on 27 December, Wakefield Trinity the next day, Hull Kingston Rovers on New Year's Day and the Lancashire county representatives on 3 January. Five matches in ten days with a playing roster which fluctuated between thirteen and seventeen as injured players battled to recover and George Gardiner served his suspension.

At least the managers and the nineteen loyal players escaped from harrowing Harrogate, the scene of so much grief, for Christmas. On Christmas Eve they travelled back to Pontypridd, where they had lost heavily to Wales in early December, and stayed overnight before beating the fledgling club by 17-8 on an overcast but dry Christmas Day. Mair was able to find plenty of positives in his match report, which was not published in New Zealand until mid-February.

'We will never forget the Pontypridd match for many a long day,' wrote Mair. 'It was the happiest time we have spent since arriving here. The host and hostess at the hotel, the Pontypridd officials, the leading artists of the place and the theatres all went out of their way to make our Christmas very happy. Before this game we had won thirteen and lost fourteen games, and the boys, imbued with the new spirit, were determined to equalise. They realised the many unfortunate difficulties they had experienced, felt that their dimmed reputation needed brightening, and to use their own words, "the best Christmas box we can give our (supporters) at home is to send them a win".

'Parkes again occupied the rake position, and is a bigger success there than on the wing. He had with him the only five forwards left in the side, and their display could be marked as the best given by a pack on the tour. Parkes' raking was a feature of the game, and he secured the ball to a much greater degree than in any previous match by the other hookers we tried. Parkes does get down low and fights for possession all the time, even when he is beaten. The forwards worked like one man.'

This time Kirwan was the makeshift fullback, Desmond switched to the wing to cover for the injured Sanders, and Cole was deemed fit enough to replace Brisbane in the centres. New Zealand led 5-3 at halftime, thanks to a Davidson try and Delgrosso conversion, against a surprisingly robust home team. The tourists were to score four of the five second-half tries, to Mason, Brown, Avery and Davidson, all of them unconverted. In what Mair described as an experiment, he said it was the first major rugby match of either rugby code to be held in Wales on Christmas Day. The gate receipts were £230.

It was not recorded how the seven banished forwards spent their Christmas, though having English-born Frank Henry in their midst would obviously have been invaluable in making contacts. It was Mair who raised the 'peculiar position' in which Henry found himself. A former rugby union representative player, Henry had switched to rugby league with York in the 1920-21 season and immigrated to

Strike! The Tour That Died of Shame

Christchurch in late 1924. Mair said that Henry's name had remained on the York club register since 1920 and had not even been erased while he was playing for New Zealand.

'After the managers of the New Zealand team suspended him for striking with six others, Henry got in touch with York, and as a result York applied at a recent meeting of the English council for permission to play him,' wrote Mair. 'The York club wanted him to play for them on Christmas Day but the English council refrained from giving the necessary permission. A further request to play him was considered at the last meeting, and in view of Henry's suspension by the New Zealand managers a peculiar position arose. The English council ruled that after the completion of the New Zealand tour in England on January 15, Henry be granted permission to play for York, and to lift their suspension, for they had unanimously upheld the suspension of the strikers by the New Zealand managers. As a result Henry will not be returning with the New Zealand team and his berth has been cancelled.'

Despite all of the upheavals which had prevented the New Zealanders from realising their potential, English club officials agreed with newspaper reports that there was considerable individual talent within the touring team. Wing Lou Brown was given a rousing reception at Wigan, where he had played previously as an amateur, and fullback Charles Gregory and centre Ben Davidson were among others to attract widespread attention from the clubs. The scouts were talking terms to some players while, in the background, lobbying continued for the removal of the two-year qualifying period for Australasian signings.

Of Brown, Mair said 'he is the speediest winger in the game here and the tries he has scored are the kind that delight League fans. Now that the prospects of lifting the ban look rosier than ever, offers are flying everywhere for the securing of players. My co-manager and I have fought strenuously against the lifting. Several of the clubs here are keen on securing Gregory. He has been the most consistent back on the tour, has the right temperament for big football and is the right type. Davidson is another player who has been approached by the clubs here. Benny has proved himself the best attacking player on the New Zealand side, and his straight running and making of tries has appealed to the officials who control clubs. However, all the New Zealanders return to New Zealand first, no matter how the decision goes.'

Victory at Pontypridd sparked a three-match winning sequence, with the New Zealanders beating Broughton Rangers 32-8 at The Cliff, near Manchester, on 27 December and Wakefield Trinity 29-24 at Belle Vue the next day. Those pleasing results were achieved despite arduous travel arrangements. The tourists actually arrived in Manchester at 1.30am on Boxing Day and kicked off at 11am the following day so they could meet train schedules and get to Wakefield for their next assignment. By necessity, the team on both days comprised Dufty, Brown, Kirwan, Brisbane, Gardiner, Hall, Delgrosso, Menzies, Parkes, Herring, Mason, Thomas and Avery.

Avery produced one of the greatest performances of an illustrious career when he scored five of his team's eight tries against Broughton Rangers. It was only 8-5 at halftime, with Avery having already crossed twice, but the All Blacks ran riot after the home side was reduced to twelve men by injury. Brown, Kirwan and Avery ran in tries in rapid succession, Mason got another and Avery finished as he had started with two more. Dufty kicked four goals. In addition to Avery, halves Hall and Delgrosso and centres Brisbane and Kirwan received rave reviews.

Only two New Zealanders have since improved upon Avery's feat, and both were also Auckland loose forwards. Rex Percy scored six tries against Central Queensland at Rockhampton in 1956 and Hugh McGahan set a world Test record of six tries against Papua New Guinea at Carlaw Park

Strike! The Tour That Died of Shame

in 1983. Ironically, Broughton Rangers was not at full strength because of a players' strike. Three Welshmen had refused to turn out in a club fixture the previous day and were suspended by their club.

When Avery touched down against Wakefield Trinity the next day, he had scored in seven consecutive matches -- against St Helens, Wigan, Yorkshire, Hunslet, Pontypridd, Broughton Rangers (five) and Wakefield Trinity. Making Avery's achievement all the more remarkable, the indefatigable captain was in the process of playing in all of the last thirteen tour matches.

Wakefield was also playing on consecutive days to capitalise on the Christmas holidays. About 6000 fans paid £430 at the gate to see the New Zealanders give 'a delightful exhibition and the best display of attacking seen in Wakefield for a long time,' according to the Press Association. Hall, Gardiner, Kirwan and Brown claimed first-half tries which, with two Dufty goals, provided a 16-5 advantage at the break. The New Zealand defence faltered more often after the resumption and the tries scored by Avery, Hall and Mason, plus two more Dufty conversions, were needed to keep the eager locals at bay.

'One try went to New Zealand under circumstances seldom seen these days in big football,' wrote Mair. 'Delgrosso kicked off diagonally towards the touch line. Thomas jumped in the air and fielded it, and after running ten yards gave to Menzies, who ran twenty yards and transferred to Mason, who brushed aside three attempts to stop him and scored. Thus the ball never touched the ground from the halfway line and was not handled by the opposition.'

Despite winning by just five points, the tourists scored seven of the eleven tries in the match. They had the satisfaction of walking off winners from an encounter with England captain Jonty Parkin, who had inspired Wakefield's comeback. 'The play of the All Blacks certainly created a very favourable impression amongst the spectators,' reported the *Wakefield Express*. 'As defenders they were not great, but as attackers they treated the onlookers to some sparkling movements in which they combined speed, strength and intelligence.'

New Year's Eve celebrations were muted by having to play Hull Kingston Rovers next day. Davidson returned to the centres, Delgrosso was given a break and Brisbane partnered Hall in the halves. But the Rovers triumphed 20-15, despite a brilliant try by Davidson and others to Brown – giving the fleet-footed wing the almost Avery-like record of having scored in seven of his last eight appearances – and Thomas, boosted by three Dufty conversions for a 15-7 halftime lead. The constant football was taking a toll, however. Hull KR levelled up at 15-15 and won with a last-minute converted try through the exhausted New Zealand defence.

'It had been a wonderfully hard and interesting encounter and as the All Blacks left the field they gave three cheers for the victors,' said the *Hull Daily Mail*. 'Few games have produced such thrilling football as that seen in the match on Saturday.' For once, the All Blacks were not able to mount one of their characteristic second-half rallies. The Saturday hoodoo had struck again.

Only forty-eight hours later they were trooping onto a very heavy Mather Lane field at Leigh to meet champion county Lancashire. It was the tourists' fifth match in ten days, and clearly one too many. Lancashire ran in eight tries and only inaccurate goalkicking restricted it to a 28-3 scoreline. The same six forwards, Menzies, Parkes, Herring, Mason, Thomas and Avery, had slogged away for the entire 400 minutes of those five games, as had Brown, Kirwan and Hall among the backs. Desmond returned against Lancashire, filling Gardiner's wing role.

With Davidson suffering a knee injury and becoming little more than a passenger, New Zealand was forced to

Strike! The Tour That Died of Shame

reshuffle the backline. It was a hopeless task, considering the *Daily Dispatch*'s opinion that Lancashire 'at the moment have at their command a team of world beaters. Lancashire commanded so much of the ball that the All Blacks had very few chances of developing attacks'. The tourists' only points were derived from a late Herring try. Brown was praised for 'superb' defence, Hall and Delgrosso given credit for 'some useful work' and Mason, Thomas and Avery were said to be 'prominent on occasions' in an overworked forward pack which was virtually on its collective knees.

'The state of the ground was the worst experienced on the tour, it being a quagmire,' wrote Mair. 'The display of the New Zealanders was easily the worst of the tour. They could do nothing right and the team was all sixes and sevens right through the game. The team played in a stale state. This is not to be wondered at in a way, for several of the team have played close on thirty matches, and their decisive defeat was a glorious failure when the inside history is known.'

How the tourists must have welcomed the five-day break before confronting another county, Cumberland, at Workington on England's north-east coast. Meanwhile the NZRL council meeting in Auckland on 6 January confirmed the suspensions imposed by the managers on Mouat, Carroll, Devine, Henry, Petersen, Singe and Wright. Managers Ponder and Mair advised by cable that a full report of the 'troubles' had been posted in late December. They were attempting to return the 'strikers' to New Zealand by the first available boat and advised that the rest of the party would sail from Marseilles on 21 January. It was not unusual for touring teams to travel overland through France and catch up with steamers which had left an English port before their final match.

Ponder and Mair attended an ERL meeting and managed to stall the bid by Britain's more ambitious clubs to lift the international transfer ban on Australasian rugby league players. As feared, the ban on rugby union signings had already been swept away and the rugby league restrictions were now under greater threat. The New Zealand managers were both allowed to speak but could lodge only one vote. Australia, the other country strongly opposed to lifting the two-year qualification period, was not represented. Wigan moved and Oldham seconded that the qualification be abolished from 1 August, 1927. The motion was lost by fourteen to thirteen, the New Zealand vote effectively ensuring the status quo remained. But Ponder and Mair knew the tide was turning against colonial wishes in this matter.

With a tour record of sixteen wins and sixteen losses, the tourists realistically had to beat Cumberland to finish with a fifty per cent winning record - even they could have given themselves little chance of upsetting England in the third Test match. The *Athletic News* agreed, reporting 'the New Zealanders made full use of their last opportunity to record success in a representative game' by winning 18-3. 'When the tourists lost the toss and were forced to play against the wind and rain victory for the county side was freely predicted.'

Gardiner burrowed back into the second-row and Herring was at hooker in place of the courageous Parkes. Kirwan reverted to fullback and Cole returned to the centres. Despite having the elements against them, the New Zealanders scored all fifteen first-half points, from tries by Hall, Davidson and Gardiner, the latter kicking three goals. Desmond went over for the tourists' sole points after the resumption. They overcame incessant rain and another sodden ground, conditions that were so bad the teams changed around without leaving the field at halftime. Mair was effusive in his praise of Kirwan's 'wonderful fullback play under such trying conditions.' At one stage, 'Cumberland's forwards came as one man, and Kirwan took the ball from their feet - he was cheered for his save'. The weather kept the attendance down to 4200 and receipts to £134.

Strike! The Tour That Died of Shame

Once again, the tourists had some respite from constant travelling and playing. They were to have the rest of the week to prepare for the third Test at nearby Leeds. At least, that should have been the situation. But this was the most imperfect of all tours and Ponder still faced the problem of dispatching the six suspended forwards to New Zealand as quickly as possible. When he approached them they refused to budge from Harrogate. Their allowances had been stopped a month earlier and they had no means of paying for even the basic necessities on a six-week sea voyage. The fireworks were far from over.

12

'LOYALISTS' THREATEN STRIKE

Minutes before kick-off in the third Test at Headingley the England players were listening intently to new captain Jim Sullivan exhorting them to complete a clean sweep over the All Blacks. In the visitors' dressing room across the corridor the mood was totally different. Instead of captain Bert Avery giving the All Blacks a stirring address about salvaging some pride from a terrible tour, he was trying to convince his team-mates not to boycott the match!

In the ultimate irony to a venture ruined by the conflict between seven forwards and Australian coach Ernest Mair, it was now the 'loyalist' players who were threatening to strike. Their action was not aimed at Mair, but at the English Rugby League councillors who they considered had taken sides with the 'malcontents'. Mair had returned from his latest stand-down the previous Monday but there was no normality within the New Zealand camp during Test week.

Manager George Ponder was by then resigned that six of the suspended players - excluding Frank Henry, who was staying in his native England - would be travelling from

Strike! The Tour That Died of Shame

Marseilles to Sydney with their estranged team-mates on board the *Narkunda* and then on to Auckland on the *Marama*. That could no longer be avoided. Although the *Narkunda* was to sail from Tilbury the day before the match, the Test players and officials could comfortably leave England on the following Tuesday and catch up with the vessel after travelling across France by train.

When Ponder arrived back at Harrogate from the Cumberland match at Workington, he was told point blank by Neil Mouat, Phonse Carroll, Bill Devine, Lou Petersen, Arthur Singe and Jack Wright that they were destitute and were not going anywhere until they received some spending money. Their allowances had been stopped weeks earlier and the prospect of a long, penniless homeward trip did not appeal to them.

On that Monday night in Auckland, the NZRL councillors were summoned to the latest of many special meetings which had plagued their summer months. There never seemed to be any good news, just a series of crises. Secretary Owie Carlaw reported that Ponder had sent yet another dire cable: 'Strikers no funds, refuse return New Zealand unless reimbursed out-of-pocket expenses. Threaten legal action. Suggest pay English League rates. Cable views urgently. Henry remaining England.'

President James Carlaw had consulted solicitors to ascertain the council's liability. He was advised that under clause five of the players' tour agreement, the 'strikers' were entitled only to second-class passages home upon termination of the agreement by the NZRL. The legal experts further recommended the conditions of the clause be strictly followed. The NZRL was required to provide a berth on board the *Narkunda* and nothing else, and that information was cabled to Ponder. The councillors decided to leave the matter of Henry until a later date.

Twelve hours later, at an English Rugby League meeting, Ponder reported the six players had refused to board the

'Loyalists' Threaten Strike

Narkunda on the following Friday, and had also refused to forward their baggage to the Tilbury docks. 'The reason they gave,' recorded ERL secretary John Wilson in his minutes, 'was that they had no money and could not undertake the six weeks voyage without some.' Having put up with the rebellious colonials for four months, the ERL was now faced with the unsavoury prospect of six of them remaining on their doorstep for an indefinite period. It was clear Ponder had his instructions and would not be doing anything to ease their plight. Any alteration to the original bookings would be at a cost to the ERL.

'In the event of the men refusing to embark it was foreseen that passage money to upwards of £600 would be lost, with the possibility of the men having to be kept here and eventually sent home,' wrote Wilson. 'The council instructed the secretary to see the six men concerned and to endeavour to get them to sail as arranged. It agreed to the sum of £10 each being paid to the men as pocket money on condition that they did so.' The ERL was not just being practical in ridding itself of what would be an ongoing problem. In the wake of their December dispute with the managers, some officials now felt a measure of sympathy for the 'malcontents'.

While the £10 per man offer ensured the six suspended forwards would agree to make their homeward journey, it caused anger among the other nineteen players. Whatever renewal of friendships had occurred during the month-long reuniting of the team had been broken apart forever. Of course, the 'malcontents' and 'loyalists' could never play together again because of the penalties which were to be meted out. But nor did they ever see eye to eye off the field in the months and years afterwards. The 1926-27 All Blacks had been split for life.

Their last official function as a team was the farewell dinner at the Griffin Hotel in Leeds on the night of Monday, 10 January. All twenty-six players, the two managers and press agent Joe O'Shaughnessy were listed on the back of the menu as being in attendance. But it was not the lavish function it might have been in other circumstances. There was a very restricted invitation list and, much to their annoyance, newspaper representatives were not included.

'I am told that the official farewell gathering at Leeds last Monday was a very happy affair,' wrote a columnist in the *Daily Dispatch*. 'If so it is about the only "happy" thing to report about the whole tour. As the council kept the function exclusively to themselves the public can only form what conclusions they like.'

Neil Mouat and Arthur Singe managed to get a few words published in New Zealand during Test week, via the Press Association. Singe told of how the 'dissentients' had been left penniless when their allowances were cut off in mid-December and thanked the English Rugby League for coming to their rescue. He also claimed the New Zealanders had never fielded their best team on the entire tour, another snipe at Mair's selection processes. Singe himself had appeared in the opening match at Dewsbury and then not again until the second Test, the eighteenth match, more than two months later when Mair was in limbo.

'Another New Zealand player, Mouat, interviewed prior to leaving for home, declares that he has no intention of publicly defending the conduct of himself and the other dissentients, but states they have been greatly misjudged.' The Press Association quoted Mouat as saying, 'Recently we stated our case to the Rugby League Council, who are now laying the matter before the New Zealand League Council demanding an enquiry into the conduct of the tour.'

The story went on to say, 'Mr Osborne, chairman of the Rugby League Council, is of the opinion that there is much to be said on behalf of the malcontents and he hopes the enquiry will be full. English rugby league circles declare that the tour had been most disappointing. The players' skill was below expectations. Enforcement of discipline was most difficult and consequently the team did not do itself justice. Instead of a surplus of £2000, there will probably be a deficit of £1500.'

On 14 January, The *Star* in Christchurch reprinted a few paragraphs from the *Sydney Referee* sporting newspaper. 'Disaster has followed in the wake of disaster in the tour of the New Zealanders. The rugby league game in New Zealand thus sustains a setback from which it may never recover. Its prestige is shattered. It is a heart-breaking experience for the English Rugby League, which saw fit to offer such conditions to New Zealand for this tour as had never been offered to any other team of football tourists.

'The worst feature is that, under fitting discipline and leadership, New Zealand is in a position to send a team abroad worthy of the country. The Dominion possesses forwards of weight, pace and strength necessary in men to stand up to the huskies of the Northern Counties, besides backs of fitting solidity. We know how players on a tour such as this improve and develop team-work or combination. It has been the experience of every well-managed organisation.'

The *Referee* finished off its comment piece with, 'It is clear that the English authorities consider Mr Mair has no likelihood of working amicably with the players concerned. It is useless to form a judgement from this end, though Australians are asking why Mr Mair was appointed coach to the players. The New Zealand Rugby League has a delicate problem to solve.'

Financial manager George Ponder took time out from his other responsibilities at Harrogate to conduct an extensive interview with the *Sports Post*, which was published on the morning of the Test. There was scant mention of the events which, the *Sports Post* said, had 'shrouded the side during its stay at Harrogate. Never has the side been able to realise its playing strength; never has it been able to settle down; it returns home known as the team which never found itself'.

Strike! The Tour That Died of Shame

Instead, Ponder accepted the opportunity at giving his views on how the sport could be improved in Britain, and he did not hold back.

After giving credit to English fans for their fairness, and referees for their impartiality, he expressed surprise at the latitude permitted scrum-halves and hookers at the scrummage. But Ponder's major theme was the dourness of the football displayed by most of the British clubs. There were exceptions, such as St Helens Recreation and Swinton, who were prepared to concede a few tries while confident of scoring even more points to achieve entertaining wins for their supporters. The All Blacks had been of similar mind and only three times failed to reach double figures in their thirty-three games.

'In New Zealand we go for the open game all the time,' said Ponder. 'Our forwards are encouraged to throw the ball about, and they do it like backs. Here, the forward seems to be used as a forward for scrummaging work first, second and last. Your teams seem to leave all their attacking movements to the backs, except, of course, for some of those fine dribbling rushes. And that is where we have been handicapped on the tour.

'When we set out for England we expected that we should find the hooker a man with duties carefully guarded. We left three hookers in New Zealand because we thought you would do things differently over here. Judge our surprise then when we found hookers being allowed far more liberty than we dreamt they would. The hookers we left behind would have been thoroughly happy here. Why, I have seen club hookers here allowed to go down on their knees for the ball.'

Asked his opinion on the financial failure of the tour, Ponder listed four reasons in the following order - the coal miners' strike, the tourists' internal trouble, the cost of admission, and unfavourable criticism by the media in the early stages of the tour. Ponder did not agree that the controversies which had blighted the tour would have an

'Loyalists' Threaten Strike

adverse effect on the game in his homeland provided the NZRL did 'the right thing' when dealing with the matters in its post-tour investigation.

Mair was also giving his views freely. He told the Yorkshire Society of Referees that, despite all that had happened, the tour had been worthwhile, saying, the generosity of the English Rugby League in financing the tour would be proved to have done good by the progress the game would make in New Zealand. At a Leeds Jewish Institute meeting, Mair commented that English and Australian tour managers had a hold over their players which a New Zealand manager could never have owing to the amateur status of the players.

The comments made by Ponder and Mair were nothing new, but there was some evidence their message was getting through. In early January, the ERL circularised its clubs asking for their assistance in stamping out the practice of hookers lying across the tunnel and preventing the ball from going in. The *Leeds Mercury* also reported that the minimum entrance fee for the third Test had been reduced to one shilling and sixpence. For those who could afford it, there were still a limited number of reserved seats at four shillings and sixpence and unreserved grandstand seats for three shillings and sixpence and two shillings and four pence.

Commentators were reviewing the tour, among them James Goldthorpe, whose by-line in the *Yorkshire Evening News* described him as 'the well-known authority on rugby league affairs'. Goldthorpe certainly had some interesting ideas, among them a belief that touring teams from Down Under should participate in the Rugby League Championship, playing all of the British clubs and being awarded medals should they top the final points table. Had it not been for the miners' strike causing Featherstone Rovers and Castleford to withdraw from their fixtures, the 1926-27 New Zealanders would have met all of the twenty-nine professional clubs.

Strike! The Tour That Died of Shame

Goldthorpe also described New Zealand captain Bert Avery as the best forward currently playing in Britain: 'In Avery, the captain, the team has a man who has throughout played a magnificent game. His skill is far in excess of that of any League forward, in spite of the weight of care which he has had to carry. He has always played whole heartedly, is ever ready and willing, and the players who have left him in the lurch must, in their hearts, be ashamed of their failure to realise that they were here to represent their country first and New Zealand football next. Men who will stand by and watch the desperate struggles of their fellow players should never be allowed to play again.'

But Goldthorpe's exhortations to the people of Leeds that they roll up in big numbers to Headingley and show the 'loyal' New Zealand players that they appreciated their struggles against adversity, even allied with the reduction in general admission prices, failed to gain much response. Only about 6000 people were in the ground while the teams went through their contrasting emotions in the dressing rooms.

England's selectors were certainly not doing the tourists any favours. Jim Sullivan was captaining the national team in the absence of an injured Jonty Parkin. Parkin's replacement at scrum-half was Bryn Evans, the mastermind behind the Swinton club's outstanding success and who was to extend his international career through to 1934. The other debutant was Salford loose forward Jack Gore, making his only appearance for his country. Jim Bacon (Leeds), a still sprightly wing from the 1920 and 1924 Lions tours, was recalled, as was Hull forward Harold Bowman, a 1924 tourist who was to return Down Under in 1928.

The New Zealand backline was missing penetrative but injury-prone Ben Davidson and also Hec Brisbane, the latter having succumbed to the rigors of appearing in twenty-seven games. In their absence, Jack Kirwan and Hector Cole combined in the centres. Jim Sanders had recovered

'Loyalists' Threaten Strike

sufficiently to be one of the wings in the farewell performance of an eight-year international career. Fellow wing Lou Brown made his fifteenth consecutive appearance on the tour, loose forward Bert Avery his thirteenth, prop Ernie Herring his eleventh, and scrum-half Wilson Hall and forwards Len Mason and Harry Thomas their ninth games without a break. Transplanted wing Jim Parkes was slotted in at hooker for the eleventh time.

Few people at Headingley were aware of the drama occurring in the New Zealand dressing room when the appointed kick-off time arrived and then passed. Official English Rugby League records later described the events which led to the match starting late:

'The final Test was delayed for ten minutes to hear representations from the New Zealand players to the English Rugby League. E C Gregory, acting on behalf of the players, said they were surprised at a statement by Mr Osborne which said, "I believe there is a good deal to be said on the side of the malcontent players, and I want them to have a full enquiry accorded to them. I appreciate that their side of the case has not been made public." Mr Gregory said that this could be construed as taking sides with those sent home. Mr Osborne denied that it could. Mr Gregory also wanted to know why the English Rugby League had given £10 each as out of pocket expenses to those who had left when nothing was given to those who stayed. Mr Osborne said the grant was made by the Rugby League Council so that they would not be without money on the journey home.

'Some players said they would not turn out unless they were promised £10 each but captain Avery persuaded them (by saying): "We feel that the Rugby League Council have done wrong in upholding these men but we cannot alter the position now. The best satisfaction we can get is to go out and beat the English team. If we cannot do that, we can at least show them that we are loyal to New Zealand".'

Having been given credit by some of his team-mates for

preventing a split in the group on arrival in England, Avery was four months later instrumental in ensuring that the final match on the itinerary actually went ahead.

The Press Association coverage of the third Test published in New Zealand contained no mention of the tense negotiations which saved the match. But the *Daily Dispatch* reported them in detail, before commenting, 'This incident shows what a trying time the tour has been for the Rugby League Council, and they must be heartily glad that the sickening business is practically over and that we can now settle down to our domestic affairs.'

The adrenalin produced by Avery's words kicked in for the New Zealanders and would have given them a useful lead had Cole not dropped the ball with the goal-line at his mercy and Brown not been dragged down just short. A Dufty penalty goal was the only positive return before England dominated the remainder of the first half. Four backs crossed for tries as it opened a 16-2 advantage. That was extended to 24-2 without England having reached any great heights. All of those watching were convinced that New Zealand was destined to suffer a trouncing. But Avery's rousing speech was not to be totally wasted. Midway through the second half the tourists staged a recovery which got them as close as 24-17.

'This match will go down as the "Ten Minutes Test",' wrote H H Nicholson in the *Leeds Mercury*. 'They occupied the middle of the second half. Previously the All Blacks had played like men weary in spirit and in body. An English side of moderate skills had toyed with them. Suddenly, like a squall bursts upon a calm sea, the seemingly moribund All Blacks raged into a fierce onslaught. What kindled the fire, I know not, but the drowsing Headingley crowd, waking up quickly, fanned the flames with yells of encouragement.

'Strong, straight dashes split the English defence. Points came teeming in at the rate of two a minute. First Delgrosso tunnelled through a rampart of English legs and arms,

'Loyalists' Threaten Strike

almost on the line. Then quick passing twice baffled the Englishmen and gave Herring and Avery clear runs to the line. The All Blacks sprang to a score seven points from that of England, and then the Englishmen, recovering from the shock, closed their ranks and the All Blacks' attack collapsed as suddenly as it had begun.

'An injury robbed them of the services of Delgrosso, and the defence, which had gathered strength, crumpled again. A host of questions spring up. Why did not the All Blacks produce this form before? Was this uprising a last bold bid of defiance, into which was bunched all their remaining strength? And, more piquant still, what would have happened to English sides if domestic trouble had not split their forces?'

Reduced to twelve fit men by Delgrosso's ankle injury, and again struggling against the tide of scrum possession, the New Zealanders could not keep the fleet-footed English three-quarters at bay and eventually lost by 32-17. Barrow centre Charlie Carr finished with three tries, and Bacon scored two down his wing. The others went to Carr's centre partner, Jack Evans, stand-off half Billo Rees and prop Harold Bowman. Dufty (three conversions and a penalty) outkicked the great Sullivan (four conversions from eight attempts) on the day.

Within one game the All Blacks had shown both their very best and their least convincing form. The Press Association gave Parkes credit for winning twenty-three of the sixty-three scrums, though the Leeds Mercury contradicted that by reporting New Zealand had the ball from only 'one scrum in six'. The true figures were probably somewhere in between. Hall and Delgrosso were reported to have made the most of their limited opportunities, Mason was rated the best of the forwards, and Kirwan and Sanders were judged to be the most effective outside backs.

'There are lionhearts among the All Blacks who have "marched breast forward" through all the discouraging dissension, loyal to their country, endeavouring their best,' wrote Nicholson. 'When one considers that the side have been without seven of their twelve forwards for most of the tour, the wonder is they have done so well.' At fulltime, players from both sides gathered together to sing 'Auld Lang Syne'. Gate receipts amount to a disappointing £562.

The New Zealanders had won seventeen and lost seventeen matches, scoring 562 points and conceding 554. Their points were made up of 132 tries and eighty-three goals; opposing sides crossed for 126 tries and kicked eighty-eight goals.

Avery finished with a remarkable twenty-three tries in his twenty-nine appearances, still a record for a New Zealand touring forward and bettered down the decades only by Kiwis wings Vern Bakalich (twenty-six tries in 1955-56) and Phillip Orchard (twenty-seven tries in 1971). Only Herring (thirty) appeared in more tour matches than his captain. Brisbane and Brown (both twenty-seven games) were the busiest backs, and forward strongman Mason played in twenty-six. Avery, Brown and Delgrosso were the only players to appear in all three Tests against England and one against Wales; they and Herring were the only players involved in all three England Tests.

The English Rugby League announced total tour receipts as £16,410 (though some English newspapers kept running totals and finished with differing amounts), out of which £2033 was paid in entertainment tax. 'New Zealand's share was £9483 and as the total costs were £10,359, the loss on the tour was about £870,' recorded ERL secretary John Wilson.

It was estimated that clubs needed to attract a £500 gate to avoid sustaining a loss on their tour fixtures. On that basis, most of them would have been out of pocket. Dewsbury and Halifax did very well and Leigh and Rochdale Hornets made small profits in the first four games, but the miners' strike, the internal dissension and the worsening weather later combined to cause heavy losses for

'Loyalists' Threaten Strike

the less fashionable clubs which had been allocated midweek dates. The Test match receipts were thousands of pounds below those taken during the 1921-22 Kangaroos tour, when total receipts topped £36,000.

Avery and his eighteen remaining team-mates went back to the West Park Hotel for the last time, with two days to get their gear together. Most had plenty of souvenirs to pack, notably the captain himself who was reported to have been presented with a jersey from every club the New Zealanders had played. There were farewells to local residents who had befriended them and last beers to be sunk in the pubs they had frequented. At the end of every tour there is an inevitable feeling of sadness, one that is quickly overtaken by the prospect of reuniting with friends and family at home. In 1927 there was a six-week sea trip between the two.

Optimistic comments by managers Mair and Ponder that matches would be played in Canada, Hawaii and Fiji should the tourists return via those stopovers came to nothing. The *Narkunda*, a seven-year-old, 16,000 gross ton P&O liner, travelled from the United Kingdom via the Mediterranean and Suez Canal to Australia with a maximum 426 first-class and 247 second-class passengers. The final public and official farewells of the 1926-27 All Blacks were held on consecutive days at the Leeds railway station and in London.

'The main party of the New Zealand rugby league tourists left Leeds today for London, whence they will go on to Paris tomorrow,' reported the *Yorkshire Evening News* of 18 January. 'They will have twenty-four hours in the French capital and will then entrain for Marseilles where they will board the *Narkunda* on Friday. This is the ship, of course, on which the malcontent players embarked at Tilbury last Friday. Thus the whole party, with the one exception of Henry, who has now rejoined the York club, will return to New Zealand together.

'A lively scene was presented at the Leeds Midland

Strike! The Tour That Died of Shame

Station in honour of the departing tourists. The members of the Rugby League Council had gone on to London in advance, with a view to according an official send-off tomorrow.' ERL secretary John Wilson was the most prominent official among a large number of rugby league enthusiasts who said their goodbyes at Leeds. The *Evening News* described the poignant scenes:

'As the hour of departure drew nigh the All Blacks, led by Gardiner, indulged in a rendering of their entertaining "war cry" for the special benefit of "Bright" Hayhurst, of Halifax, who, as trainer throughout their stay, had become a general favourite. The "war-song" over, the players hugged and kissed Hayhurst and in every possible way showed their appreciation of his services, while the tour managers (Mr G H Ponder and Mr E H Mair) both paid him the compliment of describing him as "an excellent example of a most conscientious trainer". The train had to be delayed a moment or two to permit all the good-byes to be said, and altogether it was a scene which did a little to relieve the sorrow which the unfortunate tour dissentions have created in the hearts of most people.'

Inevitably, the managerial interviews with the *Evening News* and *Daily Dispatch* got around to the internal troubles, and Mair did not hold back: 'As to the bogy put up by the malcontents about my being an Australian, I want to say that this does not hold water. I was appointed manager six months before the players themselves were chosen, and I was one of the officials who actually selected them. I have been Australian representative for New Zealand since the latter's tour to Australia in 1924 (sic), and I have been resident in New Zealand most of the time since and for six months before this tour started. I am still the representative of the Timaru League on the New Zealand council.

'In my opinion there is never any excuse for any sporting team to strike on tour. We set out fully trusting our players. We believed that their love of their country, their love of the

'Loyalists' Threaten Strike

game in New Zealand and in England, their position as guests of the English council, the opportunity of seeing the world under splendid conditions for nothing, their opportunity of showing their work to the English clubs in view of the possibility of the lifting of the ban on signing-on Colonial players, and their loyalty to their own comrades and to the New Zealand council would have been sufficient to have prevented open disloyalty.'

Despite having effectively twice been ordered by the English Rugby League to relinquish his selection and coaching duties, Mair said he appreciated the delicate position that body was placed in when 'frictionitis' hit the side. Not that Mair saw his 'suspensions' in that light: 'On two occasions I was able to make a personal sacrifice to prevent the tour being disbanded, and I have the assurance of my co-manager and the nineteen loyal players that my sacrifice was appreciated by them. The fact, too, that these nineteen players remained loyal during the whole period while the malcontents remained under the same roof speaks volumes.'

Ponder generally endorsed Mair's remarks, adding that he had 'nothing but regret for the dissensions which have marred the tour'. He went on to say that he had no doubt that a full investigation would be made by the NZRL, and, for his part, he would demand it be open to the press.

However, while the *Dispatch* gave Mair free rein, it reserved the right of reply through its rugby league correspondent. There was, he said, 'another side to the story. From the outset of the tour, it became apparent that the task of the managers was going to be a difficult and thankless one. The majority of the Rugby League Council are, I believe, satisfied that Mr Mair did not handle the situation with the tact necessary and desirable. The players - or at least a strong section of them - resented the instructions he issued. From what I have heard there have been faults and indiscretions on both sides.'

Strike! The Tour That Died of Shame

Outlining the by now well-publicised incidents during the outward voyage and at Harrogate after the opening match, the *Dispatch* writer said, 'it was then that stern authority and discipline was necessary. Not back-biting but strong and definite action. Either the men responsible should have been sent back, or the Rugby League should have advised the New Zealand council - by cable - to recall Mr Mair if they were satisfied that his managership of the team would result in chaos.

'It was too late two months later to establish harmony. The New Zealand council will have before them a detailed statement from the (English) Rugby League council, who are not likely to conceal any material facts. If what I am told is correct, all the blame will not fall on the "strikers". It is simply absurd for Messrs Mair and Ponder to pretend that good can come out of this tour. Such may be their hope, but it is difficult to see how it can.

'On the contrary, a great deal of harm has been done to the game here, and its effect in New Zealand may be worse. The Rugby League and its followers will not be greatly concerned about the £800 or so lost. What we are concerned about is the reputation of the code, which has enough mud slung at it in England without fetching it over from New Zealand. The conduct of the tourists on the field of play has been excellent. That it was not maintained in other respects is a matter for extreme regret. The Rugby League has been badly let down. New Zealand's duty is to investigate and punish those responsible.'

The *Dispatch* man had followed the tour as closely as any of the English journalists and apportioned blame to both the dissenting players and Mair. It must have come as a shock to him when he learned the seven players were suspended for life, without any right of appeal, within a day of arriving home, that calls for an open inquiry were ignored by the NZRL, and that Mair was thanked for his services.

Mair and Ponder were now set in their stance, issuing a

'Loyalists' Threaten Strike

joint statement to newspapermen at their London farewell hosted by six English Rugby League councillors. Their remarks were published in *The Press* and other New Zealand newspapers on 20 January. The managers again claimed the game would not be harmed if a full NZRL investigation was properly conducted; that future tours would be more successful if the authorities were more careful in the selection of players; that although only 50 per cent of games were won the moral success was higher because of the circumstances; and that the nineteen loyal players had proven themselves to be true sportsmen.

'Mr Mair pointed out that the managers were unable to fine the strikers, which was the English and Australian custom, because the New Zealand authorities trusted members to play the game,' reported the Press Association. 'Mr Ponder paid a tribute to Mr Mair's large mindedness in twice standing down to save the tour.' The story mentioned that Ponder had delivered sixteen addresses and Mair had given five lectures on New Zealand life while in Britain, 'resulting in many applications for passages'.

The *Athletic News* trumped its rival publications by obtaining an indepth interview with New Zealand captain Bert Avery, who until then had maintained a 'creditable reserve' because of a wish to complete the tour before talking publicly. Once it was all over, Avery penned his thoughts for Fred Marsh, who had written the official tour brochure and covered the matches under the pen-name of 'Forward'. Avery came down totally on the side of Mair and blamed his seven team-mates totally for the team's failure to repeat its success against Queensland at Auckland in late 1925.

'As a captain of wide experience, I have no hesitation in stating that Mr Mair did not exceed the legitimate function of a manager appointed by a governing football authority. I consider that in the face of unprecedented difficulties Mr Mair did his utmost, in the interests of the tour, to uphold his position,' said Avery.

Strike! The Tour That Died of Shame

'I realise I am on delicate ground but I desire to give my views as one with inside knowledge of things as they were, and have no hesitation in stating that I think the (English) Rugby League Council has been remiss in not more adequately supporting Messrs Ponder and Mair in their efforts to be managers in reality. I also think that Mr Osborne, a gentleman who I hold in great respect, was, to say the least, indiscreet in his remarks concerning recent statements by our vice-captain, Mouat.

'The action of the Rugby League Council in making a grant of £10 to each of the suspended players may have been entirely devoid of any implied support of players who had done their utmost to wreck the tour, but it was an action against which I and the other eighteen loyal players strongly protest as a matter of principle. We may be wrong in our assumption but we think the League's action has in effect implied support of the malcontents.'

Avery said the internal eruptions were not the sole reason for all of the disappointing results, conceding the All Blacks had encountered some teams which were superior in skills, but he was adamant the lack of team unity and support for the managers caused many of their losses. The captain had no sympathy for the suspended seven and left no-one guessing as to the testimony he would give the NZRL.

'I consider the attitude and actions of the suspended players and their breaches of discipline fully warranted suspension. When I get back to New Zealand my attitude at the investigation will be to support the managers. As captain I should be false to my position if I took any middle course,' said Avery.

'I regret that our tour has been spoiled by players whom one must allege were false to their trust and broke their agreements, but your public must put the blame in the right quarter and rid themselves of any misplaced sympathy. I feel my position most acutely. The tour has been a tragedy in

'Loyalists' Threaten Strike

the sense that with complete unity it might have proved a great success and a visit to England which every member of the team could treasure as a happy memory for the rest of his life.'

Moving on to 'more pleasant recollections', Avery paid tribute to Swinton, boasting brilliant backs such as Bryn Evans, 'Billo' Rees and Jack Evans, as the best club team in Britain, and rated Jim Sullivan as being the finest fullback he had seen. He had thoroughly enjoyed many of the matches - including some which had resulted in defeats - with the game against Hull being his favourite. The fans had been the fairest in the football world and New Zealand would learn much from the harsh lessons of professional scrummaging methods. 'I hope that when the miserable part of the tour is disposed of my lasting memory of England and its Rugby League clubs will be of the happy time we have had,' concluded Avery.

While not agreeing with Avery's statement in its entirety, *Athletic News* journalist Fred Marsh said that 'the All Blacks captain had opportunity for investigation and observation denied to others, and [I] accept his statements as sincere and made with the object of placing truth before rumour'. Avery's comments were not published in England until 24 January, by which time the entire New Zealand party was steaming through the Mediterranean.

13

BANNED FOR LIFE

The chances of alleged strikers Neil Mouat, Phonse Carroll, Bill Devine, Lou Petersen, Arthur Singe, Jack Wright and British-based Frank Henry receiving a balanced hearing from the NZRL council were minimal at best. Few people within the game were surprised when all seven forwards were disqualified for life little more than twenty-four hours after returning to Auckland. They were then denied the right to appeal. What is more, the whole affair was carried out in secret, and the evidence which convicted them was permanently buried.

Rugby league justice, rough or otherwise, was meted out very quickly in the game's pioneering days in New Zealand. In 1913, for instance, the entire fourteen-man Auckland Rugby League executive was disqualified indefinitely after a dispute with the NZRL which flared when the Auckland body suspended international forward Charles Savory for life! The Auckland officials were charged with defying their superiors, much as the seven 1926-27 All Blacks were accused of defying tour co-manager and coach Ernest Mair.

Banned For Life

NZRL president James Carlaw and his councillors had weeks while the returning players and officials were at sea to digest the damning report forwarded to them by Mair and financial manager George Ponder. They were also in receipt of the English Rugby League's opinions, which almost certainly attributed fault to both sides. They had nothing from the defendants apart from a few vague comments by Mouat and Singe in one brief newspaper story.

The councillors had endured months of hurriedly arranged meetings to consider Ponder's grimly-worded cables informing them of the 'troubles' within the New Zealand camp and also the increasingly disappointing gate receipts. They were well aware that a major reason for the financial downturn was the inability of the All Blacks to field their best teams. That the already broke NZRL would incur a sizeable loss from the tour would have further darkened their collective mood as judgement day approached.

Another leaked letter from one of the 'loyal' players was published in the *Auckland Star* on 21 February. It was accusatorial in its comments about the seven suspended forwards and would surely have made an impact on the entirely Auckland-resident NZRL hierarchy.

'"I want to get the first tram home without waiting for either the band to play or a civic reception," states one of the Auckland members of the New Zealand rugby league team in a letter written just on the eve of the departure of the tourists from England, and he adds he is not the only one of that ill-starred combination who is looking forward to the sight of old Rangitoto looming up on the port bow of the Sydney boat.

'The Aucklander considers that had all gone well on the tour the New Zealanders would have won the majority of the matches that were played, and would have had a sporting chance in the Test games. As it was, the split in the ranks destroyed the morale of the team, too great a strain was thrown on depleted playing resources, and the result from the playing viewpoint was only what could be expected. In a run of eight hard matches there were but seventeen players to draw upon, as in addition to the tourists who decided not to play football, several were on the injured list. "Had it not been for the fact that Bert Avery was skipper, the Aucklanders would have come home long ago", adds the writer.

'He states that apart from the schism, the New Zealand selectors made a grievous blunder in sending the team away without hookers, seeing that there were several players of merit offering. "We were never able to get possession of the ball from the scrums more than once in four times," he adds, "and although the backs played quite brilliantly and showed good combination, it could not make up for the great weakness forward. Parkes, chosen as a back, was the best hooker tried and he was an invaluable man to have on a side."

'The writer says that the star of the back division was undoubtedly Davidson, who captured the fancy of the north of England crowds with his great pace, straight running, and unfailing unselfishness in catering for the players supporting him. Brown was acclaimed as the fastest wing three-quarter in the game, and the writer's regret is that Wetherill was not there for the inside position and the finesse necessary to launch scoring movements. He says that Dufty and Gregory played the fullback role satisfactorily, while the greatest forward was Avery, who throughout the tour played magnificently and revealed a skill far in excess of any other League forward that they met.

'In conclusion, the writer says: "It was nothing short of a tragedy that some players should allow private grievances to dominate their actions. It has been a bad business, and will not help the game. But what of the players who loyally stood up to it, and saw the tragic tour through, often taking the field in a more or less injured state? The New Zealand Rugby League has a duty. What is it going to do?" That letter must have caused Carlaw and his councillors to further harden their attitudes towards those who were to appear before them.

In Christchurch, the *Star* newspaper had reviewed the tour, comparing it most unfavourably with that of the unbeaten 1924-25 rugby union All Blacks, and answering its own question of what the future held for a now embattled game: 'The effects are that public opinion in New Zealand will be influenced against the code for years to come, and the finances will suffer instead of being added to, and that a fair proportion of the touring players will probably retire from the game.'

But the *Star* did not join the media lynch mob. It pointed out that 'the manager (Mair) was also suspended by the English Rugby League' and drew on the benefit of hindsight: 'Before the team sailed from New Zealand's shores there were many who saw the possibility of trouble ahead, and they have been proved right. Numerous critics saw the unwisdom of appointing an Australian to coach and manage a New Zealand team. Sentiment and patriotism enter largely into sport on tour, and had a New Zealander, even one with less qualifications than Mr Mair, been appointed he would have felt from the start that the players were with him. The appointment of an outsider as manager destroyed any patriotic sentiment and made the tour appear more of a business than an outing.'

To accept the *Star*'s argument as a mitigating factor would have required the NZRL officials to admit they had erred by appointing Mair ahead of, say, Charles Pearce, the coach who Mair had deposed during the 1925 New Zealand tour of Australia. Of course, they knew that five of the accused forwards, Petersen, Henry, Devine, Mouat and Wright, were chosen from South Island clubs, Carroll hailed from the lower North Island and only Singe was from Auckland. If there were to be protests against strong disciplinary action they would almost certainly originate in the south and be muted by the time they reached rugby league's halls of power in Auckland.

Regular NZRL council meetings were held in the countdown to the team's arrival aboard the *Marama* from Sydney. As early as 20 January it was agreed that the services of the loyal players should be recognised. That would eventually take the form of a medallion, suitably inscribed and which, with the agreement of the various provincial leagues, would admit the recipient to any match throughout the country. Several discussions were also held between council representatives and the League's solicitor, Harry Rogerson, in matters of procedure.

The NZRL minutes of 2 February included a decision that 'immediately on arrival of the players they be advised per notice that, should they be desirous of appealing to the council, accommodation for forty-eight hours would be provided'. Three weeks later, there was another reference that 'in pursuance of Mr Rogerson's advice, Messrs Snedden and Carlaw were deputed to convey to the suspended players the information that they have the right of appeal against their suspension as made by the managers of the team'.

In the light of subsequent events, that must be interpreted as being able to appeal against the suspension imposed during the tour but not against any subsequent disqualification meted out by the NZRL itself.

The inquiry was set for the afternoon of 2 March at the NZRL rooms in the Grey Building, and notice of the time and date was sent to Ponder in Sydney to be handed to the players concerned after the ship's departure from that port. It was also decided the inquiry should be held in committee. A belated motion by one councillor to have the inquiry conducted by three appointed councillors and three 'outsiders' received a seconder but no other support.

On the morning of 1 March, the day the team was due home, the *New Zealand Herald* in Auckland reprinted James

Goldthorpe's article from the *Yorkshire Evening News*, the one which lobbied strongly for life suspensions for 'men who will stand by and watch the desperate struggles of their fellow players'. Goldthorpe concluded his piece with: 'It passes my comprehension to understand how any man who is fond of the game can keep out of harness. The loyalists will have the satisfaction of knowing that many supporters of football appreciate the efforts they have made.' The NZRL councillors digested Goldthorpe's words with their breakfast before heading down to meet the *Marama*.

The *Auckland Star* had first crack at reporting the arrival of the 1926-27 All Blacks. Its headlines included 'Open Inquiry Wanted', 'Sensational Disclosures Expected' and 'Allegations of Favouritism, Also of Mismanagement'. Despite the players having made a pact not to talk publicly about the goings-on which ruined their tour, there were widespread calls for the NZRL council to conduct an open investigation.

'The council a week ago discussed the holding of an inquiry and decided that it would be held in committee, which means, of course, that the press will not be admitted, and that all the public will get to know will be what the council cares to supply to the newspapers,' said the *Star*. 'That would be the position if the council is allowed to carry out its programme, but the players and at least one manager were emphatic that the inquiry should be open to the press. Mr Ponder, financial manager of the team, in his own words said: "Well, if the inquiry is not open to the press I am not going to say anything, and I am done with the game."

'If Mr Ponder adheres to this attitude, and he has the support of other members of the team who were questioned, then the public will get the whole facts of the case as given to the inquiry. But in addition to the manager, there are the six "strikers" - Messrs Singe, Mouat, Devine, Thomas (sic, it should have been Wright), Petersen and Carroll - to be considered. They were not inclined to discuss the troubles of the team beyond saying that they would demand that any inquiry should be a public one.'

Captain Bert Avery was quoted as saying: 'It has been a wonderful trip, but we were unlucky that there should be trouble shortly after the team left Auckland. However, I cannot say anything about that now as there is to be an inquiry. Our team was a great one if all had held together, and I think we did very well. Owing to the refusal of some players to take the field we were left with only five forwards to carry on for two months. Players were being shifted from all over the field and under the circumstances the record of winning 50 per cent of the matches must be considered satisfactory.'

'One of the "strikers" said that the trouble arose early when they were only two or three days out from Auckland. It was alleged that Mr Mair displayed favouritism towards certain players and this was objected to by others. "From that moment he had me set, and others who also took exception to what we considered, and still consider, was gross mismanagement. As a matter of fact, we (the strikers) consider the tour was mismanaged from the start."

'The nineteen loyal members of the side who saw the tour through were a bit disappointed that they had not been able to put together a better record. The one or two spoken to on board the ship this morning consider that the malcontents were quite wrong in the attitude they adopted, one saying, "There may have been conditions imposed which we did not entirely agree with, but most of us were prepared to put up with them and it was the same for all. If a player had a grievance it was always heard before the whole of the members."

One 'prominent' player told the *Star*: 'If the inquiry to be held is not going to be open to all then it is not going to do the game any good. Already the tour has done harm to the game, and to hush matters up is not going to help any with the public.' The newspaper also revealed that centre Ben Davidson, wing Lou Brown and forward Len Mason would

Banned For Life

be among those to attract offers from British clubs should the two years residential qualification be lifted.

Next morning, the *New Zealand Herald* opened its coverage by reporting the six suspended players had been officially notified about the inquiry, 'when they had the right to appeal to the New Zealand League council. Judging by comments of different members of the party there has been no exaggeration of the discord in the ranks on tour. The announcement that the council had decided to hold the inquiry in committee received a mixed reception, the general opinion being that in fairness to the players and the public and the game itself it is essential that the proceedings be open to the press.'

Neil Mouat likened Mair's management to the Star Chamber, the all-powerful seventeenth-century English court of law where sessions were held in secret with no rights of appeal, no juries and no witnesses, claiming 'that has been the trouble with the New Zealand League all along'. Mouat was emphatic that his case should be heard publicly and hinted he would seriously consider not appearing before the council if the investigation was private. 'I am not leaving the matter there. I am taking legal proceedings,' he said. Mouat's comments would not have endeared him to a NZRL which had twice issued warnings about his conduct even before the tour started. But his views on the need for an open inquiry were supported by the other suspended players, the two managers and the majority of the nineteen loyal players.

'Both Mr Mair, who at one stage was suspended by the English League, and Mr Ponder said that they preferred to remain silent regarding the discontent,' said the *Herald*. 'Mr Mair said it was a great tour spoiled. He had done his level best to treat all alike and pull with the men, but he could not contend with the personal bitterness shown to him as manager. He hoped the inquiry would be an open one.'

The newspaper took the opportunity to reprint in full Bert

Strike! The Tour That Died of Shame

Avery's interview with the *Athletic News* in which the highly respected captain placed all of the blame on the dissenting players and criticised English officials for aiding them. One of the sub-headings quoted Avery as saying, 'Mr Mair Not In Any Way Responsible'. In addition, the *Herald* published adjacent photographs of the New Zealand Maori rugby union team, showing a full complement of players arriving home on the *Tahiti*, and the New Zealand rugby league team, featuring only the nineteen 'loyal' players on the deck of the *Marama*.

While the NZRL council was able to consult its solicitors for weeks leading up to the hearing, the six accused forwards had only hours to brief Eric Inder, their appointed legal representative. James Carlaw and his councillors steadfastly adhered to their policy of holding the inquiry behind closed doors and only a brief statement was released to the journalists who kept a long vigil outside. On the morning of 3 March, the *Herald* topped its pancaked headlines by announcing the inevitable outcome - 'DISQUALIFIED FOR LIFE'.

'The inquiry was held in committee,' said the *Herald*. 'At the close the following statement was made to the press: "An exhaustive inquiry was held, lasting four hours. Mr Inder appeared with Mouat, Petersen, Devine, Carroll, Singe and Wright, as counsel. Henry, who remained in England, was not represented by counsel. Mr Inder cross-examined the managers of the team, Mr E H Mair and Mr G H Ponder, on the question of the above players refusing to play while on tour. The council decided that the suspension of the players by the managers be confirmed and, further, that the players be disqualified for life."

'Questioned after the meeting, Mr Carlaw said the disqualification would be effective in England, where Henry is reported to be playing for the York club. The players had been disqualified from the (entire) League code. Mr Carlaw also stated that the question of the suspension imposed on Mr Mair in England did not come before the council.

'In a statement after the announcement of the decision, Mouat said: "With regard to the matter of the striking, for which we were disqualified, we were refused permission to bring evidence of justification. The sole question was whether we struck or not". Asked whether he and the other disqualified men intended to seek legal advice with a view to contesting the decision, Mouat said, "Certainly".'

The *Auckland Star* weighed in with an editorial: 'We do not think that many persons will take serious exception to the penalty imposed upon the football strikers by the council of the New Zealand Rugby League. When men are chosen as members of a touring team, they represent not only the game they play, but the standards of athletic conduct and the sporting spirit of their country as well. Whatever the cause of all the friction that spoiled the tour of the League team in Britain, it is at least certain that seven members of the team arrogated to themselves the right to disobey orders issued by the officials placed in authority over them, and in our opinion disqualification for life is the only punishment that would adequately meet the case.

'At the same time we regret, in the interests of sport in general and rugby league in particular, that the inquiry was not open to the public. This is not a private quarrel between Mr Mair and the insubordinate players. Partly because the League game has a large following in New Zealand, and chiefly because the internal dissensions of this team have reflected injuriously upon the fair fame of the whole Dominion in the field of sport, we think that the public, who support the game, and who helped to pay the expenses of these representatives, are entitled to know the facts of the case. Moreover, a public inquiry would in all probability have justified the action of the Rugby League more completely in the public mind, and cleared the air by bringing the facts to light, including the defence of the men concerned.'

In just two days the NZRL had charged the seven players

with striking, convicted them at a secret hearing, disqualified them for life, and been given tacit approval by one of the nation's most influential newspapers. The only criticism was that the dirty linen had not been aired in public. In fact, no record of the hearing was even included in the official minute book. It was secluded elsewhere.

Meanwhile, in Christchurch, the *Star* canvassed prominent men in both rugby codes for their opinions of the severe sentences. 'I thoroughly endorse what the council has done,' said Dr Henry Thacker, who was both NZRL patron and president of the Canterbury Rugby League. 'The firm action will probably have a salutary effect on League football in New Zealand. It may prune it back, but pruning does good.'

Thacker had some belated reservations about Mair's appointment: 'The League men went away not under proper control. The council, rightly or wrongly, appointed as manager an Australian, Mr E H Mair, on the strength that he brought to New Zealand such a brilliant team as the Queenslanders. It might have been better to have appointed a New Zealander. I speak, however, with no knowledge of inside circumstances.'

An anonymous 'rugby union man of many years standing' told the *Star* that the NZRL had done the right thing, its firm action testifying to a desire to have the game conducted under proper control. The league code, he speculated, would undoubtedly gain much prestige through the disqualifications.

Among those branches of the game which would immediately suffer were the Marist clubs in Greymouth, Christchurch and Auckland - who between them would lose four international forwards from their ranks - and the fledgling league in South Canterbury, where former Christchurch Marist prop Bill Devine was the only player of any note. However, a Christchurch Marist spokesman said he did not expect the Marist clubs to stage a united protest and believed the strikers would receive little sympathy from their former team-mates.

One of the most outspoken comments came from prominent Canterbury Rugby League official Ernest McKeon, who said he held 'no brief for any men who go away to represent New Zealand and break their solemn contract because of a personal dispute with their management'. But he agreed with Thacker that it had been 'a mistake to have appointed a coach from outside New Zealand, for we have men who are capable of managing a tour'. McKeon also hoped the NZRL would not move on without 'conducting a searching inquiry into the action of the management to see if the men had an original justification for feeling in a mood to strike'. The name of Ernest McKeon was to feature prominently when the controversy flared again two months later.

There was, however, a dissenting voice from West Coast Rugby League president Jim Wingham, who was also a NZRL vice-president. Wingham complained the inquiry had not been conducted by a truly national administration, only by the Auckland-based delegates from the various district leagues. 'If the disqualified men appeal, the whole matter must come before a really full meeting of the council,' he said. 'Many of the delegates at Auckland do not cut much ice. I telegraphed to the council yesterday for information as to the result of the inquiry, but no reply is yet to hand. The council ignored me, and I consider the West Coast has been treated very unfairly.' In Mouat and Wright, the Coasters had lost the pillars of their provincial forward pack.

Unfortunately for Wingham, he received no support from Thacker, the other senior official in the South Island. Thacker offered the view that the disqualifications could only be overturned by the Supreme Court or by a committee of the House of Representatives. Regarding Wingham's complaint about not being invited to attend the inquiry, Thacker said even if both of them had been there it is doubtful whether they would have had any voting powers.

On the day after the disqualifications were announced,

Strike! The Tour That Died of Shame

press agent Joe O'Shaughnessy made a comprehensive statement to fellow journalists. He reviewed the conflicts which arose on the outward journey over laundry expenses, the compulsory wearing of collars and ties at meal times in the tropics, the refusal by some players to perform the haka on a near-deserted Canadian railway platform and the unprecedented fines imposed on three players for missing a shipboard training session. When the fined trio asked for their return passages upon arrival in England, they were joined by the other forwards in dispute with Mair.

O'Shaughnessy next mentioned the incident at Harrogate after the opening tour match which led to Mair ordering two players home. Once again, others demanded their return boat tickets and the order was withdrawn. O'Shaughnessy told of the English Rugby League's attempts to mediate, the refusal of the seven forwards to play under Mair's control, and the unanimous decision of all twenty-six players for Mair to relinquish his coaching and selection duties for a month from mid-November.

'On this point I am emphatic,' declared O'Shaughnessy, 'the position was to be reviewed at the end of a month. During the month the seven players resumed playing and trained wholeheartedly. However, at the end of the period named, without any review of the matter having been made, Mr Mair automatically resumed control. Upon Mr Mair taking this step, six players - Mouat, one of the original seven, being then in hospital - notified the managers that unless the matter was reviewed in the terms of the previous agreement they would once again refuse to play. The New Zealand sub-committee of the English League thereupon held a meeting and decided to suspend Mr Mair for a further period of one month. A later meeting of the English League council confirmed this suspension.

'Thereupon, Mr Ponder, financial and co-manager with Mr Mair, suspended the seven players who at the time Mr Ponder suspended them were perfectly happy to play again as Mr Mair had relinquished control of the team. Mr Ponder also stopped their allowances, this taking effect approximately three weeks before Christmas. Thus for eight weeks in England and six weeks on the boat coming home, the malcontents have had no allowances paid to them by the New Zealand managers. Rather than see these men return penniless on the voyage to New Zealand, the English League made them a grant of £10 each,' said O'Shaughnessy.

The press agent was clearly sympathetic towards the seven suspended players and blamed Mair for igniting the second 'strike' in mid-December by resuming his roles as selector and coach when the situation was to have been reviewed. In most circumstances, a man in his position would be considered unquestionably impartial. O'Shaughnessy, though, was not only a club-mate of Petersen (and previously Devine) at Christchurch Marist, in 1926 he was also an active player in the Marist B senior team, the club's secretary and its delegate to the Canterbury Rugby League. His comments might have been clouded by club loyalty and personal friendships.

Ernest Mair and George Ponder attended a boisterous meeting of the NZRL council on the night of 3 March. Frank Henry's situation was an early item on the agenda. The English Rugby League advised Henry was remaining in England, where he was still a registered member of the York club. It was decided to reply to the ERL that as it had accepted Henry as a member of the New Zealand touring team he was susceptible to the discipline of the team's managers and the NZRL, so the disqualification meted out to him should be recognised.

When Ponder stood, apparently to read his voluminous tour report, he surprised by asking to be excused from the meeting because of a private engagement. Contrary to what he had told the media two days earlier, Ponder then demanded his report be taken in committee. He even threatened to tear it up if that did not happen. A warm

Strike! The Tour That Died of Shame

discussion developed before a majority of nine votes to two confirmed the matter would not be handled in open meeting. Wellington delegate Tom Tuohy was so angered that he promptly stormed out of the room. Tuohy had argued that the public, which kept the game going, should be told the facts.

Ponder was granted leave of absence for one hour to keep his appointment. Mair began reading the report, Ponder taking over when he returned to the meeting about 9.50pm and continuing through to 10.30pm. The managers were thanked and the report was officially received. But it was held over for discussion until a special meeting on 8 March. That night both Auckland newspapers waited in vain for a statement. NZRL secretary Owie Carlaw recorded in the minutes that, after a three-hour debate, a four-man committee was elected to go through the managers' report and make any necessary abridgements before it was circulated.

There was also another reminder from the shipping agents that the sum of £53 10s 5d was owed for expenses incurred by players when travelling to Auckland for embarkation to England the previous August. The account was held over yet again, and would continue to be deferred until an exasperated English Rugby League - told by the agents the NZRL had finally refused to pay - decided to avoid further friction and settled the account. But that was not until December.

The Wellington *Evening Post*, in a report sent from Christchurch, quoted Lou Petersen saying 'nobody has heard our side of the story yet. Reporters everywhere we have been have been chasing us for it, but it has not come out yet. When it does it will create a big surprise, and I think it will be the means of those life disqualifications being removed.' Petersen had just arrived in his home town and was clearly of the opinion that the case was far from finished.

'Mouat and Wright are up in Auckland now,' he said, 'making arrangements for a further inquiry. That inquiry they held was no good. I think there will be another all right. We were disqualified without being heard. We had no chance to defend ourselves. It was an inquiry into the so-called strike. What we want is an inquiry into the management of the whole tour. Anyway, there was no strike; not one man in that team refused to play. We have been disqualified for striking, and we didn't strike at all; that's the position.

'When we arrived back in New Zealand the people said that it was only right that we should be disqualified. That was because they had not heard our side of the story. We were bound by a written agreement to give nothing to reporters anywhere on the tour; we didn't either - but Mr Mair and Mr Ponder were giving the other side of the story at every opportunity,' said Petersen.

'Nothing of our case has been published. We don't want it published yet; it will come out at the inquiry. It is such a good case that when it does come out the public will change their views. With regard to that other inquiry, it was hopelessly unfair. If a man commits murder or theft he gets a chance to defend himself, but we didn't. We can defend the charge against us with a substantial case. Those disqualifications will be removed.'

Joe O'Shaughnessy described the inquiry as 'a farce' in an interview with the *Star* in Christchurch. 'The alleged strikers in the New Zealand rugby league team did not have a chance to call witnesses in their defence,' he said. 'The team's managers, Messrs E H Mair and G H Ponder, were also represented by a solicitor and were allowed to call witnesses on their behalf. The inquiry was, in my opinion, a farce. The basis of the whole dispute seems to be whether the seven players struck or did not strike. This point will be settled at a later date.'

Comments made by prominent Canterbury Rugby

Strike! The Tour That Died of Shame

League officials in support of the life disqualifications had been made before the southern members of the side arrived back in Christchurch, said O'Shaughnessy. The officials had not heard from the players. As a former city mayor and Member of Parliament, Dr Thacker should have had sufficient knowledge of inquiries 'to know that some were not really inquiries at all. When only one side of a case was known, a wise man would never pass judgement.'

Others were being welcomed home as heroes. Veteran back Jim Sanders was the guest of honour at a function attended by more than 100 fellow workers from the Addington railways workshops and residents of Riccarton, the Christchurch suburb where he lived. Also present was Harry Thomas, the only Otago representative in the team, who was travelling on to Dunedin the next morning. The Mayor of Riccarton, Bert Kyle MP, said it was gratifying to know Sanders and Thomas had been 'loyal to their team, their captain and their country'. Canterbury Rugby League chairman Winter Cole made similar comments.

In England, the *Daily Dispatch* raised the dilemma of Frank Henry, who had signed again for York on 14 January, 1927, giving his address as the West Park Hotel in Harrogate. The York club argued Henry had never officially qualified to play in or for New Zealand under the two-year rule, so was still a legitimate club member. The ERL originally decreed that his suspension, imposed by Ponder and ratified by the ERL, would end when the tour finished.

'Henry has remained in England and is now playing for York, for which club he was a registered player before going to New Zealand,' claimed the *Dispatch* after the life disqualifications were announced. 'The point therefore naturally arises whether the New Zealand suspension will prevent Henry from playing football in England. On the face of things it will, though the English council - a good many of whom had a lot of sympathy for the strikers - may consider Henry's case on its merits, more particularly as he has not had the chance of defending the charges against him before the body which has disqualified him for life.

'On the other hand, if his suspension is not upheld here it will appear, at any rate in New Zealand, as tantamount to supporting the "strikers" against the managers and New Zealand council. The (English) Rugby League have a standing order that a person suspended by a governing body must make personal application to the council before taking part in rugby league football. In this case the New Zealand council is an affiliate as well as a governing body, so their decision must be given very serious consideration.'

(But York club records disclose that Henry did not play again until the 1929-30 season, and then only four times. In the space of eight days in September 1929 he appeared in the York team beaten at Huddersfield, the decisive loss to the touring Kangaroos and a home win over Bradford. His final game was a narrow home defeat by Dewsbury two months later).

The NZRL council had agonised long and hard over the managers' report in March 1927. It initially agreed to make it available for perusal by delegates at the annual meeting, and that copies be given to all district leagues and to the press, the latter with a proviso it be published in full or not at all. However, a cautious James Carlaw then successfully moved the report first be shown to the NZRL solicitors 'in respect to any contentious or libellous content'.

There was also a vote of appreciation to Ernest Mair, in recognition of his services to the game in New Zealand, wishing him a pleasant holiday and an early return from Australia.

One week later, NZRL council member Cyril Snedden, himself a lawyer, advised that the league's solicitor, Harry Rogerson, found 'the managers' report contained matter which could be libellous' and 'the publication thereof would give grounds for action against the council'. Rogerson further believed that no newspaper would take the risk of

Strike! The Tour That Died of Shame

publishing the report. After an in-committee discussion, the 17 March motion authorising publication of the report was rescinded. It was instead decided to make no mention of the managers' comments in the NZRL annual report. Those decisions were then announced to the waiting newspapermen and the sections of the report by Ponder and Mair about the 'troubles' were buried forever.

Mair had written his newspaper tour review before leaving England. Published it mid-March, it generally followed the theme that, 'had the team been given a fair crack of the whip, had the seven forwards thought more of their comrades, their country, their game, their hosts etc., we would have had more of the ball (being a knitted pack) and brought back thousands of pounds to further help the game in New Zealand'.

But Mair did make one unsubstantiated accusation: 'From the time of leaving Auckland, right through the piece, my first duty to my council compelled my silence. Despite the misunderstandings this attitude has probably created, of the losses of my personal property on two occasions, of physical attack on myself etc., my only regret is that I was denied the opportunity of making good for a country that has so signally honoured me.' That was the only reference by Mair claiming to have been the victim of theft or assault.

On 31 March the NZRL council received letters from Phonse Carroll, Arthur Singe and Lou Petersen appealing against their life disqualifications. They asked that the appeals be heard before the provincial delegates at the annual meeting in early April. It was decided to tell the appellants that 'there is no appeal against a decision of the council as per clause thirty-two of the constitution of the NZRL'. It is known that Jack Wright, and probably also Neil Mouat and Bill Devine, wrote to the council and received a similarly negative answer. Tom Tuohy, the Wellington delegate who walked out on 3 March, had not attended any subsequent meetings and his seat was declared vacant.

Banned For Life

On 1 April the *New Zealand Herald* reported the NZRL had informed the Auckland Rugby League of the life disqualifications and requested it ban the disqualified players from attending matches at Carlaw Park. Chairman Bill Hammill said because the national council had no jurisdiction over any grounds it was compelled to seek the assistance of its provincial affiliates to enforce the terms of the suspensions. Debate on the legality of barring players from other than the privately-owned Carlaw Park, and the failure of the NZRL to furnish a managers' report, occupied much time before it was decided the sole Auckland-based player (Arthur Singe) would be 'warned off Carlaw Park during the pleasure of the Auckland executive'.

The *Auckland Star* was not satisfied with the NZRL decision to shelve the managers' report. Under the heading, 'Why This Silence?' a *Star* editorial asked when the public was to be taken into its confidence regarding the punishments. 'It is a matter of grave public interest and by its failure to realise this aspect of the case the League has done a great deal to injure the reputation and the prospects of the game which it controls,' it said. 'The public which supports the game here has a right to demand that it shall be acquainted with all the facts of the case, and to know that the League management is not only willing and able to dispense even-handed justice, but to protect all its loyal players, and to maintain its reputation and dignity as a powerful and influential athletic body'.

That plea was ignored, and the NZRL kept a tight rein on tour comment at its annual meeting in Auckland on 7 April. Although the English Rugby League had financed the actual tour, there were items of expenditure dealing with the pre-tour preparations listed on the balance sheet as, 'trial games in south £354 13s 4d and English tour expenses £1876 18s 2d'. It was explained the latter was the actual cost to the NZRL of sending the team to England.

'The English tour can be said to have cost us in the

Strike! The Tour That Died of Shame

vicinity of £2000,' said the financial report. 'This is largely accounted for by the fact that whereas the English League allowed £1 per man when they were travelling and £2 per week whilst on tour, your council augmented the English allowance so that each player received as out of pocket expenses the sum of £3 per week for single men and £4 10s per week for married men for the whole time they were away from New Zealand. During the year the council obtained a loan of £850 from the Otago Rugby League, without which the players and their dependents would not have received their full allowance.' The NZRL assets at season's end amounted to £352 18s 6d.

James Carlaw had already made it known at the Auckland Rugby League annual meeting the previous night that he was standing down as NZRL president, saying, 'I am so disappointed that I do not like to touch on the matter at all. I would like, however, to thank the players who remained loyal. I feel sure they will have their reward'.

The *New Zealand Herald* summarised Carlaw's comments to the NZRL annual meeting: 'Last year was the most disastrous in his experience. After years of anticipation the New Zealand council had accepted an invitation to tour England. Unfortunately, internal troubles developed, and, instead of an expected profit of £7000 being made, a serious loss has to be faced. However, he had no fear for the future of the game.' Carlaw, his dream shattered, then retired from office and was succeeded by Cyril Snedden.

In late April, almost two months after the team's return, the NZRL released to the media a comprehensive 'portion' of the report written by managers George Ponder and Ernest Mair. But it dealt only with the financial losses and match results, and not the 'troubles'. It was not the 'portion' that the newspapers were keen to sight.

Ponder listed the contributing factors towards the financial deficit as: (1) the general coal strike in England; (2) the adverse press criticism at the beginning of the tour; (3)

the prices charged for the various games; and (4) the internal trouble in the team.

Mair gave the following reasons for the modest playing record: (1) the lack of a hooker; (2) the failure of the forwards to pack properly and put their weight in the scrum; (3) the failure of the forwards to adapt themselves to English conditions, breaking too quickly and being too eager to function as backs; (4) the failure of the backs to adapt themselves to English conditions, particularly in defence; (5) bad goal-kicking; (6) the failure to secure the ball from scrums; and (7) the lack of keen team spirit due to internal trouble in the side.

The partial report then expanded on all of those items, apart from the 'internal trouble' which was the last-mentioned in each section. Having fed these titbits to the newspapers, the NZRL believed nothing more would be heard of the tour, at least in the public domain. It was wrong.

14

THE AFTERMATH

Some of the other provincial leagues were not as compliant as Auckland and Canterbury in accepting the seven life disqualifications and agreeing to ban the players from their grounds. Wellington decided to wait until a managers' tour report was received from the NZRL before warning off Phonse Carroll. West Coast reflected the anger of its president, Jim Wingham, and fired in a strong protest that the sentences on Neil Mouat and Jack Wright had been imposed without a full public inquiry. But, as with the suspended players' individual appeals, the protest was rejected.

That feelings were still running high among the returning players was illustrated by the usually mild-mannered Wally Desmond's comments to delegates at the Wellington annual meeting, held in early April. Desmond had been accorded a hearty welcome home and was praised for 'upholding the honour of the League on and off the field'. He replied that he was looking forward to passing on the experience he had gained on the tour, then moved on to more contentious matters.

The Aftermath

'Personally I had a very enjoyable time,' he said, 'and I have no complaint to make of any kind either with the managers or players. So far as the management was concerned, it was a bit slack in parts. The only thing I have to say against the strike is that the players, in my opinion, got what they deserved, absolutely, because they didn't play the game over there in any shape or form.'

'The tour was very hard because of the strike,' the *Dominion* newspaper quoted Desmond as saying. 'If there had been no strike and everything had gone smoothly the New Zealand council would have made £8000, and the team would have won 80 per cent of the games. The team enjoyed themselves and there was no ill-feeling among the nineteen players. They had to contend with the disloyal players, who made it hard as far as training and playing the game was concerned.'

When the NZRL circulated the portions of the managers' report dealing with finances and playing performances to its affiliates, it enclosed the following message: 'We regret that, acting on the advice of our honorary solicitor, we are unable to make public the full details of information in our hands.'

Meanwhile, the enterprising Auckland Rugby League - basking in the glow of having enjoyed a financially lucrative 1926 season - had beaten its parent body to the punch by arranging an early-season fixture between its representatives and the Auckland members of the New Zealand team at Carlaw Park. The NZRL discussed the possibility of requesting a share of the gate receipts before relenting and approving the match.

The New Zealand XIII included Charles Gregory at fullback, Lou Brown, Ben Davidson and Frank Delgrosso in the three-quarters, Jack Kirwan and Hector Cole in the five-eighths and Stan Webb at halfback. The forwards were Joe Menzies, Jim Parkes, Ernie Herring, Craddock Dufty, George Gardiner and Bert Avery, the only time that transplanted backs Parkes, Dufty and Gardiner all played together in the same pack. The sole Aucklander missing from the nineteen loyal players was Hec Brisbane, who was still recovering from the injury which kept him out of the third Test at Leeds. Menzies, from South Auckland, was the single non-Aucklander. Those not called up were Desmond (Wellington), Len Mason, Wilson Hall and Jim Sanders (Canterbury) and Harry Thomas (Otago).

Captained by Maurice Wetherill, the man who was dearly missed by the touring All Blacks, Auckland won 24-21, scoring the winning try in the last minute to delight the 14,000 fans. The individual star, however, was Brown, who displayed the speed which had thrilled the British crowds and attracted the Wigan talent scouts as he raced away for three tries. Menzies and Parkes also scored tries for New Zealand and Gardiner (two) and Dufty kicked goals. The rising Auckland stars had the better of their rusty New Zealand rivals at crucial moments.

'The form of the returned New Zealand players was watched with great interest, and although defeated - chiefly through failure to win the ball from the scrum - the play of several of them has generally improved,' reported the *New Zealand Herald*. 'From almost any position on the field the New Zealand team attacked by quick passing and splendid backing up of the player in possession, thereby retaining the ball. It was only because of weak handling by the New Zealand inside backs that the movements did not achieve full success.'

While the New Zealand scrum formation was praised for its tight packing, the forwards were haunted by hooking problems to the very end. Auckland was well served by hooker Neville St George and Devonport prop Jim O'Brien, two of those left behind when the All Blacks had sailed for England the previous year. The backs stationed around Wetherill - Tim Peckham, Stan Prentice and Claude List - would all make their New Zealand debuts in the Test series against the 1928 British Lions.

The Aftermath

That game should have lifted the curtain on a season of consolidation as the NZRL council, now chaired by Cyril Snedden, put the horrors of 1926-27 behind it. But the whole saga was to be dredged up again in May; and that other distasteful subject, the attempt by Wigan and other ambitious and cashed-up British clubs to abolish the two-year qualification period for Australasian players, was to bite severely in June.

Ernest McKeon was an outspoken Canterbury Rugby League official at a time when that body was embroiled in its own internal strife over the financing of its Monica Park ground. He sprang to national prominence at the 1927 NZRL annual meeting by presenting a remit calling for the national headquarters to be moved to the South Island. McKeon argued that Auckland was strong because the NZRL was based there, and moving the governing body would have a similarly beneficial effect on growing the game in the south. The remit was beaten by eight votes to five. One who voted against was George Rhodes, the Aucklander who represented Canterbury on the NZRL council. Rhodes told an angry McKeon he was acting in the best interests of the game.

But McKeon brought more than a disappointing result at the ballot box home from Auckland. He waited a few weeks before telling the *Star* newspaper in Christchurch that while at the national conference he had cross-examined All Blacks manager George Ponder, claiming, as the *Star* headlined, that the 'League Players Did Not Refuse To Take Field'. The sub-headings read, 'Management "Often Inefficient," Declares Canterbury Official', and the third line was, 'Reveals Inner History Of Tour, And Suggests Commission Of Inquiry Be Set-up'.

'That the seven disqualified rugby league players had not refused to take the field when called upon, that the English League council had suspended Mr E H Mair twice for alleged mismanagement of the tour, and that a full inquiry into the disqualifications was bound to come, were statements made yesterday by Mr E L McKeon, the Canterbury representative who recently returned from the annual conference of the New Zealand Rugby League in Auckland,' said the *Star*.

'Mr McKeon said that he had obtained his information from a cross-examination of one of the joint managers, Mr G H Ponder, at the conference. In answer to a question whether he thought he was taking a Sunday School class to a picnic instead of a team of virile footballers on a tour, Mr Ponder had said that he did not see any difference between the two. McKeon was then quoted as saying: 'There were no specific charges against any of the seven players in the joint managers' report, which I read, and therefore I don't see that the New Zealand council had any cause to hold an inquiry at all. Mr Ponder admitted that in one case the men did not strike, but that he locked them out and forthwith issued the suspensions.'

McKeon said he would reveal nothing that was done in committee but felt, having read the managers' report, that he was justified in revealing certain aspects. Neither the players nor the general public was satisfied with the current situation. McKeon advocated the establishment of an independent commission to examine the players, managers and the English Rugby League, and to investigate other sources of information, with the NZRL and the accused players first agreeing to accept its decisions.

In answer to a question, McKeon said the first report of the managers had evidently been amended. There were, in the report, absolutely no charges whatever against any of the disqualified players of having refused to play when called upon. On the contrary, there was conclusive evidence to prove that some of the disqualified men were admitted to be in training and perfectly fit, yet the managers saw fit repeatedly to omit these players from matches. This had undoubtedly led to dissatisfaction.

'Another reason, continued Mr McKeon, was the

The Aftermath

apparent inefficiency of the management. These two factors had combined to create so much dissatisfaction on the tour that it culminated in a meeting of players, managers and the English Rugby League council. As a result of this meeting, one of the managers was suspended for a month because, according to the English council, he had mismanaged the tour. The managers' report to the New Zealand council, however, had said that "Mr Mair had voluntarily made a personal sacrifice in standing down for the good of the game".' McKeon then told the *Star* the ERL had made it a condition that the situation would be reviewed at the end of that month and all parties agreed.

'Mr Ponder admitted, said Mr McKeon, that Mr Mair handed over control of the team to him, but that two days before the month had expired he (Mr Mair) posted a notice on the board at the team's headquarters at Harrogate that he had again taken up the management. This was on a Thursday morning, two days before the big match against Wigan. One of the now disqualified players, on coming down the stairs and seeing the notice, drew Mr Ponder's attention to the fact that Mr Mair's action was a breach of the agreement. A little later the seven players told Mr Ponder that the agreement had been broken. However, not wishing to let the team down, they said they would play against Wigan on the Saturday, but would not take the field again until the position had been reviewed in accordance with the agreement. Mr Ponder then issued the seven suspensions which, because he was acting on behalf of the New Zealand League, the English council had to endorse in the meantime. Immediately after the Wigan match, and prior to the next game taking place, the English council again met and further suspended Mr Mair for another month. No mention whatever to this effect is made in the joint managers' report. I feel certain that had these facts been known to the New Zealand council at the time of the inquiry, a different result would have been arrived at.'

Strike! The Tour That Died of Shame

McKeon claimed that no specific charges were laid against any of the disqualified players in the second managers' report. He said only one name was mentioned throughout the whole report, for a trivial offence. That player was not called before the council and was not one of the suspended men. Further questioned, McKeon admitted he had not only strongly opposed the appointment of Mair for the tour but had warned the council that in appointing him they might be courting disaster. 'As Mr Mair did not wait in Auckland for the conference, but returned to Australia, I had no opportunity of questioning him,' said McKeon. 'However, from the cross-examination of Mr Ponder I am satisfied that he at least was not the right type for a manager. Footballers are good fellows at heart but are hard to manage if not taken in a human way.

'Further cross-examination revealed the character which Mr Ponder ascribed to Mr Mair. One day at Harrogate Mr Mair, coming out of the hotel with his bag and seeing one of the now disqualified players who, by the way, is about fifteen stone and well over six feet, towering above him, ordered him, "Carry my bag to the station". One can well imagine the reply of this burly, virile New Zealander who, had he been approached in a spirit of good fellowship, would probably have been willing to have carried to the station both the manager and the bag. While I am prepared to admit that there might have been breaches on the part of the players generally - and not exclusively the disqualified ones - that required some form of discipline, I consider that in respect to the so-called charges against the disqualified men, the greater censure should have been meted out to the management. It has all been a case of want of tact.'

McKeon said Ponder had admitted it was Mair, and not the head steward, who had issued the order for players to wear collars and ties for meals on board the *Aorangi* because Mair felt he could do what he wanted with the team. It was only a small point, but one of a number which eventually led

The Aftermath

to disaster. Recalling he had made a statement when the team returned to New Zealand that any touring footballer who refused to play should have no sympathy, McKeon said he still emphatically held to that opinion.

'I have found out since, however, the disqualified players did not strike but that, according to Mr Ponder, Mr Mair created what could be termed a breach of the agreement. The disqualified players should not have been punished for striking when they did not do so. As a matter of fact, Mr Ponder admitted in cross-examination that the men did not strike, at least on that occasion, but that he locked them out and forthwith issued the seven suspensions. The meagre information at my disposal several months ago led me to believe that the players were in the wrong. The public still think so, and I therefore feel justified in throwing more light on the matter. The whole miserable business must inevitably affect the good name of the code, and the sooner the council act upon my suggestion of a commission, or something equally acceptable, the better it will be for all concerned,' concluded McKeon.

Ponder felt compelled to defend himself against McKeon's allegations, so much so that he had three of the players, Charles Gregory, Lou Brown and Jim Parkes, with him when he made his reply. Gregory, an Auckland Marist club-mate of the suspended Arthur Singe, had become something of a spokesman for the nineteen 'loyal' players, for it was he who had put their case to English Rugby League officials in the dressing room at Headingley.

'I am disappointed and surprised with Mr McKeon breaking faith with the New Zealand council,' Ponder told the *Star*'s Auckland correspondent. 'As all the inquiries were held in committee it is therefore not surprising that his remarks are inaccurate and in fact could almost be termed slanderous. I have attempted at all times to keep faith with the wish of the majority of the New Zealand council. I feel that I now have my back to the wall and must make a statement.'

Strike! The Tour That Died of Shame

The 'Sunday School' charge was described by Ponder as 'ludicrous in the extreme. For one thing, the question was never asked. Anyhow, be they Sunday School children or virile footballers, the least that could be expected of them was to play the game in the best interests of New Zealand and the good name of rugby league footballers. As for the matter of carrying the bags, this was absolutely incorrect, for taxis were hired, and there was only one occasion there was not a taxi, and that was when the car had broken down. For Mr McKeon to say there were no specific charges in the managers' report is nonsense. He must have been asleep, for they were spoken of in a general manner throughout. It is interesting to note that Mr McKeon very shrewdly started his attacks as regards the position in the middle of the strike, for be it known that a strike had taken place twice previously.'

Ponder then assumed the role of interviewer, asking Gregory whether the seven disqualified men went on strike at any time while on tour. 'Yes, certainly,' replied the fullback. 'They went on strike three times. The first was shortly after arriving in England when three or four of the players got into a dispute with Mr Mair and refused to play. The English League then arbitrated and after a while the thing was washed out and the men took the field again. A week or two later the same trouble cropped up again, and they refused to play. Once more the English League stepped in, and this time Mr Mair voluntarily stood down for one month, he himself stating that at the end of that time he would come in again. He was accepted, but as soon as he did actually come in and take control the troublesome players refused point blank to play. Matters now looked bad, and the next step on the part of the managers was to put up a notice to the effect that any player in the team in future refusing to play would have his out-of-pocket expenses stopped. Upon this the mentioned players in a body refused to play. The notice was ripped and torn around as soon as it was put up.'

The Aftermath

The question-and-answer series then went:

'Mr Ponder: To the best of your knowledge, did I ever lock out these players?

'Mr Gregory: No, not as far as I know.

'Mr Ponder: In your opinion, did I at any time do anything to hinder the success of the tour in the interests of the game itself and New Zealand?

'Mr Gregory: Certainly not.

'Mr Ponder: Were you ever ordered to carry bags to the station?

'Mr Gregory: No.

'Mr Ponder: Did you consider it reasonable that the players should go to bed at night at eleven o'clock?

'Mr Gregory: Yes, it was absolutely essential, especially when there was a game to be played on the following day. After all, we were in training.'

The interview then reverted to being one-on-one with Ponder, who explained why he not only changed his mind about requesting a public inquiry but threatened to destroy his report rather than read it in open meeting. During the inquiry which resulted in the seven players being disqualified for life, their counsel, Eric Inder, had threatened Ponder with court proceedings in connection with the managers' report. At the following night's NZRL council meeting he took Inder's remarks into consideration and refused to read the report in open meeting, as had been demanded by some members.

'The first proof that there were members antagonistic to the managers was borne out by one member leaving the room,' said Ponder. 'The New Zealand council then went into camera again. After the reading of the managers' report the meeting was adjourned for four days. At the subsequent meeting the managers were cross-examined for nearly four hours on their conducting of the tour. At the conclusion of the examination the council passed a resolution of appreciation and confidence in the managers. They also set up a committee to edit the managers' report for publication in the local papers.'

Ponder revealed that he had been in Wellington and missed the meeting when the NZRL's solicitors advised against publishing the report. Similarly, discussion of the report at the NZRL annual meeting was also held in camera, though Ponder had no say in the matter. South Auckland was then represented by a direct delegate and Ponder, its resident delegate, had relinquished his speaking and voting rights to him.

'I therefore could not protest against the action of the New Zealand council in refraining from publishing the report as promised; neither did I have a voice in connection with the resolution sending the council into camera. In conclusion, as I am honour bound to respect the rulings of the majority of the New Zealand council while a member of that body, my only method of stating the above position to the public - and this is necessary in justice to myself - was to resign my position as the South Auckland delegate and to take steps to publicly reply to allegations that were made against me.'

McKeon was also criticised by his own provincial colleagues. Sid Richardson, the Canterbury Rugby League secretary, told journalists he was "astonished' a member of his executive should so far forget himself as to reopen in the press a matter which both the New Zealand council and Canterbury saw fit to take in committee. Richardson said Canterbury was in accord with the council's action in disqualifying the seven players. It did not want the matter reopened, as practically all the members, with the apparent exception of McKeon, were satisfied the players received no more than their just deserts.

Neil Mouat, Phonse Carroll, Bill Devine, Lou Petersen, Arthur Singe and Jack Wright never set foot on a rugby league field again. In England, Frank Henry made a brief reappearance for the York club early in the 1929-30 season.

The Aftermath

He could not have done that without the blessing of the English Rugby League, which appears to have initially supported the NZRL action before lifting the disqualification after thirty months. The West Coast Rugby League did not concede easily. It sought to have Mouat, in particular, reinstated on several occasions over the next decade, without success.

Little more than a week after Ponder's response to McKeon's criticisms it was revealed by the *Auckland Star* that international wing Lou Brown had requested a clearance from his City club to sign for Wigan. That was the tip of the iceberg. It soon emerged that Wigan was also on the trail of Brown's club-mate and centre Ben Davidson and Hornby forward Len Mason. Brown and Davidson had been the most incisive outside backs during the All Blacks tour of Britain and Mason emerged as a strong man in a severely depleted forward pack. All this was happening while the two-year residential qualification clause was still in place. City passed the applications from Brown and Davidson on to higher authorities. On consecutive nights, the Auckland and New Zealand Leagues refused to grant clearances.

No-one could blame the players for being attracted by offers of as much as £800 for a season with one of the code's most famous clubs. After all, they had just slogged their way through a thirty-four match campaign while being paid a comparative pittance. Brown was especially aware what they were in for, having spent a season with Wigan as an amateur. All that was holding them back was the two-year stand-down and both the Australian and New Zealand Leagues were fighting tooth and nail to have it retained to protect their playing resources. But there was no international federation to legislate such matters in those days. England was very much the boss.

On 11 June, the news broke that England had cancelled its transfer agreement with Australia and New Zealand. Within hours Brown received a cable from Wigan: 'Ban removed. Am booking passages for Davidson and self, first available boat. Inform Davidson.' On the same day the obviously much in demand Davidson also received a cable from the Hull club: 'Two years ban removed. Do you accept my terms? - Dannatt, Hull.' But Hull was too late, for Davidson had already signed with Wigan. On 15 June, Brown received another cable: "Have booked passages for Davidson and self by *Corinthic*, leaving Wellington June 29. Inform Mason - Taylor, Wigan.' Only then was it publicly known that Len Mason would be part of a New Zealand trio at Central Park.

Rebuffed when the New Zealand managers effectively had what amounted to a casting vote during the tour, Wigan had this time pushed through a twenty-to-nine majority decision among the British professional clubs. Aware it had Brown, Davidson and Mason in the bag if it succeeded, Wigan was not to be denied and convinced the majority of its rivals the British game needed rejuvenating with an influx of overseas players. Reaction was mixed in New Zealand on the day the news broke.

'It might even mean the breakaway of Australia and New Zealand from the English Rugby League,' speculated one newspaper. 'Supporters of the agreement between the three parties would see in it the death-blow to their hopes to keep the game up to international standard in the Dominion. Naturally, there is considerable satisfaction among those who have supported the granting of the transfers.' It quoted a well-known supporter saying, 'If the New Zealand council had let these two (Brown and Davidson) go, this ban would not have been remitted. It shows how powerful these English clubs are. Both these players would sooner have gone with the consent of the New Zealand council.'

Auckland Rugby League officials made it known they were still opposed to granting transfers as a matter of principle, but felt it was now only fitting the services Brown and Davidson had rendered to the game in Auckland should

The Aftermath

be recognised by a suitable presentation. Both the Australian and New Zealand Leagues asked England to delay the lifting of the ban until a conference was held with the managers of the 1928 Lions touring team. The NZRL also sent a message direct to England expressing its disapproval. President Cyril Snedden told the media that consideration would be given to cancelling the Lions tour and seceding from the English administration. All of that sabre-rattling had no effect and the three Wigan-bound players departed on schedule. In all, five 1926-27 All Blacks signed for British clubs.

Mercurial wing Lou Brown scored 106 tries in 130 appearances for Wigan. The most famous of those tries assisted Wigan to beat Dewsbury in the 1929 Challenge Cup final, the first to be held at London's Wembley Stadium. From 1930 to 1932 he scored thirty-three tries in forty-three games for Halifax. After a short term with York, Brown returned to New Zealand and played Test football against the 1935 Kangaroos and 1936 Lions. For the next two years he was with the Bordeaux club in France, before finishing his professional career at Bramley from 1939 to 1943. Brown died only four years later, after a long illness.

Centre Ben Davidson played sixty-seven matches for Wigan from 1927 until 1930, scoring thirty-one tries. Despite that satisfactory strike-rate, he never consistently reproduced the form displayed for the All Blacks and ended his contract by mutual agreement. Davidson returned to Auckland but was not finished with big-time football. In 1932 he scored a try for Auckland in its 19-14 loss to the Lions, and was recalled for the second Test match at Christchurch.

Marathon man Len Mason was a team-mate of Brown in that first Wembley Cup final, a highlight of an amazing professional career which stretched to 475 club appearances for Wigan (from 1927 to 1935, 365 games), Keighley (1936-37, thirty-six games), Bramley (1937-39, sixty-four games) and Keighley again (1939-40, ten games), before retiring when close to his thirty-seventh birthday. Mason also represented

Strike! The Tour That Died of Shame

Other Nationalities on four occasions and played twice for a Dominion XIII against France. He returned to New Zealand after the Second World War and settled back in his native Waikato district.

Scrum-half Wilson Hall, who only two days before the two-year qualification was lifted had told the *Star* in Christchurch that he was unemployed and might need to return to the North Island to find work, joined Hull, the club which had unsuccessfully pursued Davidson. Hall played forty-four times for the club before moving on to find greater fame at Castleford (1929-1934), where he scored twenty-four tries in 175 appearances. He had one game for Dewsbury in 1934, returning to Castleford in retirement and living out his life in England.

Versatile back Wally Desmond met his future wife, Norah, during the All Blacks tour and was eager to return to England. The removal of the ban was a godsend for him. Desmond signed for Leeds in October 1927. Over the next two years he made forty-two appearances for the Headingley-based club and crossed for ten tries. Like Hall, Desmond made England his home, serving as a referee and touch judge, working at a school for the blind and being a lifelong rugby league and Yorkshire cricket fan until his death at the age of fifty-three.

Of the other 'loyal' players, captain Bert Avery, Ernie Herring and Jim Sanders - who could all trace their international careers back to 1919 - and rugby union recruit Jack Kirwan had all retired from the representative scene before the next New Zealand team was selected to play the 1928 Lions. Recognised as the greatest player of his era and inducted into the NZRL Legends of League in 1995, Avery served as an Auckland and New Zealand selector. Sanders coached and selected Canterbury and South Island sides and Kirwan was secretary of the Auckland Marist club from 1932 to 1950.

George Gardiner went on to a colourful career as a

The Aftermath

professional wrestler in Australia under the ring name of George Tiki. He was killed while serving with the Australian army in the Middle East during the Second World War. Hector Cole, Joe Menzies, Jim Parkes, Stan Webb and Harry Thomas did not play for New Zealand again, though opportunities were limited. The only international fixtures during the next eight seasons were home Test series against the 1928 and 1932 Lions and a non-Test tour to Australia in 1930.

Hec Brisbane carried on in fine style, appearing in the second and third Tests in 1928, touring Australia two years later and bowing out after playing in all of the three 1932 Tests. Frank Delgrosso played in two 1928 Tests, represented Auckland until 1930 and wore Ponsonby's colours through to 1934. Craddock Dufty's tenure in the forwards was to be short-lived. Dufty was fullback in all three 1928 Tests and also toured Australia in 1930, when the New Zealand captain was fellow fullback, long-time rival and occasional team-mate Charles Gregory.

Three years after the All Blacks tour, press agent Joe O'Shaughnessy was suspended for two years by the Canterbury Rugby League after chairing a meeting of allegedly rebellious players during the ongoing dispute between the CRL executive and the Monica Park trustees. O'Shaughnessy claimed the players were just acting as a buffer between the warring parties and were not disloyal. Christchurch Marist, the club which evolved out of the Payne Trophy affair in 1924, folded after the 1930 season. O'Shaughnessy was Greymouth reporter for *The Press* newspaper when he enlisted for war service in 1939. After being stationed in the Pacific, the Middle East and North Africa, Lance-Sergeant O'Shaughnessy accompanied his infantry battalion to Italy. He was killed at Cassino on 3 April, 1944, aged forty.

Neil Mouat, the vice-captain accused by Ernest Mair as being the 'strike' leader, was killed in a work accident near Westport in May 1967. The *Westport News* obituary said he

Strike! The Tour That Died of Shame

had been engaged in farming, coal mining and timber milling. In addition, Mouat owned a contracting business which had been responsible for road construction and river protection work on the West Coast. Harness racing was his major sporting interest in later life. The only obituary reference to the 1926-27 tour said the team 'did not prove to be a happy or successful party'. Mouat was described as 'a splendid type, he would have graced any forward pack, league or union, in the country, right up to the present time'. Tributes included a description of him being 'a colourful and strong character in his own right' and another from a business rival who 'fought him on many issues in industry and sport, but we always finished up good friends, that being his nature'. Local legend has it that he worked hard and played hard.

Ernest Mair was welcomed home by the Valley Football Club in March 1927, and signified his intention to stay in Toowoomba. A few days later the Toowoomba Rugby League made him a selector for the district team. When Duncan Thompson announced he could only coach the team on a part-time basis, delegates decided the captain would be responsible for the coaching when Thompson was absent. Mair apparently had no further appetite for coaching. In April, Mair's role within the Toowoomba executive was questioned by a delegate. The chairman replied that according to the constitution Mair held no official position. But in 1925 Mair had guaranteed a bank overdraft on a grandstand and was empowered to vote on questions of finance. Mair was elected a life member of the Toowoomba Rugby League in November 1927, and the following February he guaranteed the league up to £1000 for improvements to a new ground at Queens Park.

There was to be another meeting between Mair and Ted Osborne, whose term as chairman of the English Rugby League had been turned into a nightmare by the 1926-27 All Blacks. It occurred midway through the 1928 season when

The Aftermath

Osborne again managed an England team to Australasia. Mair presented Osborne with a silver kangaroo at the post-match function after the Lions had beaten Toowoomba 17-12. By then Mair was also president of the Queensland Amateur Swimming Association, and in that capacity he welcomed home competitors from the 1928 Olympic Games in Amsterdam. Mildred was still at his side, handing out bouquets, and they remained in the hotel industry.

But in September 1929 Mair's fortunes took a nosedive when he was charged with attempting to persuade two men to set fire to one of his less profitable businesses, the Commercial Hotel in Cunnamulla. The case received extensive coverage in Queensland newspapers. Mair was thirty-nine years old and described as a hotelkeeper. Bail was allowed, Mair being required to pay £70 and arrange one surety of £70. After two remands, evidence was given in the Police Court on 8 October.

Plainclothes constable J F Buggy outlined the police case that Mair hired Charles Ernest Smart and George Fraser to put a match to the Commercial Hotel as the first of a series of arsons. When Fraser said he would not do such a dirty trick on the licensee, Charlie Pye, who lived on the premises with his wife and child, Mair replied it was their own fault if they got burnt to death. Mair told Smart and Fraser if they did the job they would be set up for life, offering to 'put them in a pub or anything they wanted'. Buggy testified that three days later Mair called Smart and Fraser to his bedroom at the hotel, and recommended they get plenty of benzene and soak the bed and a corner recess before torching it. Claims were made that Mair gave Fraser a sum of money before catching a train from Cunnamulla and, after arriving in Charleville, wired more money to Smart. Instead of doing the deed, Smart and Fraser decided to return to Brisbane.

Mair appeared again on 15 October, when Smart told the court he and Fraser were originally hired by Mair for an undisclosed job. On 12 August the three of them travelled

Strike! The Tour That Died of Shame

together from Ipswich to Toowoomba, before Smart and Fraser went on alone to Connamulla and booked into the Commercial Hotel, which Mair had told them he owned. Mair instructed them not to recognise him when he arrived five days later until given a casual introduction which he would arrange. Smart said he was using the name of Burr.

Smart confirmed that Mair had shown no regard for the hotel managers and that Mair had shown them how to set the fire 'because he wanted the centre of the building to go up first'. Mair had wrenched the catch from the door of his room to allow Smart and Fraser access. Smart quoted Mair as saying, 'Now just come round from your room, open the door, fix it up, and away she goes'. He detailed two payments made by Mair via wire from Charleville.

In what was becoming a weekly soap opera for the *Brisbane Courier* readers, Fraser stepped into the witness box on 22 October and confirmed the evidence already given by undercover constable Buggy and Smart. Walter Everard Foote recalled driving Mair to Connamulla, and being told the Commercial Hotel was not paying its way and that something would have to be done about it. Some weeks later the defendant asked the witness to burn the hotel down, but he refused. When it was realised Foote was talking about an incident in 1928, not 1929, the magistrate reserved his decision on whether the evidence would be accepted.

After two more remands, the case eventually reached the Supreme Court - before Chief Justice J W Blair no less - in late November, where Mair's counsel challenged the evidence of three lower court witnesses, including Foote, as being so remote and unconnected by point of time with the actual charge as to be inadmissible. When the prosecutor did not press for the evidence to be allowed, the Chief Justice ruled it out. The prosecutor then announced he did not wish to continue, and the jury was recalled and informed they would not be required to give a verdict. Despite the damning evidence against him, Mair was discharged.

The Aftermath

In the 1936 Queensland electoral rolls, Mair's address was given as the Empire Hotel, The Valley, Brisbane. He had obtained some mining licences and his occupation had changed to mine manager. There was no mention of Mildred.

The previously diehard Queenslander moved to Darwin in September 1940, and was the subject of an extensive article in the *Northern Standard*. It reported he had recently been elected a life member of the North Queensland Amateur Boxing and Wrestling Association, 'a body he was the prime mover in founding twelve months ago. Mr Mair is connected with the company in Darwin who are about to erect buildings to house the machinery that will arrive by the first boat for a modern steam laundry and dry-cleaning concern, and is associated with the management of the Chung King Café in an advisory capacity'.

Mair told the newspaper he intended forming boxing, wrestling, swimming and rugby league organisations in the Northern Territory. In the latter case, that did not occur until 1950, well after he had returned south. By 1943 Mair, described as a shopkeeper, was living at Kedron in Brisbane with his second wife, Grace. Their electoral-roll details were unchanged in 1954. Ernest Hartley Mair died on 12 January, 1957, from injuries suffered when struck by a car on Lutwyche Road, The Grange, Brisbane.

Five years after Mair's death the seven life disqualifications which followed the 1926-27 All Blacks tour of Britain were re-examined by the New Zealand Rugby League.

15

DISQUALIFICATIONS 'UPLIFTED'

The 'life' disqualifications imposed on Neil Mouat, Phonse Carroll, Bill Devine, Frank Henry, Lou Petersen, Arthur Singe and Jack Wright lasted for thirty-five years, six months and twenty-two days. They were officially 'uplifted' at a NZRL council meeting in Auckland on 24 September, 1962, as the result of a campaign mounted by council member Geoff Plant.

Plant had a personal interest in the case of the 1926-27 All Blacks. Singe had died from an illness in 1936 and his widow later married Plant. The termination of the life bans was the culmination of several discussions at NZRL meetings and consultations with 1927-37 NZRL president Cyril Snedden and veteran Kiwis selector and coach Thomas 'Scotty' McClymont.

The NZRL chairman in 1962 was Dr Leo Cooney, and Plant convinced him the seven players had been harshly treated. At a meeting on 28 August, Cooney moved and Plant seconded a notice of motion, 'that the decision of the council of management of 1927 suspending certain New Zealand

Disqualifications 'Uplifted'

players be rescinded'. But when the motion was raised at the next meeting on 11 September it was deferred until the 1927 minute book could be located and studied.

Secretary Ted Knowling noted in the minutes of 24 September that, 'the minute book covering the years 1926-27 had been returned to a past president of the New Zealand Rugby League, Mr Cyril Snedden, and had been perused by the chairman and secretary for the purpose of locating the actual minute dealing with the disqualification of the players following the tour of England in 1926. This disqualification had apparently been the subject of a special meeting and no formal minutes were recorded in the minute book of the New Zealand Rugby Football League.

'Correspondence was received from Mr T A McClymont, and members spoke of the information which was now available. The discussion was held in committee, and when the meeting resumed in open meeting the following resolution was carried: "That any disqualification placed upon players as a result of the tour of England in 1926 be uplifted". Moved Dr L J Cooney, seconded Mr G G Plant, and carried on voices.'

The Carlaw duo, James and Owie, had buried all written record of the disqualifications so deeply that James Carlaw's successor as NZRL president, Cyril Snedden, had no inkling where it might be found when approached in 1962. McClymont had been a member of the 1926 national selection panel and effectively replaced Mair as the New Zealand coach when the 1928 Lions toured. He served on selection panels alongside All Blacks captain Bert Avery and would have had many opportunities to discuss the tour with those who were there.

Unfortunately, it was too late for at least four of the suspended men. Jack Wright had died of tuberculosis only two weeks after Singe in January 1936. Bill Devine died in 1956 and Lou Petersen in 1961. The fate of Englishman Frank Henry has not been recorded. The only two 'malcontents' alive in New Zealand in 1962 were Neil Mouat, who died in May 1967, and Phonse Carroll, who died in December 1974.

The lifting of the disqualifications received little publicity, certainly nothing to match the headlines when they were originally imposed. The *New Zealand Herald* and *Auckland Star* covered the NZRL meeting but their reporters did not understand the historical background or the ramifications. Both newspapers ran smallish articles from the meeting but led with other items of business.

The *Herald*, however, did quote Dr Cooney explaining that because there was no trace of the appropriate minutes there was no question of the council 'rescinding' the disqualifications. 'It was merely a question of whether the council would now agree or not to terminate the suspensions,' he said. So Mouat and Carroll had to settle for their disqualifications ending on 24 September, 1962, and not rescinded from when they were handed down on 2 March, 1927.

A short Press Association message from the *Herald* was followed up by *The Press*, which obtained a brief response from All Blacks financial manager George Ponder, who was then living in Christchurch. The entire news item read:

'The recent decision of the New Zealand Rugby League council to lift the life suspensions imposed on seven members of the New Zealand rugby league team at the conclusion of its tour of England in 1926-27, suggests that something new was revealed to the New Zealand council which was not made public, said one of the team managers, Mr G H Ponder, of Christchurch, yesterday. "I would be intrigued to know why the issue was opened up again," said Mr Ponder. Dr L J Cooney, chairman of the New Zealand council, had no comment to make when Mr Ponder's remarks were referred to him in Auckland yesterday.'

Appropriately, the re-investigation had also been held in committee and the last words on the whole sad saga were 'no comment'.

Disqualifications 'Uplifted'

CONCLUSIONS

Despite hints from various sources that there was a darker, deeper cause of the split between the seven 'malcontents' and their Australian co-manager and coach, Ernest Mair, nothing of the sort was ever revealed. Several loyal players ignored the supposed vow of silence to condemn the actions of their disqualified team-mates but did not accuse them of any previously unknown crimes. Official press agent Joe O'Shaughnessy, viewed by some as a spokesman for the rebellious players, did not disclose any radical new information. Nor did the investigative British press uncover anything more serious than the incidents which began soon after the boat left Auckland and continued on at the team's Harrogate headquarters.

Mair made one vague reference to having property stolen and being assaulted but never mentioned either accusation again. That was surprising for a man whose management style was seriously questioned by an English Rugby League which was initially reluctant to get involved but was forced to mediate. Surely Mair would have pushed his case to the limit, not only when told to stand aside by the ERL but also in the face of criticism from some NZRL councillors and others who had questioned his appointment and management methods.

There was one newspaper reference to religious differences between the suspended players, who were all Catholics or played for Marist clubs, and managers Mair and George Ponder, both Freemasons. Religious clashes were not uncommon in Australasian sport in that era, the best known being that between Australian cricket legend Don Bradman, a Freemason, and his Catholic team-mates, Jack Fingleton, Bill O'Reilly and Stan McCabe. But there were three Auckland Marist backs who did not join the revolt. One of them, Charles (nicknamed Pope) Gregory, was a spokesman for the loyal players and publicly supported financial manager Ponder.

No suggestion has ever surfaced that Mildred Mair

Strike! The Tour That Died of Shame

became involved with any of the players, though her presence must have been a distraction. It was certainly not in the best interests of the tour that one man should be accompanied by his wife while all others spent seven months away from their own loved ones. Ernest and Mildred Mair subsequently returned to Toowoomba and stayed together - at least until Mair was accused of attempting to burn down one of their less profitable hotels.

From comments made, the NZRL inquiry largely centred on whether the players had gone on strike, or whether they were locked out. There seems to be no doubt that they threatened to strike soon after arriving in England and then did so for five matches beginning with the Oldham game on 23 October. By 8 November, early in the week of the second Test, the ERL felt it had no choice than to use the mandate given it by the NZRL and take action.

ERL chairman Ted Osborne reported to his council meeting two nights later that Mair had 'eventually' offered to withdraw from the selection committee and fill only a passive role in the team management. The players then unanimously agreed that Ponder, captain Bert Avery and vice-captain Neil Mouat be the selectors for one month. The ERL minutes went on to say that 'the position (was) to be reconsidered and reviewed at the end of that period'. It would be very surprising if that condition was not known by Mair and Ponder, especially as the players were aware of it.

The lack of any reconsideration or review was the crux of the final split in the camp. Mair and Ponder claimed there never was any agreement to review the situation, while the players counter-claimed they were not striking but objecting to management breaking the agreement. Ponder, they said, then locked them out and stopped their allowances. When the ERL attempted to stand Mair down for another month, Ponder refused to comply and there could be no reconciliation. In sympathy, the ERL gave each of the suspended and destitute players £10 spending money for

Disqualifications 'Uplifted'

their homeward journey, almost sparking a sit-in by the 'loyal' players in the Headingley dressing room on the day of the third Test match.

Where, then, did the fault lie in the sorry saga of sport's most infamous tour and the equally shameful aftermath of trial without appeal? The only logical conclusion is that all the major parties, with the probable exception of the English Rugby League, were at fault.

James Carlaw and his fellow NZRL officials were largely responsible for the debacle, both before and after the tour. Mair dazzled them with assurances he could lift the New Zealand team to higher levels despite not having any proven coaching credentials. The fact that he was a Queenslander in an era when Queensland ruled the rugby league world seemed to be enough recommendation. His so-called professional methods clashed with the amateur approach of his players, many of them comparatively recent converts from rugby union. In a nutshell, New Zealand's naive rugby league administrators were conned.

Just as critically, the NZRL not only refused pleas and advice from all quarters to hold its post-tour inquiry in public but subsequently refused to release any of the details. The seven players hardly had time to meet their lawyer, let alone prepare a case, before they were in the dock for a trial they could never win. Their basic right of appeal, either to rugby league or independent authorities, was denied them. The haste with which the matter was dealt with, and all details buried deeply, also suggested the case for the prosecution was not as strong as it might have been.

When, in 1962, another NZRL council revisited the matter it consulted former president Cyril Snedden and former national selector and coach Scotty McClymont, two men who were close to the scene in 1926-27, and terminated the disqualifications. Obviously neither Snedden nor McClymont disclosed anything to persuade them to reinforce the suspensions.

Strike! The Tour That Died of Shame

The NZRL council blundered in appointing Mair and also by knowingly sending some acknowledged troublemakers on tour. When the inevitable divisions arose on the outward trip neither the players involved nor the managers showed the diplomacy needed to restore harmony. What began as a series of minor spats grew into an irretrievable chasm.

Relishing the power of his position, Mair responded by refusing to select certain players and wanting to banish them from the tour. The seven rebellious forwards firmed in their resolve not to play or train for him, confident the tour could not continue without them.

Mouat could only have been appointed vice-captain in the hope that responsibility would moderate the behaviour which had already earned him two reprimands from the NZRL. Instead, it gave him a form of officer rank in the uprising.

Four of the seven 'malcontents' had become rugby league players in the midst of the Payne Trophy dispute with rugby union authorities, and the other three were also code jumpers. Mair gave a potentially rebellious group a cause, and Mouat emerged as its leader. He was the mutineers' Fletcher Christian to Mair's Captain Bligh.

Mouat and his sidekicks had done the sums - without them there would be only five forwards left - and responded to what they regarded as Mair's unfair treatment and overbearing authority by attempting to hold the tour to ransom. They had not counted on the courage of backs such as Jim Parkes who were prepared to go far beyond the call of duty.

Declining to represent one's country on home soil, as Mouat did by missing the Queensland games at Carlaw Park in late 1925, is one thing. Refusing to train or play while on tour - when no replacements could be summoned, and sick, injured and ill-equipped team-mates were forced to fill the gaps - was inexcusable and merited a strong

Disqualifications 'Uplifted'

punishment. But the seven players involved should have received a fair trial, not a kangaroo court.

The English Rugby League wanted to take firm action some time before it was given a NZRL mandate to do so. When armed with that permission, the ERL decided there were faults and a poor attitude on both sides of the dispute and hoped to save the tour by sacrificing one coach to retain seven forwards.

But that compromise was accepted by co-manager George Ponder, captain Bert Avery and the other eighteen players only for so long, until the 'loyals' also demanded the 'malcontents' be punished. The ERL was then in a no-win situation and confirmed the players' suspensions on condition Mair also stood down for a second time. It finally wanted rid of them all, Mair as well as those who opposed him. From that point it was inevitable the tour would limp to its inevitable conclusion and disgraceful aftermath.

The ERL tour report to the NZRL blamed poor management as well as the rebellious players for what occurred. Although the NZRL - then at loggerheads with its English counterpart over the abolition of the two-year international transfer qualification - chose to ignore that, the ERL suspensions of Mair, as well as the 'malcontents', proved there were eight villains on the 1926-27 All Blacks tour and not just the seven who were consigned to rugby league's Hall of Shame.

Images from the final trial ahead of New Zealand's 1926-27 tour, in which North beat South 31-22 in an inter-island game at Carlaw Park. 1: Jack Wright scores for South. 2: Frank Henry fields a kick. 3: North captain Bert Avery. 4: The winning team, from left, Tim Peckham, Ben Davidson, Wally Desmond, Alf Townsend, Hector Cole, Jack Kirwan, Ivan Littlewood, Ernie Herring, Arthur Singe, Craddock Dufty, Alan Clarke, Lou Hutt, Bert Avery. 5: A South try to Len Mason. 6: Davidson tackling Henry.

16
STATISTICS

TOUR RESULTS

Date	Opponent	Result	Score
September 11	Dewsbury	Won	13-9
September 15	Leigh	Won	23-16
September 18	Halifax	Lost	13-19
September 22	Rochdale Hornets	Won	11-9
September 25	Barrow	Won	19-16
September 29	Widnes	Won	15-5
October 2	First test at Wigan	Lost	20-28
October 6	York	Won	19-11
October 9	Warrington	Lost	5-17
October 13	Bramley	Won	35-12
October 16	Hull	Won	15-13
October 20	Bradford Northern	Won	38-17
October 23	Oldham*	Lost	10-15
October 27	Leeds*	Won	13-11
October 30	St Helens Recreation*	Lost	14-28
November 3	Salford*	Won	18-10
November 6	Huddersfield*	Lost	10-12
November 13	Second test at Hull	Lost	11-21
November 17	Wigan Highfield	Won	14-2
November 20	Batley	Lost	17-19
November 23	Keighley	Won	21-3
November 27	Swinton	Lost	14-16
December 4	Wales at Pontypridd	Lost	8-34
December 8	St Helens	Lost	12-22
December 11	Wigan	Lost	15-36
December 15	Yorkshire*	Lost	16-17
December 18	Hunslet*	Lost	12-13
December 25	Pontypridd*	Won	17-8
December 27	Broughton Rangers*	Won	32-8
December 28	Wakefield Trinity*	Won	29-24
January 1	Hull Kingston Rovers*	Lost	15-20
January 3	Lancashire*	Lost	3-28
January 8	Cumberland*	Won	18-3
January 15	Third test at Leeds*	Lost	17-32

*denotes matches while seven forwards were not available.
Totals: Played 34, Won 17, Lost 17. For: 132 tries, 83 goals, 562 points. Against: 126 tries, 88 goals, 554 points.

Statistics

PLAYERS' PERFORMANCES

Player	Games	Tries	Goals	Points
H Avery	29	23	0	69
H Brisbane	27	6	0	18
L Brown	27	15	0	45
A Carroll	17	3	0	9
H Cole	14	1	0	3
B Davidson	23	14	0	42
F Delgrosso	20	4	6	24
W Desmond	15	8	0	24
W Devine	9	2	0	6
C Dufty	19	2	42	90
G Gardiner	20	10	10	50
C Gregory	15	0	6	12
W Hall	22	4	0	12
F Henry	12	2	0	6
E Herring	30	6	0	18
J Kirwan	18	5	0	15
L Mason	26	8	3	30
J Menzies	12	1	0	3
N Mouat	10	3	16	41
J Parkes	17	5	0	15
L Petersen	8	2	0	6
J Sanders	15	5	0	15
A Singe	6	1	0	3
H Thomas	18	2	0	6
S Webb	7	0	0	0
J Wright	6	0	0	0
Totals	442	132	83	562

TOUR RECEIPTS

The *Yorkshire Evening News* compared the tour receipts with those of the 1921-22 Kangaroos.

Opponent	1921-22 £	1926-27 £
Dewsbury	720	965
Leigh	507	540
Halifax	1130	1034
Rochdale Hornets	1210	587
Barrow	810	477
Widnes	580	460
Test in Lancashire	2536	1650
York	421	269
Warrington	1689	601
Bramley	136	87
Hull	1338	857
Bradford Northern	219	275
Oldham	1601	1136
Oldham (second game)	303	not played
Leeds	1558	269
St Helens Recreation	400	347
Salford	931	230
Huddersfield	1303	370
Test at Hull	2924	592
Wigan Highfield	not played	82
Batley	647	222
Keighley	305	293
Swinton	524	641
Wales	991	700
St Helens	462	163
Wigan	2625	620
Yorkshire	742	186
Hunslet	308	277
Pontypridd	not played	230
Broughton Rangers	1031	340
Wakefield Trinity	668	423
Hull Kingston Rovers	1338	430

Statistics

Bill Devine, left, and Wilson Hall were respectively the biggest and smallest members of the 1926-27 All Blacks.

Opponent	1921-22	1926-27
Lancashire	947	460
England	827	not played
Cumberland	459	134
Test at Leeds	3891	552
Totals	36,081	16,069

New Zealand's first home Test win over England, at Carlaw Park in 1924. Top: Scrum-half Scotty McClymont passes to Terry Gilroy.

Left: Neil Mouat (right) prepares to collect the ball.

Left: Bill Te Whata, Jim O'Brien, Bert Avery, Hec Brisbane, Neil Mouat, Ernie Herring, Craddock Dufty, Maurice Wetherill, Bill Stuart, Terry Gilroy, Charles Fitzgerald, Sam Lowrie, Scotty McClymont (capt).

Left: Additional seating was needed for a capacity crowd.

TOOWOOMBA'S LEADING HOTEL,
The
NEW GLOBE,
Ruthven and Bell Streets.

Hot and cold water and electric appliances in every room. Everything in hotel new and up-to-date.

E. H. MAIR,
Proprietor.

'Phone 299.
P.O. Box, 191.

Left: Newspaper advertisement for the Mair-owned New Globe Hotel.

Left: 1925 Tour montage: Oval-shaped photo was taken at the Sydney Cricket Ground. Back, from left, Bert Laing (captain), Charles Pearce (coach), Bert Avery (vice-captain). Front, from left, Nelson Culpan (financial manager), Ernest Mair (NZRL representative on ARL), Jim Wingham (team manager). Right: Ernest Mair's portrait, a further part of the montage he presented to the New Zealand Rugby League.

BIBLIOGRAPHY

E Bennetts, 1933, *New Zealand Rugby Football League Annual*, NZ Newspapers, Auckland.

J Coffey, 1987, *Canterbury XIII*, Canterbury Rugby League, Christchurch.

J Coffey and B Wood, 2007, *The Kiwis: 100 Years of International Rugby League*, Hodder Moa, Auckland.

J Coffey and B Wood, 2008, *100 Years - Maori Rugby League 1908-2008*, Huia, Wellington.

J Coffey and B Wood, 2009, *Auckland - 100 Years of Rugby League 1909-2009*, Huia, Wellington.

R Davis, 1985, *Great Britain Rugby League Tours*, BRL Lions Association, England.

R Gate, 2008, *Rugby League Lions: 100 Years of Test Matches*, Vertical Editions, England.

I Heads, 1990, *The Kangaroos*, Lester-Townsend Publishing, Sydney.

T Hyland, 1969, *Marist Memories 1919-1969*, Marist Old Boys RL Club, Auckland.

Bibliography

B Montgomerie, 2004, *Those Who Played*, Montgomerie Publishing, Sydney.

G Moorhouse, 1995, *A People's Game: The Official History of Rugby League*, Hodder & Stoughton, London.

G Morris, 2009, *Destination Wembley: The History of the Rugby League Challenge Cup*, Vertical Editions, England.

G Morris and J Huxley, 1983, *Wembley Magic*, Evans Brothers Ltd, London.

Australian newspapers: *Brisbane Courier, Northern Standard, Queensland Times, Sydney Morning Herald, Toowoomba Chronicle*.

British newspapers and periodicals: *All Sports Weekly, Athletic News, Batley Reporter, Daily Dispatch* (Manchester), *Daily Express, Daily Telegraph, Evening News, Halifax Courier, Hull Daily Mail, Hull Evening News, Keighley News, Leeds Mercury, Oldham Standard, Rochdale Observer, St Helens Reporter, Sporting Life and Sportsmen, Swinton Journal, The Sports Post, Wakefield Express, Warrington Guardian, Widnes Weekly News, Wigan Observer, Yorkshire Evening News, Yorkshire Herald, Yorkshire Observer, Yorkshire Post*.

Canadian newspaper: *Daily Star* (Montreal).

New Zealand newspapers and periodicals: *Auckland Star, Auckland Weekly News, Evening Post* (Wellington), *Grey River Argus* (Greymouth), *New Zealand Free Lance, New Zealand Herald* (Auckland), *New Zealand Sporting and Dramatic Review, New Zealand Truth, Rugby League News* (Auckland), *The Press* (Christchurch), *The Star* (Christchurch), *Weekly Press and Referee* (Christchurch), *Westport News*.

Past deeds. Present voices.

Introducing Rugby League Classics - an ongoing series of historically significant rugby league books - rediscovered, rebranded and republished in paperback, often after having been long out-of-print.

Each edition comes complete with the original manuscript intact, and contains a wealth of new and updated material, including an introductory overview written by a relevant modern-day expert, evocative photographs, appendices, an index and the modern-day recollections of those closest to the book's primary subject, i.e. family members, former team-mates and other contemporary figures.

It is anticipated that at least one such title will published every year, covering a wide range of eras and celebrated rugby league personalities.

To stay right up to date with news of all our latest releases, simply drop an email to **news@scratchingshedpublishing.com** and we will add you to our mailing list.

Rugby League Classics

OUT NOW - Numbers 1-6
- Gus Risman
- Lewis Jones
- Eric Ashton
- Eddie Waring
- 1926-27 NZ Tour

COLLECT THE SET!

Visit our website:
www.scratchingshedpublishing.co.uk

Scratching Shed Publishing Ltd

Treasure the old. Embrace the new.

When rugby league changed forever

XIII Winters, XIII Worlds

A classic collection of rugby league essays
Edited by Dave Hadfield

Published for the first time ever in one 496-page volume

ISBN: 978-0956007551

In *XIII Winters*, Dave Hadfield contributes to an entertaining and memorable collection of essays in which an assortment of writers reflect upon a particular season in the history of their favourite club. First published in association with *Open Rugby* magazine, *XIII Winters* boasts chapters by the likes of Harry Edgar, Martin and Simon Kelner, Paul Wilson and Huw Richards. Its writers may not have realised it at the time but, in the mid-1990s, when a switch to summer was just around the corner, rugby league's long-standing association with the depths of the English winter would soon be lost, presumably forever.

Such was the chord struck by *XIII Winters* that it was soon followed by *XIII Worlds*, a lively, quirky celebration of rugby league's much maligned international dimension. Subsequent events and the passing of the years have rendered this entertaining, witty and often overlooked collection equally worthy of reappraisal.

Here, with a new introduction penned by Dave Hadfield himself, *XIII Worlds* and *XIII Winters* have been combined as part of Scratching Shed's Rugby League Classics series. Together, they are a high-water mark in the development of quality rugby league literature.

Scratching Shed Publishing Ltd

Treasure the old. Embrace the new.

Stay up to date with all our lastest releases at
www.scratchingshedpublishing.co.uk